DESIGNING
Australia's cities

Robert Freestone is Professor of
Planning and Urban Development in the
Faculty of the Built Environment at the
University of New South Wales.

ROBERT FREESTONE

DESIGNING
Australia's
Cities

CULTURE, COMMERCE AND THE CITY BEAUTIFUL, 1900–1930

A UNSW Press book
© Robert Freestone 2007
First published 2007

Simultaneously published in

*Australia and New Zealand and their
dependent territories, Papua New Guinea and
Fiji by*
University of New South Wales Press Ltd
University of New South Wales
Sydney NSW 2052
AUSTRALIA
www.unswpress.com.au

National Library of Australia
Cataloguing-in-Publication entry:

Freestone, Robert.
Designing Australia's cities: culture,
commerce and the city beautiful 1900–
1930.
Includes index.
ISBN 9780868408118.
1. Cities and towns - Australia. 2. City
planning -Australia. 3. Environment
(Aesthetics). 4. Australia - Civilization
- Philosophy. I. Title.
307.1416

Cover design Di Quick
Cover image Lloyd Rees, 'Imaginary
City' (1918), ink and wash. Bequest of
John Sailer, 1970, The Howard Hinton
Collection, New England Regional Art
Museum, Armidale, NSW, Australia and
Viscopy.
Printer Everbest, China

This book is printed on chlorine-free
paper.

The UK by
Routledge
2 Park Square, Milton Park, Abingdon
Oxfordshire, OX14 4RN

The USA and Canada by
Routledge
270 Madison Ave, New York, NY 10016

*Routledge is an imprint of the Taylor &
Francis Group*

A catalogue record for this book is
available from the British Library

A catalog record for this book has been
requested from the Library of Congress

ISBN 978-0-415-42421-9 (hardback)
ISBN 978-0-415-42422-6 (paperback)

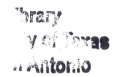

Contents

Acknowledgments

The core research for this book was made possible by grants from the Australian Research Council. Sharon Veale's diligence as primary research assistant and collaborator from 1993 to 1996 laid the foundations. Publication has been made possible by grants from the Australian Academy of Humanities and the assistance of the Faculty of the Built Environment at the University of New South Wales under the research leadership of Peter Murphy and Martin Loosemore.

Colleagues in a variety of scholarly networks – notably the International Planning History Society (IPHS), Society for City and Regional Planning History (SACRPH), and the Australasian Urban/Planning History conference series – have contributed insights and information in numerous ways over many years. Individually, I acknowledge international colleagues: Arnold Alanen, Genie Birch, Ray Bromley, Robert Bruegmann, David Gordon, Peter Hall, Michael Hebbert, Ken Jackson, Richard Longstreth, Caroline Miller, Mervyn Miller, Ernest Morrison, Jon Peterson, Ted Relph, John Reps, Christopher Silver, Bruce Stephenson, Tony Sutcliffe, Wallace Van Zyl, Stephen Ward, Bill Wilson and Jeanne Wolfe. My key Australian informants and critics have included Richard Aitken, Elias Duek-Cohen, Graeme Davison, Zeny Edwards, Christine Garnaut, Robert

Gibbons, Ian Hoskins, Alan Hutchings, David Jones, Jon Lang, Stuart McKenzie, Colleen Morris, Don Newman, David Nichols, Stefan Petrow, Ken Taylor, Christopher Vernon, Martyn Webb, James Weirick, and Georgina Whitehead. A cohort of UNSW planning students undertook historical research projects under my direction which have shaped the scope and content of this book. My thanks to Stuart Carr, Felicity Chan, Clayton Davidson, Murray Donaldson, Phoebe Ikladios, Anna Michalandos, Aneesh Singh, Theresa Smyth, Kasanita Vave, Debby Wong and Natalie Yezerski. A catalogue of librarians and archivists on several continents are the unsung heroes.

My thanks also to John Elliot of UNSW Press and his colleagues Heather Cam, Di Quick and Neil Thomson at all stages of the publication process.

Sections of the book have been adapted from previous publications: 'Melbourne and the city beautiful movement 1900–30', in Dingle, T (ed) *Proceedings of the Third Australian Planning History/Urban History Conference*, Monash University Office of Continuing Education, 1996, pp. 223–32; *The Federal Capital of Australia: A Virtual Planning History*, ANU Urban Research Program, Working Paper No. 60, June 1997; 'The City Beautiful: Toward an Understanding of the Australian Experience', *Journal of Architectural and Planning Research*, 15, 1998, pp. 91–108; 'International influences on early metropolitan planning: Sydney, Australia 1908–09', Paper presented to the SACRPH Conference, Washington, DC, November 1999; 'The Civic Centre in Modern Planning History: General themes and Australian interpretations', Paper presented to the IPHS Conference, Helsinki, August 2000; 'Town, Gown and the Campus Beautiful', in Garnaut, C & Hamnett, S (eds) *Fifth Australian Urban History Planning History Conference, Conference Proceedings*, University of South Australia, Adelaide, 2000, pp. 182–92; 'From city improvement to the city beautiful', in Hamnett, S & Freestone, R (eds) *The Australian Metropolis: A Planning History*, Allen and Unwin, Sydney, 2000, pp. 27–45; 'Imagineering the City Beautiful: Parks, Gardens and Town Planning Thought', in Whitehead, G (ed), *Planting the Nation*, Australian Garden History Society, Melbourne, 2001, pp. 159–86.

The author and publisher are grateful to the following for their permission to reproduce illustrations:

California Historical Society (p. 43)

Chicago History Museum (p. 23)

City of Sydney Archives (p. 289)

Fawkner Crematorium and Memorial Park (p. 218)

Fryer Library, University of Queensland Library (pp. 203, 205)

JS Battye Library of West Australian History (pp. 186–187)

Mitchell Library, State Library of New South Wales (pp. 49, 230, 262)

National Archives of Australia (pp. 66, 82–83, 115, 116, 216)

National Capital Authority (pp. 101, 290)

National Library of Australia (pp. 86, 90, 98, 100, 110)

Perth City Council (p. 63)

Royal Australian Institute of Architects (WA Chapter) (p. 154)

University of Western Australia Archives (p. 200)

Woods Bagot (p. 201)

US Fine Arts Commission (pp. 26–27)

Every effort has been made to trace copyright holders for illustrations. Unattributed photographs are by the author.

CHAPTER 1

Introduction

The city beautiful era was an influential chapter in the history of 20th century urban planning. It helped define and refine an agenda for an emergent profession by highlighting both the possibilities and limitations of planned aesthetic interventions in the processes of urban development. Its vision was wide-ranging, from definitive place-making grand gestures to more humdrum improvements to the everyday environment. Its legacy is palpable in the administrative apparatus of planning and in the many historic buildings, parks, and streets that contribute to urban character. Conceiving the city as a work of art is a time-honoured tradition but the special contribution of the city beautiful movement was to link public improvements and interventions to broader notions of comprehensive planning. Many of the first urban plans were city beautiful inspired and captured the power of conveying visions through imagery. The 3-D bird's eye perspective was a staple technique.

Anthony Sutcliffe has written that 'although aesthetics greatly strengthened the appeal of planning, it nearly swamped it in the process'.[1] But ultimately city beautiful thought lacked the inclusiveness of a genuine planning paradigm, being largely silent on issues of social welfare, failing to address more pressing issues of transportation and land use regulation, and demonstrating a seemingly greater concern with the luxury of culture than the necessity of commerce. Nevertheless, the role of an aesthetic sensibility as one component of planning's mission was firmly signalled.

The city beautiful movement had world-wide impacts in the early 20th century. This book explores how planners and civic leaders in Australia responded to the opportunities, challenges and constraints shared with urban reformers around the world. They spoke a common language but the Australian story was distinctive and produced urban landscapes whose common lineage has not been widely appreciated. This is a fresh look at an old but enduring approach to city-making.

My treatment is informed by three themes. The first embeds city beautiful ideas within the wider context of the early town planning movement in Australia – its central ideas, personalities and institutions. The second acknowledges not only the importance of American precedents and parallels but a global movement for reform of some diversity – contrary to the conventional wisdom. The third theme is how projects inspired by the city beautiful movement always struggled to satisfactorily combine aesthetic improvement with more utilitarian ends to win general community acceptance; in a broader sense, this relationship between culture and commerce was frequently troubled. I expand on each of these dimensions in turn.

The Australian context

The evolution of modern urban planning as a force for shaping Australian cities has many parallels in other western nations, particularly the United Kingdom and the United States. The basic chronology is well established.[2] Responses to problems thrown up by rapid urbanisation at the end of the 19th century included both new public health legislation to regulate streets and buildings and utopian tracts promoting completely new communities. Incremental city improvements were pursued in hit-and-miss fashion. A more integrated and coordinated approach slowly emerged in the early 1910s that transcended but built upon existing built environment professions such as architecture, engineering and surveying. Early calls for action by middle class reformers and professionals led to a variety of innovations, including new statutes to enable local

authorities to plan their territories in advance of settlement, formation
of planning commissions to oversee preparation of comprehensive city
plans, provision of new open spaces, slum clearance, and building of
planned communities. From a protracted period of experimentation
and voluntary advocacy came the institutionalisation of planning
controls at different tiers of government, particularly after World War
II as the state acknowledged the necessity of regulation in the interests
of economic, social and environmental health. An accumulation of
problem-specific initiatives ensued as planning powers and techniques
expanded to address diverse policy objectives.

The distinctiveness of the Australian experience is rooted in the
framework of a federal system of government, weak local government,
capital city dominance, the tyranny of distance from overseas sources
of innovation, a small population, modest-sized economy, and the early
dominance of British conceptual and legal precedents in responding
to urban issues. A heavy dose of pragmatism ruled city development,
with the demands of capitalism pre-eminent. Different waves of
enlightened approaches were felt. In the early 1900s the British garden
city movement with its roots in housing and land reform had a
major impact in tidying up existing suburbanisation trends into new
model house-and-garden suburbs. By the 1920s the cutting edge was
comprehensive city planning with a strong bias towards American city
functional thought, but the legislative innovations arriving belatedly
at a national scale in the 1940s followed British town and country
planning precepts based largely around municipal land use control.

The early mantra was for the simultaneous achievement of
convenience, health, and beauty. A substantive scholarly literature has
deconstructed many aspects of this agenda in every Australian state.[3]
The aesthetic strain has been less diligently pursued, perhaps because
it was the weakest dimension, routinely sacrificed, compromised
or ignored for more pragmatic ends. There is also a surprisingly
ahistorical approach in modern Australian urban design that tends
to look overseas when it looks to the past. Yet the city beautiful idea
nurtured both rhetorically and practically a nationally distinctive
strain of early planning advocacy. In professional discourse as much
as the popular imagination, first thoughts turn to Canberra and the
1912 plan by Walter Burley and Marion Mahony Griffin. Recognising

its eclecticism and humanity, Hall describes it as the blueprint for the 'City Beautiful Exceptional'.[4] But there was much more to the city beautiful in Australia. Set within the wider movement for planning in every state, the range of urban plans and landscapes, which influenced directly and indirectly to the 1930s and beyond, is remarkable.

America and global meanings

The city beautiful is most often boxed as a purely American phenomenon animated by an over-the-top neo-baroque style. There is some truth here but this clichéd textbook dismissal does not do justice to an inherent progressiveness and complexity. Some urban reformers may have tended towards an 'imaginary form of the city, to the ideals of unity, harmony, and perfection envisioned in a dream of a classical Olympian city'.[5] More often, reform aspirations were embedded in wider fields of action embracing public education, higher standards of suburban development, strategic planning, and vital infrastructure provision. The finer grain of politics, aesthetics and ideology in this more empathetic view is well captured in case studies of particular cities.[6] William Wilson convincingly argues for the city beautiful as a grassroots political and cultural movement as much as an elite aesthetic and environmental one.[7] Jon Peterson also provides a compelling perspective of a multi-faceted movement integrating various 19th century urban reform threads into the birth of comprehensive city planning in the United States.[8]

Apart from acknowledging the inspiration of European cities such as Paris, Vienna and Rome, what is missing from many accounts is a true sense of international mindedness. The American city beautiful was only one, albeit very influential, strand of a global turn to civic art in the late 19th and early 20th centuries. Stephen Ward records comparable agendas in many countries as well as the transnational diffusion of influences and ideology.[9] Peter Hall, reminds us that the 'city of monuments' was as much about Berlin, New Delhi and Moscow as Chicago, Washington, and Cleveland, and that the phenomenon 'manifested itself, over a 40-year period, in a great variety of different economic, social, political and cultural circumstances'.[10] Gilbert Stelter encapsulates the city beautiful as a movement embodying 'some very positive planning ideas' and reaching to Canada, Japan, and South America.[11] The international manifestations of an aestheticised planning were the product of a globalisation of ideas responding to shared problems and opportunities, with actual origins and outcomes refracted through a diversity of national and regional planning cultures and circumstances.

The term city beautiful is attributed to New York artists and art critics in the late 1890s and it soon became the catchphrase for a new civic enthusiasm. Taking off worldwide in the early 1900s, it often braided into complementary planning paradigms such as the garden city movement to capture a politically middle-of-the-road manifesto to make cities better by being more beautiful. Similar aesthetic solutions surfaced even when the phrase was not in common use. My references to the city beautiful and the city beautiful movement in this book connote the wider international rather than narrower American definition, with their actual meanings contingent upon specific circumstances and contexts.

The city beautiful idea as an international force sought to reorder and improve the urban environment for economic and moral betterment. By fusing aesthetics, civic design and municipal improvement, the movement strove 'to improve the utility as well as the comeliness of cities, to elevate urban citizenship, and to fulfil human needs for transportation, recreation, and residential environment' in response to modernisation.[12] The role of an ingrained urban beauty was to inspire civic pride and patriotism, resulting in increased productivity and an improved urban economy. At the 1910 Royal Institute of British Architects conference on town planning, the British politician John Burns argued that an artistic city was also a prosperous, progressive, and socially cohesive one:

> Cities are not only emporiums for goods, centres of commerce and trade. They are something more than a mere cash nexus; they are places where utility, comfort, and beauty can be and ought to be combined.[13]

The monumental may have been the ideal but the city beautiful was often more readily realised in small-scale, piecemeal, often quite pragmatic civic improvements. Street tree planting, street furniture, parks and gardens, the eradication of ugly billboards, beautification of public utility works, and endorsement of sundry civic embellishments, including war memorials, statuary and fountains, were just as desirable. Contemporary discourse about design principles used phrases and keywords such as balance, harmony, symmetry, uniformity, dignity, unity, and strength, but without ever really defining these attributes. Formal and informal responses were evident. The formal ultimately drew on sources such as Baron Haussmann's rebuilding of Paris under Napoleon III and Pierre L'Enfants's 18th century plan for Washington, DC, with their diagonal avenues, vistas, and dominating buildings and landmarks. Architecturally, major inspiration came from beaux arts principles of symmetry, hierarchy, and balanced order. Informality was a counterpoint, most evident in the treatment of parks and small open spaces.

Wilson identifies ten major tenets of the American movement, all of which resonate singly or in different combinations in other nations:

- Recognition of the aesthetic and functional shortcomings of cities.
- Positive endorsement of urbanisation and urban life.
- Undiluted belief in social progress.
- Europhilic.
- Technocratic pathways to realising an unambiguous public interest.
- Acceptance of existing social, political and economic arrangements.
- Class-conscious moral obligation to civic duty.
- Gospel of efficiency for increased production and wealth.
- Environmentalism through the ameliorative power of beauty.
- The synthesis of beauty and utility.[14]

Politically, these aims were pursued through different models. Stelter identifies three types of leadership: 'the baroque cult of power', with authority (and patronage) exercised top-down; the 'professional and bureaucratic', mostly associated with architecturally inspired planning; and 'populist initiative' forged through civic and commercial coalitions. The third model links to the regimes of public officials, reformers, businessmen, newspapers, professionals, and city planning commissions most associated with the American experience.[15] Techniques of implementation varied to match structures of governance, from the ineffectual sentiments of advisory committees through to brutal enforcement by dictatorships. A plan was mandatory but the environmental setting ranged across different scales: regional, metropolitan, capital city, central city, suburb, town and village. The Australian experience exemplifies this spectrum of responses from the design of small public spaces to entire metropolitan regions.

The quest for beautility

The tension between beauty and utility in the city beautiful era connected into more fundamental dimensions in cultural life between romanticism and rationalism, art and science, and 'commerce and civilisation', as the *Sydney Mail* put it in 1909.[16] The contemporary consensus was that, desirably, such values should be captured simultaneously. 'Beauty and utility were always emphasised simultaneously as interdependent goals', argued Emily Talen, because the city beautiful constantly endeavoured to find 'a more utilitarian basis for its existence' than aesthetics alone.[17] City beautiful advocates

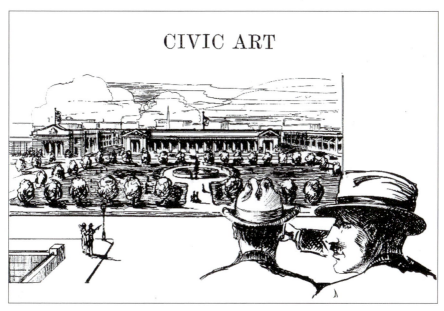

City planners and civic art. *Harland Bartholomew, Memphis Plan, 1922*

saw beauty as more than surface ornament; beauty had to be more than skin-deep. The genesis of these ideas was the work of 19th century landscape designers led by Frederick Law Olmsted, who argued the societal role of beauty in securing a contented workforce, enhancing property values, and promoting local civic and economic development. Later, as Wilson has noted, the nexus between beauty and utility came to denote something 'more palpable, direct, and design-related'. The values were inseparable, for 'no structure or scene could be truly beautiful without being functional as well'. In an address to the American Civic Association, the architect-designer Arnold Brunner coined a new term to express the desired fusion of beauty and utility in design projects: 'beautility'.[18]

Beauty as an expression of pure artistry symbolising divine intervention has long had its advocates. The artist and critic John Ruskin was dismissive of the idea that the beautiful had to be useful. 'Remember that the most beautiful things in the world are the most useless; peacocks and lilies for instance', was a well known quotation from *The Stones of Venice* (1851). According to Ruskin, to hold that beauty is derived from usefulness was 'to confound admiration with hunger, love with lust, and life with sensation; it is to assert that the human creature has no ideas and no feelings except those ultimately referable to its brutal appetites'.[19] Ruskin's views were complex for his writings in other ways anticipate the precepts of modern urban planning, holding elsewhere that 'what is most adapted to its purpose is most beautiful'.[20] This stance more clearly aligned with the ideas of other philosophers, such as 18th century English philosopher David Hume, for whom works of art were only judged beautiful 'in proportion to their fitness for the use of man'.[21]

This notion of linking aesthetic value to use value is a time-honoured credo in many aspects of everyday life and goes back centuries. The view that 'usefulness is the standard of beauty' is attributed to Socrates.[22] A key ancient source is 1st century BC Roman architect Vitruvius in his classic text *Ten Books on Architecture*. Vitruvius claimed architecture rotated around the interplay of utility, strength, and aesthetic effect, translated in the 17th century by Sir Henry Wotton, the English writer and diplomat, into commodity, firmness, and delight. As will be seen, this could have urban planning connotations, but in architectural terms it meant that beauty became a by-product of structure. This was a preoccupation of American architectural critic FW Fitzpatrick (whose writings also circulated in Australia) whose formula was 'Be natural, logical, direct, refined and sane and your design, whatever it is, will be beautiful'.[23]

An evolving locus of the beauty versus function debate can be tracked through contemporary American writings. The prominent early advocate Charles Mulford Robinson 'made civic art especially appealing to his countrymen by telling them that it joins utility to beauty'.[24] In books such as *The Improvement of Towns and Cities* (1901), a consistent theme of Robinson's was the practical benefits of beautification. No opportunity was too small: 'If drinking fountains, for man or beast, band stands, or lavatories have the conspicuousness in site of a public statue, their artistic character should be scrutinized as rigidly. Utility should not excuse ugliness'.[25] In *Modern Civic Art* (1903), beauty was inseparable from the other two essential needs of cities: circulation and hygiene.

American architect John Carrère's three essentials of city planning were identical. In *City Improvement from the Artistic Standpoint* (1910), he advocated their thoroughgoing integration. 'In our cities, and in fact in our whole mode of life, we separate work from pleasure, the practical from the beautiful, instead of blending them as is so skilfully done by the older nations of the world'. There was no reason, for example, why thoroughfares could not also be 'breathing spaces and pleasure grounds all in one'. Paris was the exemplar.[26] Carrère also articulated the evolving discourse that beauty not decoration had to be inherent in a city plan. 'I hold ... that it is cheaper to develop a city artistically than otherwise. By artistically I mean not surface ornament and display, but logically planned, well-proportioned arteries, parkings with proper provision for monuments, public buildings and private buildings of importance, work done with foresight – which means with imagination'.[27]

Modern American planning pioneers provided a more analytical foundation for this position. In 1917 FL Olmsted Jr wrote that:

The demands of beauty are in large measure identical with those of efficiency and economy, and differ mainly merely in requiring a closer approach to perfection in the adaptation of means to ends than is required to meet the merely economic standard. So far as the demands of beauty can be distinguished from those of economy, the kind of beauty most to be sought in the planning of cities is that which results from seizing instinctively, with a keen and sensitive appreciation, the limitless opportunities which present themselves in the course of the most rigorously practical solution of any problem, for a choice between decisions of substantially equal economic merit, but of widely differing aesthetic quality. Regard for beauty must neither follow after regard for the practical ends to be obtained nor precede it, but must inseparably accompany it.[28]

From the outset of his professional career the city planner John Nolen sought 'to blend functional considerations with beautification' in the context of dynamic city growth 'whose basic workings must be understood'.[29] In a 1922 address to the National Conference on City Planning, he articulated the relevance of the Vitruvian essentials of utility, strength and aesthetic effect to city building, with its parallels in structural integrity, social function, and desire for beauty. The key argument was that planning makes cities beautiful, not beautification:

The city plan provides the location and arrangement, the elevation or gradient, the foreground and background, the vistas, balance and symmetry, the street scenes; it provides a proper sense of scale, the broad relationships, the environment, and the opportunity for the grouping, assembling and composition of such works under conditions that make them truly and permanently beautiful.[30]

This idea that beauty was the product of utility came to define a central thrust of planning in many western nations in the 1920s.

Beauty and utility were interlocked in an evolving relationship. Trawling through contemporary ideological statements and the wordings of actual plans suggests an interrelationship working on three main levels, which can be noted in turn.

The first rhetorical-level sustained, long-standing ideological arguments justifying a reordering of the urban environment for moral and economic betterment. The fusion of artistic design and rational physical improvement targeted, often nebulously, nationalism, citizenship, patriotism, economic productivity, social cohesion, and the quality of life. For FW Fitzpatrick, city beautifiers were doing 'more real good work to advance Culture, Civilisation, and Christianity than are the missionaries sent at infinitely greater cost, into far distant lands'.[31] Ceremonial design could also convey legitimating messages for specific ideologies and power systems in physical form. Never too far away, were frequent appeals to the imperatives of capital accumulation. A key argument was encapsulated in the American architect and urban planner Daniel Burnham's statement that 'beauty has always paid better than any other commodity and always will'.[32] The general economic value of beauty in this sense lay in increased productivity, stimulating investment, and attracting tourism.

Over time, these general assertions were not enough. An Australian commentator noted in 1911 that 'Were any of the Australian cities to project uncommonly large loans for the sole purpose of beautification, and offer as the only explanation that civic beauty was an asset which would account for more population and an enhanced public spending capacity, the next polls would tell the inevitable story'.[33] Hence, a suite of more pragmatic arguments was needed to lock in grander sentiments. Wider city streets not only lent themselves to boulevard treatment, they also improved traffic flow. Parkways were not just attractive pleasure drives but mechanisms for transforming unsightly corridors into impressive civic showpieces, as well as buffers against the spread of fires and disease. The grouping of major public buildings was more than symbolic of civic citizenship and the rise of the modern state, it also responded to the need to improve communication within the bureaucracy and the spatial confinement of government functions for the good of the private land market.

The third level was the bottom line: the demand for specific architectural and urban design projects to deliver multiple collateral benefits, preferably quantifiable. Aesthetic projects unless very special in a commemorative way should have some extra practicality. At the same time, utilitarian projects should ideally embody aesthetic content. 'Commercialism is not to be decried', an Australian commentator noted, 'but cannot a utility product be cloaked by an artistic housing, thereby creating a pleasing combination of the two?'[34] These views not only raised the design stakes but ensured that the costs of and returns from projects needed to be carefully scrutinised. Returns from projects involving compulsory government resumption of property for redevelopment were of particular interest. The discourse of utility was often reduced to pure economics, and proposals that went nowhere near recouping their costs were easily jettisoned.

These three levels could be found combined in many planning statements, so pervasive was the importance attached to the beauty-utility tradeoff in different settings. In a loose sense, we can see them almost as phases in the development of planning ideology through the early 20th century as it moved from a conspicuous mission of idealistic civic aesthetics to working more quietly for efficient city forms that could be inherently beautiful.

Arnold Brunner's term beautility brilliantly sensitises us to how proposals under the city beautiful banner might be both more successfully marketed and scrutinised by governments and the wider community. A simple model to make sense of this contemporary concern is to see a conceptual spectrum of project values from unalloyed priceless beauty at one end to a hard-nosed utilitarianism on the other. The city beautiful message delivered professionally sought an appropriate combination of these values. However, a linear scale objectively measuring the right combination of aesthetic and functional values is too simplistic; these were relative not absolute values. Constructions of what was 'beautiful' and what was 'utilitarian' differed. The right mix determining the acceptability of a project was shaped by numerous factors, including:

- Nature of the proponent (technical and artistic credibility, power).
- Nature of consent or approval mechanisms (simple, complex).
- Nature and variety of stakeholders (private, public, intergovernmental).
- Nature of project (scale, significance, location, cost)
- Timing of the project (era, circumstances).

Controversy could be sparked and linger if commitments to proceed were made before the right combination was achieved. Assessments or perceptions of the right combination could also shift over time. A whole complex calculus of consensus was often at work. Cumulatively these decisions – be they fleeting judgments as much as formal assessments – helped define the public mood. While early city beautiful advocates were aware of the importance of delivering utilitarian benefits, it seems clear that their integration of these values did not go far enough, and the cutting edge of planning soon shifted toward a city efficient philosophy. By this time, the ruling creed was less that beautiful things could be useful and more that useful things could be beautiful.

The planning proposals coming under scrutiny ranged from site-specific development projects to city plans. But there was one class of project which confounded the dominant desideratum of combining beauty and utility. This was the war memorial, often a major element of artistic local improvement immediately after World War I. This reflected more deep-seated social attitudes, certainly in Australian and American society. There were vigorous debates between the merits of purely commemorative statements versus more practical memorials such as hospitals and returned servicemen's clubs. However, even when the more reflective artistic option was preferred this was arguably less an outright rejection of the value of utility than its redefinition into rhetorical qualities of remembrance and collective memory that had an important social function.

In Australia, the contemporary planning and design literature in journals such as *Building and Architecture* carried frequent references to the desirability of combining beauty and utility in projects, without precisely defining these values. Being alive to their importance now provides one useful perspective for surveying the nature, breadth and depth of the artistic turn and its evolutionary path in early urban planning. Without blocking out other important political, institutional and socio-economic issues, it is the major theme pursued here to:

- Highlight cleavages in the planning movement around artistic versus economic values.

- Enable a closer scrutiny of the actual design and economics of projects.

- Reveal new factors of importance in the acceptability and implementation of projects.

- Add a dimension in understanding the politics of contested projects.

Urban drama: A new approach to Sydney from Central Railway Station by
John Sulman. *Royal Commission on Sydney Improvement*, 1909

In fact, many of the stories of individual projects can be represented as
an ongoing negotiation between shifting and multiple understandings
of beauty and function in search of community consensus about
their optimal combination. These stories variously carry elements of
success, failure and contestation.

The differential valuation of beautility provides a means of
exploring the aims, issues and problems of a wide variety of projects
in a way which links them to an evolving discourse of the scope,
limitations and methods of city planning globally. The key point is
that beautification of the city was not conceived as an end in itself.
Artistic ideals had to be, and for the most part were, propelled by more
than aesthetics alone. In 1916, the leading British urban reformer JS
Nettlefold captured a universal understanding: 'The City Beautiful will
be of no practical value unless it is also the City of Commonsense'.[35]

Designing Australia's cities

The early 1900s witnessed a 'world-trend of civic planning'. Endorsing 'civic beauty as an asset', The journal *Building* reported that 'The "new birth" of cities is world wide. It is for beauty as well as convenience and comfort. The poetic outcry from old Vienna for the material conveniences of a new age is equaled by the materialistic cry from new cities for the artistic overlaying of their modern devices'.[36]

Australia was caught up in this movement under the banner of the city beautiful. This book attempts to provide an exploration of the phenomenon: its origins, ideology, impacts, and legacy.

The approach is infused with the expansive notion that the influence of the city beautiful has been extensive and that it has informed 'in a variety of ways the ideas, practices and accepted symbolism of nineteenth-, twentieth- and twenty-first century city-centre design and architecture'.[37] A critical perspective is adopted that seeks to avoid a celebratory tone that might ignore the social, economic and environmental disbenefits of location, design and development decisions. The approach is to understand why things did not happen as much as accounting for why they did. In this way, the book contributes to an established historical discourse on cities 'that might have been'.

As the first book to try and capture the national dimension of the city beautiful, this work inevitably will be seen to complement my earlier history of the Australian chapter of another of the great global forces for urban reform, the garden city movement.[38] It is similarly concerned with setting the Australian scene in an international setting, concentrates on the years before World War II, and provides a typological and geographical matrix to help chart the extent of impacts on the ground. But whereas the garden city influence was predominantly suburban, the city beautiful idea, while embracing the suburbs, tended to focus on the central business district and environs. In strongly monocentric cities, here were the flagship urban spaces which represented the centre of both commercial power and cultural activity. This book also differs from the earlier work in eschewing an all-encompassing documentation in favour of a more representative treatment. Much of the detail awaits further research. Without making this a history of urban beautification in the widest possible sense, this stance acknowledges the importance of local action and the many more stories awaiting recapture. This book hopefully provides an initial framework in which they might be situated.

Designing Australia's Cities draws on numerous primary and secondary sources. Two key journals were *Architecture* (from 1917), which begun publication as the *Journal of the Institute of Architects of New South Wales* in 1904, and *Building* (from 1907), a Sydney-based commercial publishing venture started by George Taylor.[38] None of the projects recorded in these and other historic documents was the singular outcome of city beautiful thinking, and outcomes often involved convoluted sequences of events over several years if not decades. The primary interest here is how ideas that can be associated with the larger aesthetics and ideology of the city beautiful movement helped shape, if only momentarily, the pathway toward realisation. While the intention is to provide a national coverage, there is some skewing towards my home base on the east coast, which also happens to be where some of the biggest stories unfolded.

The scene is set in the next chapter through first reiterating the international context of the city beautiful and then in an overview chapter surveying the way in which Australia prepared itself for the new aesthetic makeover promised by the emergence of the modern town planning movement. A closing chapter considers continuities and discontinuities beyond the city beautiful heyday as well as the fate of the aesthetic thrust in the later planning movement. The core nine chapters of the book survey manifestations in theory and practice, primarily from the early 1900s into the early 1930s when city beautiful ideas were at their most popular and the planning movement was a

Beautifying the commonplace: former electricity substation,
Carlton, Melbourne

relatively coherent mix of shared ideas and values, personalities, and institutions. This stability would be terminally ruptured, first by the Great Depression and then by World War II. The old guard would be largely forgotten as new advances in planning theory were adapted to a new set of circumstances.

The thematic organisation of chapters is informed by *The American Vitruvius: An Architects' Handbook of Civic Art* (1922) by Werner Hegemann and Elbert Peets. This book appeared when the city beautiful movement was past its prime in the United States, but offered a remarkable compendium of projects with high aesthetic content extending well beyond superficial monumentalism into college campuses, civic centres, street art, city plans, residential communities, and park systems. A similar typology is employed here. The classification of certain schemes proves a little difficult in some cases, as centres segue into spaces, memorials feature in parkland settings, and multi-purpose schemes are hatched. The complexity and contestation of some projects will be apparent, and some of these narratives are pursued for bigger projects. But the major aim is to interconnect projects large and small in a way that has never been done to reveal shared common values and aspirations, and refresh them as part of a broader social movement of historical significance in the shaping and making of Australian cities and planning.

CHAPTER 2

America
and the world

The Town Planning Conference of the Royal Institute of British Architects (RIBA) held in London in 1910 brought together for the first time many of the leading global players in the emergent profession, including the Americans Daniel Burnham and Charles Mulford Robinson, the Frenchman Eugène Hénard, the German Joseph Stubben, and the British Raymond Unwin, Ebenezer Howard and Thomas Mawson. The proceedings are a rich record of papers, reports, and speeches defining the state of the art of the fledgling global planning movement and revealing different national planning cultures. There are diverse concerns, including design of public spaces, town-extension planning, garden suburb development, provision of open spaces, civic ornamentation, regulation of advertising, and legislative approaches. John Simpson, RIBA secretary-general, noted that planning 'has different meanings in different mouths' but that a key role of the planner is to satisfy all these various requirements 'and to create in doing so a work of art'.[1] The conception of the city as a work of art was not new.[2] Delegates could have identified some major landscapes in world cities that all would have found memorable: Domenico Fontana's axial thoroughfares slashed through late 16th century Rome, John Nash's regency planning in London from the late 18th century, Karl Friedrich Schinkel's neo-classicism in early 19th century Berlin, and

Baron Haussmann's celebrated Parisian boulevards from the 1870s. All had powerful patrons but what surfaced in London in 1910 was a wider interest in less authoritarian models.

The rise of interest in interrelating beauty and planning as a global movement had different strands, including civic art (major buildings and public spaces), civic design (master planning), and civic improvement (upgrading of towns).[3] These different responses took shape via a global diffusion and adaptation of ideas facilitated by study tours, conferences, international consultancies, books and journals. This chapter surveys this internationalisation. It devotes most attention to the United States, the exemplar of the city beautiful in the crusade against ugliness coinciding with the emergence of modernist urban planning, and Great Britain, where the approach to aesthetic questions would constitute an influential force as Australia's 'mother country'.

The American city beautiful movement

City beautiful thinking surfaced enthusiastically in the United States around the turn of the 19th century as a middle-class 'clean-up, paint-up, fix-up' idea propelled by the ugliness of the American city. It interconnected with other reform impulses to lay a foundation for the emergence of comprehensive urban planning. For reformers, the problems were self-evident:

> Our American cities are lacking in unity of purpose and harmony of design. The desire for immediate pecuniary results, the dominance of commercial motives, the assertiveness of powerful individuals, lacking artistic education, and the scorn of public supervision have made of the typical American city a miscellany of dingy warehouses, tawdry shops, squalid tenements, tasteless mansions, usually monotonous but sometimes variegated streets. There is not unity, but neither is there pronounced individuality, only restlessness.[4]

The aesthetic commitments of the city beautiful were an eclectic mix of mannered formality and natural beauty. Trees, parks and other informal green spaces were indispensable, as CM Robinson conveyed:

> In the mental picture of a beautiful city or village, the tree has

'Chaos': the artistic tragedy of ad hoc building development. *Architectural Review (New York, 1904) in W Hegemann and E Peets, The American Vitruvius, 1922*

an inseparable part. Tree-lined avenues, tree-arched streets, the background of foliage to well-placed sculpture, the softening of stern facades, the play of light and shadow on the pavement, the screening of the sun's glare upon walk and window, the lovely chronicle of the season's progress as it is written on the tree where all can read it – these are factors of beauty thrusting themselves at once upon the mind as requisite to success. They are universal in appeal.[5]

Architecturally, inspiration was drawn variously from Renaissance geometry, the imperialism of ancient Rome, and the haussmannisation of Paris. The preferred neo-classical architecture offered continuity with the grand civilisations of the past as well as a link to the contemporary monumentalism of European cities. Many of the leading city beautiful architects studied at the esteemed École des Beaux Arts in Paris. Here they acquired the requisite design skills of composition, regularity, rectilinearity, and symmetry to visually express unity, order, power, and control.

But there was more at stake than aesthetics. Efforts were directed ultimately to renewal of the urban fabric in the interests of social stability and economic development at a time of rapid urban growth. This aligned city beautiful aspirations to the Progressive movement in urban politics, with its wider agenda of efficiency, technocracy, morality and loyalty. The link was made between a city's moral state and its physical appearance. There was a strong environmentalist belief that beauty had the ameliorative power to improve human thought and behaviour, but that was about as radical as it got. Promoters of civic art and design were content to work within existing power structures. Capturing this acceptance of capitalism were city plans which outside the set design pieces left the city to market forces. Public education to improve receptiveness to and understanding of aesthetic improvements was a vital cog in the city beautiful movement. J Horace McFarland, a Harrisburg businessman and leading light in the American Civic Association, tirelessly travelled the country on a crusade against urban blight and disorder, delivering 400 lectures between 1904 and 1924.[6] Even critics of the message conceded that an interest in civics stirred by city beautiful plans 'played an indispensable part in promoting the general idea of planning'.[7]

Events and trends pointed the way through the 19th century. There was no single wellspring. Visions of better ways of citymaking came first hand from travels through European capitals and were also conjured up by utopian novels like *Looking Backward* (1888) in which Edward Bellamy envisaged a future Boston divorced from contemporary ugliness and social ills:

> Miles of broad streets, shaded by trees and lined with fine buildings, for the most part not in continuous blocks but set in larger or smaller enclosures, stretched in every direction. Every quarter contained large open squares filled with trees, along which statues glistened and fountains flashed in the late-afternoon sun. Public buildings of a colossal size and architectural grandeur ... raised their stately piles on every side.[8]

The World's Columbian Exposition staged to celebrate the 400th anniversary of the European discovery of the Americas captured this image. Held on the Chicago lakefront in 1893, it was staged in purpose-

World's Columbian Exposition, Chicago, 1893. *Photographer - CD Arnold.*
Chicago History Museum, ICHi - 25216.

built but temporary buildings designed largely in neo-classical style and arranged artistically around public spaces, water basins, lagoons and sculpture. Local architect Daniel Burnham choreographed the whole affair with assistance from landscape architect Frederick Law Olmsted, sculptor Augustus Saint-Gaudens, and a bevy of heavyweight architects. 'Nowhere, at no time that history has any record of, was there ever grouped together so perfect and impressive an array of structures … the very apotheosizing of art', gushed FW Fitzpatrick.[9] In dramatic contrast to the chaos of the commercial city beyond the site of the fair, it sent a powerful message about the possibilities of artistic city planning:

> The secret of its perfection was not so much the beauty of the individual structures as their perfect and studied relation to each other. They were so planned that each building held an integral relationship to the ground scheme of the whole.[10]

Chicago's Michigan Avenue as the Champs Élysées of the American
Midwest. *Plan of Chicago, 1909*

The leading architectural critic of the day, Montgomery Schuyler, recognised its aesthetic power in dreading copycat reproduction of 'a miniature plaza, with a little Administration Building and a little Machinery Hall' across urban America.[11] This did happen and the so-called 'White City' also set the mould for later expositions to make their mark as model urban environments. The St Louis Fair of 1904 was dubbed the 'Ivory City'.

Jon Peterson identifies other early strands energised in different towns and cities across America: the municipal art movement based around designer adornment through sculpture, murals, and stained glass; civic improvement expressing populist moves toward clean-up campaigns in which women played a leading role; and outdoor art which bridged the rise of landscape architecture and the parks movement.[12] These elements came together through the 1890s. As important as the Chicago exposition, came a second watershed in the US Senate Park Commission plan for Washington, DC in 1902. Burnham was again the central figure, alongside Saint-Gaudens, Frederick Law Olmsted Jr, and the New York beaux arts architect Charles McKim. Seeking inspiration for its resuscitation of the L'Enfant plan, the commission journeyed to Europe to take in Paris, Venice, Vienna, Budapest, Frankfurt, Berlin, Rome and London. Their proposals had two main elements: a replanned ceremonial core and an extensive metropolitan park system. Applied to a real city, albeit the special case of a national capital, this exercise in the collaborative arts signposted a comprehensive planning formula taken up through the 1900s.

A third trophy event came at the end of the 1900s: the landmark Plan of Chicago prepared for the Commercial Club of Chicago by Burnham, again, and his partner Edward H Bennett. It appeared on 4 July 1909, American Independence Day. The plan transcended the limitations of the Chicago gridiron by supplying the major missing features: artistic landmarks, radial avenues, lakefront park, cultural and civic centres, forest preserves, and a park system. Firmly on the commercial side were extensive transportation proposals including a regional highway system, improved public transit, and freight-handling centres. Expunged from the final report was a concern for the everyday city, including housing.[13] The sumptuous plan set new production standards. It was more like the catalogue of an art

exhibition than a planning report. Nearly half of over 140 illustrations were specifically prepared. Strikingly original illustrations by École des Beaux Arts-trained artist Jules Guerin evoked a magical future city. Peterson nonetheless judges the plan a failure through Burnham being unable to fully reconcile 'his functional ethic with his civic-aesthetic sense'.[14] The rationality of the transportation infrastructure proposals were overpowered by the utterly unrealistic civic centre and didactic symmetrical remodelling of the central city. Nonetheless, many of the street, bridge and park elements of the plan were implemented to 1930 under the supervision of Edward H Bennett for the Chicago Plan Commission.

Through the 1900s came a string of city beautiful-style city plans, usually commissioned by business and voluntary organisations. The spectrum of styles is best defined by the contrasting approaches of Burnham and Robinson. As is evident in both his Chicago and earlier San Francisco (1905) plans, Burnham was the 'Olympian Ideal-

Senate Park Commission replanning of Washington, 1902.
US Fine Arts Commission

ist' striving for the grand statement and pitching to the top end of
town. 'Make no little plans', he wrote, 'they have no magic to stir men's
blood'. By contrast, CM Robinson appealed to the higher calling of
moral improvement. His interventions were more modestly scaled. He
favoured a more 'relaxed formality' than Burnham. With his roots in
small-scale urban improvement, he endorsed more 'naturalistic' and
'attainable' goals, being especially fond of park-like street vistas.[15]

There were six recurring elements in city beautiful planning: the
civic centre, the gateway railroad station, the processional boulevard,
the belt parkway, the outer park system, and the public playground.[16]
Such attributes defined 'the structural skeleton of the city beautiful'.[17]
Alongside, came a standard list of small-scale physical improvements
like public squares, new street furniture, civic embellishments such

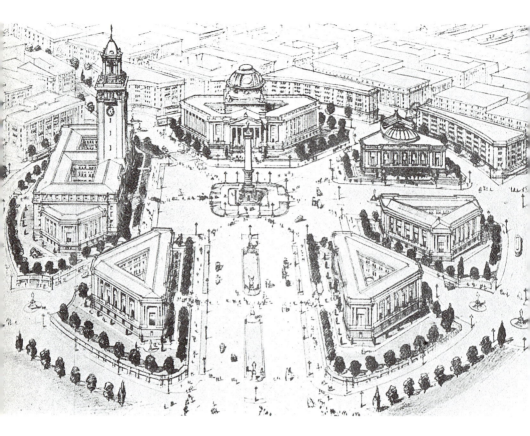

Civic Centre project, Seattle.
J Sulman, Town Planning in Australia, 1921

as statuary, fountains and triumphal arches, tree planting, and more regulatory elements like building-height and billboard controls. War memorials as civic improvements also 'would not have been possible without the City Beautiful ideology'.[18]

The civic centre was the city beautiful *par excellence*. Along with belief in the importance of neo-classical architecture and reverence for natural beauty, grouped public buildings have been described as the third 'major aesthetic commitment' of the city beautiful movement.[19] The civic centre captured all the broader aesthetic, ideological, and functional goals of the planning movement, and was a veritable simulacrum of the ideal city. By the 1910s it had become 'a passion' in American cities.[20] The architect Frank Koester wrote in 1915:

> The advantage of the planning of a city on the principle of civic
> centers is indeed so great, that no other kind of plan receives any
> consideration. The fundamental principle of city planning is the civic
> center, and when the center has been properly planned and placed,
> the remainder of the design is readily worked out.[21]

The dominant image is of a beautiful ensemble of classically-inspired
structures grouped around open spaces or at the intersection of axial
boulevards according to beaux arts principles. But there were many
variations on this theme. The development of some centres spanned
decades and involved many of the most famous names in planning
history. The Cleveland 'Group Plan' (1903), by the ubiquitous Burnham
in association with fellow architects John Carrère and Arnold Brunner,
was the first significant city beautiful plan after Washington.[22] The
realisation of Frank Lloyd Wright's 'dream civic center' in Madison
was an extraordinary decades-long saga of big names and matching
egos, personality clashes, delays, and design and cost blow-outs which
mired the civic centre idea deeply in urban politics.[23]

At the other end of the impact spectrum, and in a more low-key
way, the implementation of controls on advertising billboards from the
1900s also registers the influence of the city beautiful. Billboards were
frowned upon 'for their lurid content, their pervasiveness, their scenic
desecration, their physical danger, their threats against the home,
their encouragement of littering, and their invitation to criminality'.
Few advocates believed there could be an 'easy resolution of commerce
and comeliness' in this campaign and worked for state regulation.[24]
Billboards did not disappear, but the crusade spawned special zoning
and other regulations as the climate of public and industry opinion
changed.

The city beautiful also made for the suburb beautiful as idealistic
developers pursued above-average standards of development to
boost real estate values. Showpiece developments incorporated
elements such as geometrically contrived street systems, major public
squares, grouped civic buildings, internal parkways, and public art.
Examples include JC Nichols' Kansas City Country Club district
(from 1905), Edward Lewis' University City (c1905) near the site of the
World's Fair in St Louis, complete with a cylindrical beaux arts office
building headquartering his publishing empire, and George Merrick's

Mediterranean-style Coral Gables in Florida, with its 'alternation of myriad real estate lots with broad open spaces earmarked for gardens and other public amenities'.[25] Grand public building groups, crescent-shaped roads and generous open spaces were also accommodated in special-purpose industry towns such as Warren (1906) in Arizona.[26]

The city beautiful was the touchstone of the American planning movement in the early 1900s, but the lustre faded. The first National Planning Conference on City Planning in 1909, marking the beginning of professionalisation, was a decisive turning point. Speaker after speaker plumped for the city practical. The anti-congestion campaigner Benjamin Marsh said:

> The grouping of public buildings, and the installation of speedways, parks and drives, which affect only moderately the daily lives of the city's toilers, are important, but vastly more so is the securing of decent home conditions for the countless thousands who otherwise can but occasionally escape from their squalid, confining surroundings … to experience the aesthetic delights of the remote improvements.[27]

Thereafter the phrase city beautiful lost currency and credibility, at least among planners. The foundation of the American City Planning Institute in 1917 closed the door, at least in name. In 1922 John Nolen observed that 'beauty' had been scarcely mentioned at planning conferences for years, suggesting three reasons: fear of popular confusion with a superficial 'planting of geraniums' approach; concern that business interests and city government were antagonistic or apathetic to beauty, and the view that beauty denoted extravagance.[28]

The wider community certainly shared the latter viewpoint, despite the best efforts of city beautiful advocates to sell the 'beautilitarian' basis of their proposals. Some of the more extravagant proposals stretched both credulity and budgets. In the late 1920s while the leading trans-Atlantic planner Thomas Adams and celebrated urbanist Lewis Mumford were at loggerheads over the growth and planning of mega 'dinosaur cities' like New York, they did agree that the city beautiful was by then marginal to urban debates. Adams saw its message as creating a public misperception of planning as representing high expenditures on fanciful luxuries rather than addressing more basic needs of shelter and sanitation. CM Mumford regarded city beautiful plans as 'all form and no content' – cosmetic follies ignoring real community needs and problems.[29]

The city beautiful lacked the comprehensiveness to which city planning aspired. It tended to ignore social welfare concerns and left issues like affordable housing for others to solve. Proponents promoted beauty as an inherent social right while at the same time they consistently upheld 'utility as the foundation of their efforts'.[30] But their balancing of beauty and utility was ultimately flawed. Beauty was code for a range of values: local pride, patriotism, cleanliness, social caring, good government, and morality. Yet no such enumeration of rhetorical social benefits could counter the huge expenditures sometimes involved. The pioneers realised this but were remarkably coy about cost details, usually deflecting criticism by advocating incremental implementation over long time periods.

Some advocates stuck to their guns. École-trained Edward Bennett left Burnham to establish his own practice in 1910 and produced a series of plans for cities, including Portland (1913), Minneapolis (1917) and Pasadena (1923), embodying his philosophy that the highest calling of planning was to craft beautiful settings for human society. His 1921 plan for Joliet on the banks of the Des Plaines River in Illinois conveyed all the right sentiments that 'city planning is economy' but the images of a European-style river city underscored his final word: 'to make our city loved we must make it lovely'. Joan Draper concluded that Bennett never satisfactorily integrated the aesthetic and the scientific. While 'zoning and traffic studies issued forth from the office ... Bennett frequently occupied himself at the drafting table or in the conference room with upholding the ideals of the City Beautiful Movement'.[31]

Supplanted by more pragmatic paradigms through the professionalisation of the planning movement, the city beautiful endured as a city planning issue into the 1930s in the subsidiary realm of 'civic art'. Harland Bartholomew's stock-standard city planning methodology revolved around investigation of six key issues: streets, transit, rail and water transportation, public recreation, zoning, and, lastly, civic art.[32] He wrote in his plan for Memphis (1924) that the fundamental issues were economic and social, but initiatives such as the grouping of public buildings, regulation of poles, wires, signs and billboards, and street

A global city beautiful:
the World Centre for
Communication project,
1913. *G Taylor, Town
Planning for Australia, 1914*

Culture versus commerce: the Dewey Arch in
Madison Square, New York. *Municipal Affairs,
June 1900*

tree planting – provided they were not too costly – could contribute to the city's appearance – and hence add to its 'drawing power'.[33]

Completion or incremental realisation of earlier projects sustained the spirit of the city beautiful into the 1930s and even 1940s. Parkways became state-of-the-art road engineering (until the arrival of the interstate highway system). The design of structures such as bridges, buildings and railway stations perpetuated a beaux arts flavour also evident in projects of the federal Works Progress Administration. In New York city, the architect Robert Stern has traced how the city beautiful idea was reshaped 'to meet the functionalist challenge of European International Style Modernism'.[34] The massing and symmetry of the Rockefeller Center is the outstanding example. The New York Regional Plan released on the eve of the Depression was the successor to the 1909 Chicago plan, with its own expansive prospectus of public works, including visionary civic centre and river transformation proposals. The same vision of a region – not just a city – as both beautiful and useful can also be traced into the Tennessee Valley plan under the New Deal.

Continental Europe

Nineteenth century continental European cities were a key source for the American city beautiful movement. A considerable theoretical body of work on city design had already been evolved by urbanists such as Charles Buls, author of *Aesthetics of Cities* (1898). There were spirited debates on urban form and structure, the most iconic between the Viennese contemporaries Camillo Sitte and Otto Wagner. As a 'conservator-protagonist of an artisan-made environment', Sitte seemed unable to satisfactorily reconcile the modern and the artistic. He saw modern city planning as too geometric, formulaic, materialistic and bureaucratic. By contrast, Otto Wagner looked to the future rather than the past, valuing rationality, functionality, and uniformity. Sitte saw the Ringstrasse in Vienna as 'a cold sea of traffic-dominated space'. Wagner like many others saw it as a step toward the planned modernisation initiated in Paris by Haussmann.[35]

The de-medievalisation of Paris had commenced before Baron Haussmann was appointed Prefect of the Seine in 1853 to oversee arguably the greatest urban renewal project in history. But his name is inseparable from the memorable assemblage of wide streets, star points and monumental vistas that defined planning in the grand manner. Paris was transformed into an almost permanent construction zone, with implementation of Haussmann's work continuing into the 1920s. Haussmann was a classicist in architectural taste, but the significance of his large-scale interventions lies more in the all-of-a-piece aesthetic uniformity imposed through regulation. Using secret and unorthodox financing methods, which created a massive long-term debt for the city, Haussmann's work also confirmed the embourgeoisation of the central city with the working class displaced to the suburbs; tourists became more visible than the poor.[36]

Exporting the city beautiful

The Haussmann approach was copied in other French cities, such as Marseilles, Lyon and Lille, as well as being exported abroad. Haussmann was consulted by mayor Jules Anspach of Brussels about that city's plans to cover over a waterway through the city centre with a boulevard flanked by apartment blocks. Through a variety of cultural and colonial linkages, cities such as Rio de Janiero, Hanoi, and Thessaloniki looked to France for planning inspiration. Without leaving Paris, Joseph Antoine Bouvard reconceived Istanbul through an arbitrarily artistic plan based around a disconnected series of set-piece monuments.[37] Into the 1920s grand manner plans could mingle various influences – evident in JCN Forestier's projects for Buenos Aires (1924) and Havana (1926), which drew upon both Haussmann and the American city beautiful.[38]

The turn-of-the-century presidency of Theodore Roosevelt cast the United States 'as a civiliser of the world'.[39] Opportunities arose for architects and planners to export their expertise via city and institutional plans, engineering works, and architectural commissions. City beautiful influences inevitably surfaced through its American heyday. In the thick of things again was Daniel Burnham, lured on an imperial mission to the Philippines in 1904–05 to prepare plans for the redevelopment of Manila and the hill town of Baguio, which he conceived as a Washington in miniature.[40] Elsewhere in Asia, Chiang Kai-shek's vision for Shanghai as a premier world city drew upon Washington and New Delhi with its cruciform axes, memorials and crescents of public buildings. The master plan was the work of Chao Chein, a graduate of the University of Pennsylvania.[41] Working more unobtrusively were other Americans such as Henry Murphy, a member of the Municipal Society of New York, who prepared city beautiful-style plans for Guangzhou and Nanjing in 1927–28, along with college campus plans merging Chinese and western influences for Beijing, Shanghai, Suzhou, Fuzhou and Nanjing.[42]

Such direct impositions were resisted in continental Europe. Steeped in their own traditions, European cities shared little enthusiasm for re-importing the ersatz inspirations of the New World. The French were completely unimpressed, although the pillaging of beaux arts principles had not gone unnoticed.[43] Up to World War II, the United States 'had little to offer Europe'.[44] Nevertheless, the projects of Burnham and others may have been a timely reminder for Europeans as to 'the qualities of their own towns'.[45] The American emphasis on parks, park systems and parkways in ordering the city, the production of handsome planning reports, and community-driven civic improvement campaigns were being noticed.

The authoritarian landscape

Authority everywhere was receptive to bombast, with planned capital city landscapes disarmingly sharing the rationality and modernity of more democratic conceptions, albeit in overdrive. Largely designed by British architect Edwin Lutyens, New Delhi was to be the showpiece of the British Empire on the sub-continent. A formal classical plan of fanning radial boulevards and polygonal geometry suggested 'uncanny similarities with L'Enfant's plan for Washington'.[46]

The recurring design vocabulary of authoritarian planning was an assemblage of ceremonial axes, lavish neo-classical buildings, and nationalistic artwork, breaking with historical continuities to showcase political prestige and power in new, monumental settings. Massed structures and grand spaces had an obvious appeal to authoritarian regimes seeking to transcend the fragmentation and backwardness of the old order. The centrepiece of Albert Speer's New Berlin for the Third Reich was a five-mile-long, 400 feet wide north-south boulevard, with an associated Great Hall and triumphal arch.[47] Mussolini's new Roman empire was headquartered at the Esposizione Universale di Roma, an efficient and clinical town centre of muted classical inspiration. A 'pall of repugnant ideological implications' may well have helped to suppress civic art enthusiasm for a generation as designers became more circumspect about such projects.[48]

Canada

One country destined to be influenced by American city beautiful developments was its northern neighbour. Similar stimuli inter-mingled – the Worlds Columbian Exposition, the repulsion at urban ugliness, and most certainly the inspiration of Paris. Interest was fostered by top-down political interest, professional encounters, and popular involvements.

Political patronage drove the replanning of Ottawa, which was ordained rather than conceived as a capital city, and a city beautiful ethos with beaux arts themes characterised its early 20th century development. The Frederick Todd plan of 1903 with an emphasis on boulevards, parkways, open spaces, and natural beauty sought to align the industrial and aesthetic development of the city. Edward Bennett's plan for Ottawa and adjoining Hull (1915) recommended a major government centre near the parliamentary buildings. A proposed national war memorial drew a memorable and revealing quotation from the 1930s prime minister, McKenzie King: 'I saw at once that I had my Champs Élysées, Arc de Triomphe and Place de la Concorde all at a single stroke'.[49] Jacques Greber's regional plan of 1950 also had its monumental qualities. David Gordon argues that these early plans are often too easily dismissed; the background studies for Bennett's plan were 'the basis for plans which transformed the Canadian capital forty years later'.[50]

The aesthetic principles that preoccupied professional architects were coherence (harmony and uniformity), visual variety (vistas and variation in street patterns), and civic grandeur (civic centres and campus plans).[51] These were expressed in tangible form in developments such as Maissoneuve, a new suburban town from 1912 in Montreal, and University Avenue in Toronto, created by a 1929 city plan.

The activities of amateur beautification groups, horticultural societies and improvement associations in street tree planting, public grounds beautification, vacant-lot gardening, and clean-up campaigns were a third, more grassroots, strand to the Canadian city beautiful. Their efforts were spurred not only by the desire to beautify but 'the persuasive reforming zeal of the period', and carried on when official programs failed.[52]

Gilbert Stelter's summation is that the city beautiful in Canada helped foster beauty as a desirable urban characteristic, promoted citizen action, introduced the idea of unified city planning, and produced some solid results on the ground. Its mission was undermined by naiveté in the ways of urban politics, the disruptive and draining impact of World War I, a lack of financial realism, and the pull of competing urban visions.[53] Aesthetic reforms also tended to ignore other pressing demands such as housing shortages and the need for better subdivision regulations. The trend of planning in Canada from the 1910s shows the same shift toward a more utilitarian, pragmatic emphasis as in the United States. Planners sought a new conception of beauty integrated within the city plan. The dominant mainstream voice of Thomas Adams argued in 1920 that 'orderly development' through planning and zoning 'will produce beauty without seeking beauty as an end in itself'.[54]

New Zealand

New Zealand as another British dominion had its quota of city beautiful rhetoric, civic centre proposals and war memorial projects.[55] The architect JF Munnings addressed the First New Zealand Town Planning

Conference on 'The City Beautiful', adopting an eclectic definition from 'the smallest article of use' to 'the greatest and noblest conceptions of man' and exhorting his peers to expend 'every effort' to make the country's existing towns 'more beautiful in every respect'.[56]

A national network of town-based beautifying, conservation and scenic protection societies was a distinctive element in New Zealand. These emerged in the late 19th century, became loosely connected with the emerging town planning movement, and subsequently evolved toward gardening and horticultural societies.[57] The Christchurch Beautifying Association campaigned against public advertisements and for tree planting, promoted private and public gardening, and urged the beautification of public squares. From 1924 it issued a journal called *City Beautiful*, comprising a mix of articles on practical gardening and beautifying issues with the odd contribution on town planning and architecture. The core aim was 'to make life a brighter and sweeter thing for the citizens of Christchurch' through advocacy in which 'no matter will be too small'.

Great Britain

The history of planning in Great Britain is dominated by public health reforms, the garden city movement, the passage of town planning legislation, and countryside preservation. Aesthetics were allied but more muted, and more obviously associated with the architectural profession. Civic art and design were almost invisible in Patrick Abercrombie's *Town and Country Planning* (1933) except as historical preamble, but they gathered more visibility from the 1930s as notions of townscape became more compelling, in part as response to the spread of garden suburbs.

The vision of a city beautiful as a planning goal was promulgated by early leaders in the field. The distinguished architect Sir Aston Webb assembled contemporary ideals in a word picture of the ideal city to be built 'under the guidance of a Commission of leading citizens and artists':

> The centre is on an eminence facing south. Round it are grouped the municipal buildings ... the centre is laid out in terraces and

flower gardens with fountains ... the buildings have statues of famous citizens forming part of their architectural decoration. Trees are planted around .... From an archway in the centre of the south side of the square a great avenue some 200 feet wide starts ... The great avenue forms also a park-like promenade for the citizens and binds the whole city together as a unit ...Outside this avenue lie the professional and commercial centres. The streets running east and west ... are the shop streets with tramways ... Further south is a belt of park land with a drive round the city in which are theatres and refreshment rooms ... the residential streets running north and south, so that the houses may get all the sun, for in 'the city beautiful' the inhabitants believe 'where the sun does not enter the doctor does'. The residential portion is small in proportion, for with increased locomotion facilities, more people live away; and for the same reason no huge barracks of dwellings for the working classes are required ... Two railway stations off the centre Mall, with large places in front, stop important vistas ... Churches and other places of worship are all given important positions, ending vistas or marking the junction of important roads ... In the residential quarter there is a total absence of front walls and railings, but instead grass margins to footways, and hedges mark the boundaries ... No advertisements are allowed except on special places appointed for them, and even shop names and signs have to be submitted to the commission, as do all lamp posts, letter boxes, and other designs.[58]

Webb did his personal best to dress-up central London in grand fashion in his work at Buckingham Palace, Admiralty Arch, and The Mall. His vision of the ideal city was shared by many of his peers, nowhere more so than in Liverpool, which emerged as an extraordinary locus of activity.

Britain's first degree in planning was established within the Department of Civic Design at the University of Liverpool in 1909. The *Town Planning Review* under the founding editorship of lecturer Patrick Abercrombie became a vital organ on all aspects of planning and design. These initiatives were underwritten with a generous endowment by the local businessman William Lever, whose own Port Sunlight model village bore the impress of a city beautiful-style classicization at a time when suburban planning was dominated by a more informal aesthetic.[59] Liverpool staged a 'City Beautiful' conference in 1907, formed a pioneering City Guild to work for city improvement in 1910, and the city engineer, John A Brodie, who was involved in the planning of New Delhi, worked towards a city-wide system of ring boulevards. Perhaps Liverpool's status as an Atlantic port served as a conduit for the introduction of progressive American ideas.

A key figure at Liverpool was architecture professor Charles Reilly. With an urbane and cosmopolitan view of city life drawn from the inspirations of Paris, the beaux arts, and the Worlds Columbian Exposition, he conceived the emerging discipline of planning as an aesthetic activity working in partnership with concerns of traffic and sewerage 'which have till now completely held the field'.[60] His colleague Stanley Adshead, the first Lever Professor of Civic Design, shared these views. Adshead contributed a series of articles on 'The Decoration and Furnishing of the City' to the *Town Planning Review* in 1912–14. His discussion of even the humblest 'utilitarian furnishings' such as telephone boxes, newspaper kiosks and public lavatories lamented how such items were 'thrown about' with no connection to a city plan. The distinguished landscape architect Thomas Mawson also lectured part-time at the University of Liverpool. His background was as a nurseryman and garden designer and he equated planning as civic art. Mawson was offered prestigious commissions, including Lord Lever's 'Beautiful Bolton' campaign, and was active in 'stirring up an interest in civic betterment' through many public addresses. He was active abroad, particularly in Canada where he produced a number of overly ambitious civic centre and campus plans. Mawson admired the American city beautiful; he personally found Burnham an individual 'with all the simplicity and modesty of those truly great' and regarded his Chicago plan as 'stupendous'. He felt CM Robinson had authored 'the most delightful works on modern civic art in the English language'.[61]

The maintenance of high aesthetic standards of development could be delivered by different mechanisms. The president of the local government board, John Burns, in introducing the *Housing, Town Planning Etc Act 1909* into the British Parliament saw its gains in 'the home healthy, the house beautiful, the town pleasant, the city dignified, and the suburb salubrious', although in practice it became enmeshed in administrative regulation. Voluntary organisations such as the

A British civic complex: Cathays Park, Cardiff.
Architecture, March 1938

Birmingham Civic Society worked locally for more beautiful towns in the manner of American improvement associations.[62] Following the example of the Commission of Fine Arts for Washington, DC (1910), royal fine arts commissions were instituted for England (1924) and Scotland (1927) to report on matters of public amenity and 'artistic expression' referred to them, such as the design of monuments and modification of public buildings. Early members of the English body included Aston Webb, Edwin Lutyens, and Thomas Mawson.[63]

City beautiful ideas were also expressed in various development projects. The two most notable were the Kingsway in London and Cathays Park in Cardiff. The Kingsway project, carried out by London County Council in 1905–20, was the most significant civic improvement undertaken in London since the construction of Regent Street in the early 19th century. It involved a new thoroughfare, three-quarters of a mile long and 100 feet wide, a subway for trams and underground railway line, and sites for new commercial buildings in a slum clearance involving the displacement and re-housing of thousands of people at a net cost of £2 million. The aesthetics of the project drew inspiration from imperial London as well as the stripped neo-classical commercial architecture of the late city beautiful. In spirit there was also a debt to Haussmann's work, 'to such an extent that it became the kind of location an impoverished film crew might choose to make a Maigret film without going to Paris'.[64]

Cathays Park was a grouping of major public buildings on a prominent 58-acre site acquired by Cardiff City Council in the late 1890s. It was a grand gesture expressing how the city saw itself – as the Chicago of Britain. The complex was initiated with the new City Hall and Law Courts by Lanchester, Stewart and Rickards, in the Edwardian Baroque style. Adshead criticised what he saw as ill-informed departures from the original site plan, but Mawson's judgment was more favourable: 'Unquestionably the finest example of forethought, enterprise and grasp of the underlying principles which make for civic art which this country can at present show'.[65] Other civic centre complexes would follow, including Southampton and Nottingham (both from 1929), but the real enthusiasm awaited the end of World War II.

Despite these ventures, compared to continental Europeans and the Americans, the British generally seemed more interested in municipal housing schemes than civic splendour. Australian planner John Sulman observed this in the early 1920s. He characterised the British planning movement as 'rather humanitarian than artistic … the artistic self-expression of the town or city taking a secondary place', noting only some attempts to give new town halls 'a proper setting'.[66] A British engineer explained this lukewarmness as a national trait: 'We are proud to consider ourselves a practical people, and, unfortunately, ideas of beauty are not bound up with this. Anglo-Saxons are too prone to consider art as a luxury'.[67] Lawrence Weaver in his book on the house and landscape art of Lutyens put it more eloquently:

> The English character does not happily consort with visions of the Grand Manner. We are so desperately afraid of being pompous that our schemes generally issue in a small banality. Much, however, is due to a difference in general attitude towards the fine arts, and to a desperate unwillingness to spend money freely and gracefully on any object which is not utilitarian.[68]

The end of the city beautiful: Demolition of the Panama Pacific International Exposition, 1915. *LA Craig, et al, The Federal Presence, MIT Press, 1984*

Conclusion

The idea of a beautiful city as central goal – or at least a significant by-product – of the emergent profession of modern city planning was an international mission in the early 20th century. An utter surrender to urban artistry proved beyond all but the most authoritarian regimes. The high costs, real and perceived, of this style of urban development, was one constraint, just as the silences on certain urban problems were another. Others had to do with competing political objectives, hostile systems of governance, and obstacles to implementation. Advocates tried to stress both the broader social and immediate tangible benefits that would accompany aesthetic reforms. But after the initial flowering of city beautiful rhetoric, the relationship between beauty and utility was more rigorously scrutinised, with a prioritisation of utilitarian aims widely evident by the 1920s. Nevertheless, the impact on the urban environment was profound, albeit refracted through a diversity of planning cultures as each nation 'drew according to its own needs and possibilities'.[69] The city beautiful idea is connected with landmark public buildings, civic spaces and park systems as well as numerous small-scale beautification impacts in many cities around the world.

For inspiration in the early 20th century, Australia could look to many countries. The glamour cities of continental Europe could not help but provide a benchmark for the city as a work of art. The United States boasted brash projects and at the same time an underlying strength in community engagement. Pulling in a different direction, Great Britain was more restrained but sporadically produced impressive statements of imperialistic design. Other British dominions picked and mixed, with Canada in a comparable position to Australia in its openness to both new world and old world influences. Many other countries were doing similar things to reinforce a global phenomenon, but geographic and cultural distances made them less influential. The international federal capital design competition of 1911–12 which produced Canberra did provide a lens on what the rest of the world was thinking, but at the end of the day the planning agenda had still to be written locally.

CHAPTER 3

The Australian scene

When the planning advocate Charles Reade noted that 'the early conception of Town Planning ... manifested itself not at all dissimilarly to antecedent developments in America and Europe', he was referring to the global impulse toward 'spectacular conceptions' of town design.[1] In Australia, the goal of the city beautiful was articulated through various channels, with professional and bureaucratic discourse staking out the main turf. Top-down endorsement facilitated initiation and at least partial implementation of some projects, but lacked the sustained patronage that was so often the clue to success abroad. A host of local organisations periodically pursued urban beautification: chambers of commerce, Rotary clubs, local councils, and sundry town planning, progress and improvement associations. While individuals interconnected through professional, political and social networks, there was no organised populist, political movement – no networked 'league of civic aesthetic self respect' that art critic JS MacDonald (who had lived in New York in the early 1900s) had anticipated in 1913.[2] The aesthetic turn which arose in the 19th century and segued into the urban planning rubric of the early 20th was a more informally shared impulse of connected plans, ideas, patriotism, ideologies, and civic pride dominated by built environment professionals with a supporting but shifting cast of progressive state and local officials.

The term city beautiful helped organise and consolidate moves toward city improvement. It was never precisely defined, and was easy pickings for a city like Adelaide wanting to hype its municipal beautification and parkland policies. A lecture by the town clerk, TG Ellery, on 'The City Beautiful' in the Adelaide town hall in August 1904 was a standing-room-only affair: 'If the lecturer had withheld his explanatory remarks some of his auditors might have imagined themselves gazing on Parisian landscapes!'[3] The term was often used by the media in reporting design issues up to World War I. It was shorthand for the planning cause generally, and its distinctiveness from the garden city movement blurred in the popular imagination. Herein lay a strength in promoting public interest in and support for town planning. This was picked up by an editorial in *The West Australian* in June 1912:

> It is only of later years that the idea of the city beautiful has impressed itself firmly on the civic imagination. Even now, in many instances, it is but the germ of an idea, not the branched tree that has fructified into realization. But the seed has been planted, and there is no municipal ground so stony that it will refuse to blossom.[4]

This chapter, the longest in the book, provides a national overview of the origins and major aesthetic and ideological elements of city beautiful thought. It introduces some of the main actors and promotional methods to set further the scene for the more thematic and place-based chapters which follow.

Origins of an Australian city beautiful ethic

The city beautiful was not an overnight sensation and can be thought of as the culmination of several developments going back to the early colonial period. These included inspirational and utopian visions for better planned cities, increasing professional concern over the general aesthetic condition of cities, the beautification possibilities raised by special events, the interest of entrepreneurs, and local beautification efforts. I look briefly at each in turn.

Visions of better cities went back to the earliest days of settlement. Convict architect Francis Greenway imagined a future Sydney Town

19th century dreams: Victoria Square proposal for city markets site, Sydney.
Australasian Builder and Contractors' News, May 1887

with radiating avenues from the principal 'metropolitan church' (the present site of St Andrew's Cathedral) and Hyde Park as a 'grand quadrangle' surrounded by public buildings. Allen Francis Gardiner (aka TJ Maslen) in *The Friend of Australia* (1830) foreshadowed an ideal colonial town not unlike Adelaide, encircled by parkland with a hierarchy of verandah-ed and tree-shaded streets, elegant public edifices, wide and spacious squares, freestanding churches. One of the most extraordinary tracts was the anonymous 'Melbourne as it is, and as it ought to be' (1850). This indictment of the city's rectilinear plan substituted an array of new principles for a better city layout, drawing from sources such as Wren's 1666 plan for rebuilding London, and European towns such as Bologna. The ideal was a central piazza surrounded by major public buildings from which broad boulevards radiated and intersected with other principal streets to form a network of public squares. Underlying this new geometry was a seminal statement of 'oneness in the requirements of beauty and utility'. 'Beauty is not superadded to utility', stated the anonymous author, 'but arises necessarily out of it'.[5]

With shades of Edward Bellamy's futuristic *Looking Backward*, Australian authors imagined future cities of stately edifices. The writer Ethel Turner turned her imagination to Sydney in 2000. Its green harbour foreshores had gone and a grand statue greeted seafarers at North Head, but the overall scene was of a 'beautiful, spoiled city. Great squares with fountains and statuary occurred at regular intervals; great buildings reared handsome fronts in places here and there – the State Museum, Library, Picture Gallery, the State Stores'.[6] A similar utopian vision continues into the early 1900s and the work of writers such as Louis Esson and artists such as Lloyd Rees, whose *Imaginary City* transformed Brisbane into an antipodean Paris.[7]

More down to earth, concern with the architectural state of the late-colonial city dominated professional journals such as *Australasian Builders and Contractors' News* and *Building and Engineering Journal*. Materialism, apathy, shortsightedness, political interference and indifference were blamed for an increasing catalogue of aesthetic woes, from inharmonious street architecture to tasteless statuary and unsightly telegraph wires. Concern with street advertising was already evident: 'The Bill-poster is in all cities a hideous satire upon our nineteenth century civilisation, and offends against the decencies of appearance as boldly as space and licence will permit him'.[8] A whole culture of city remodelling proposals was cultivated, most dealing with important urban spaces, artistic solutions to transportation problems, and aimed ultimately at enhancing economic competitiveness.[9] Proposals for grand public structures to lift standards were also reported.

Since the Duke of Edinburgh's Australian tour in the late 1860s, state occasions had been catalysts for not only impressive street decorations but also more permanent civic improvements. In Sydney

An Australian Statue of Liberty: 'Australia Facing the Dawn' monument project by John Sulman, 1888. *Mitchell Library, State Library of New South Wales*

a rash of projects was mooted to mark the centenary of British settlement in 1888, including a national monument, state house, new houses of parliament, new public spaces, new streets and statuary. Centennial Park was the outstanding legacy. Ruling artistic tastes were captured fleetingly in elaborate triumphant arches and street pageantry.[10] The 1901 Federation celebrations festooned all state capitals and many smaller regional cities with architect-designed decorations. These events demonstrated the possibilities of more permanent and dramatic city improvement, although the lasting impacts were usually restricted to ceremonial park plantings and modest beautification works such as stabilised embankments and street gardens.

Entrepreneurial interest in urban aesthetic questions did not extend far beyond commercial architecture. But there were projects which indicated a nascent interest in wider questions, such as the design competition for the Kensington Model Suburb in Sydney. The winning design by a team involving architect Walter Liberty

Vernon featured a grand parkway and public squares. The growth of community civic pride in existing suburbs cast a wider social net. The ambitious mission statement of Melbourne's Kalizoic Society picked up a pot-pourri of improver aims:

> The encouragement and cultivation of the beautiful, the planting of trees and flowers in promenades, and also in the city, suburbs, places of public resort, and the laying out of reserves; the protection of all ornamental plants, flowers, trees ... the encouragement of window, cottage or front gardening, the prevention of the pollution of our streams and reservoirs to enlist the sympathies of the professional and general public in improving the appearance of our city and its suburbs by the creation of an artistic taste, and by constituting every citizen a custodian of our gardens, trees and birds.[11]

Named from the Greek words for beauty and life, the Kalizoic Society attracted high-profile support from the artist Tom Roberts, landscape gardener William Guilfoyle, and art critic James Smith.[12] While local community action never expanded into the national networking seen in America, it did constitute a stratum of civic awareness conducive to beautification objectives. Some groups went beyond the usual local amenity concerns. A notable Tasmanian example was the Launceston City and Suburbs Improvement Association (1899), which opened up and maintained Cataract Gorge (the Cliff Grounds). Local memorials erected with public subscriptions and donations were a sporadic form of early civic art that escalated into a nationwide activity after World War I.

Elsewhere, by turn of the 19th century, there were grabs of urban beauty: individual public buildings, botanic gardens, avenues of trees, elite suburbs, and the serendipity of attractive river and harbour settings. Three particular achievements were early beacons of inspiration. One was the King's Parade-Machattie Park complex in Bathurst, in regional New South Wales, based around a government building group designed by Colonial Architect James Barnet. Ballarat's Sturt Street with its central landscaped plantation was also widely cited. And of the capital cities, only Adelaide with its ring of parklands dating from the 1830s had a memorable planned urban form which made a strong case for the benefits of comprehensive civic design.

The approach of modern city planning ideology was signalled by moves to integrate many of the otherwise fragmented concerns of physical urban reform. The major theme was the need for better regulation over buildings and open spaces. The two most visionary statements were by the surveyor John Keily and the architect John Sulman. Apart from a strange diversion into mythological symbolism, Keily's paper read before the Victorian Institute of Surveyors in 1889 provided a scientific treatment, introducing quantitative standards, hierarchical typologies, and technological fixes. He railed against the random scatter of the 'chance system' of town building and endorsed the 'harmonious whole' of planning. All communities should have 'a predominant central feature' in the form of a major public square and grouped civic buildings. This would be supplemented by a series of smaller squares at major intersections, not only for ornamental effect but to accommodate rising traffic volumes.[13]

The seminal critique of chessboard planning was British expatriate architect John Sulman's paper on 'The Laying Out of Towns' delivered to a scientific meeting in Melbourne in 1890. He advocated the alternative radial-concentric lines of the 'spider's web' pattern as a more sensible alternative for both the possibilities of beautification through placement of buildings and the convenience of movement. Street width should be 'ample, both on the score of health and beauty' and tree planting was encouraged as 'a wise sanitary precaution'.[14] Surveyor-statistician George Knibbs developed Sulman's radial city into a rigorous mathematical statement in 1901.[15]

City themes

Most capital cities had their own artistic preoccupations. For example, in Perth, the targets of early city improvement measures were quite diverse and included more parks and gardens, shade trees, the need for foreshore reclamation, and the search for alternatives to an ugly proliferation of verandah posts. The propelling force behind these concerns was the imperative to retain population and wealth created during the gold rush years as the West Australian capital transformed from a big town to the metropolis of the west.

As Brisbane steered into the 20th century, a recurrent concern was how the development of the city centre had failed to realise the opportunities of a splendid riverfront site. Its motley mix of buildings saw undistinguished structures – 'mere shells of small value' – compromising grander public buildings to spoil the outlook to the city from the west.[16] A city so 'artfully set by Nature ... should have given the inspiration for better deeds'.[17]

Sydney developed from the outset as a dense old world seaport rather than a spacious new world settlement, more akin to a Boston than a Chicago. The outcome was evident for all to see: the city was a 'tangle of mean streets and distressful architecture and lost opportunities'.[18] To the rational geometric mind of the early 20th century planner, the incoherent street pattern in the central city was being extended chaotically to the suburbs without producing one notable planned urban space or vista. An underlying tension in Sydney planning in the early 1900s was between the formal remodelling promoted by modern planning and conservation of the informal natural beauty based on the harbour setting. Ad hoc encroachment of the harbour foreshores and ocean beaches – the natural elements that really delivered Sydney's unique beauty – was also lamented.

The fundamental problem in Melbourne was the 'rectangular grimness' of the right-angled gridiron plan of long unbroken streets laid down by the surveyor Robert Hoddle in 1837. In 1901 the horticulturalist Charles Bogue Luffman argued that Melbourne had 'the most uninteresting streets and surroundings of any great town in the world – convenient and clean – nothing more. No view points, no internal spaces, no dignity, no powers of revealing what we are or whence we came'.[19] The main problem according to John Sulman was 'well displayed' but scattered government buildings and 'no definite centre'.[20] The absence of any suitable public square was an almost universally agreed shortcoming among the urban cognoscenti.

Post-colonial aspirations

Informed opinion in architectural and artistic circles held that Australian cities had squandered opportunities to become refined, virtuous and artistic centres of urban civilisation. For all their brash dynamism, Australian cities seemed ugly, dull, and lacking civic pride. They boasted few noble vistas, architectural squares, or open spaces. The emerging central business districts were a chaos of uncoordinated development. The colonial ways of city development were seen as outmoded in the new industrial era. No longer could the activity of expanding cities be facilitated by the inherited roads and buildings of the 'casual and slummocky pioneers', as *The Bulletin* magazine put it. Essential town building and infrastructure needed to be taken care of. The accompanying aesthetic critique sharpened at the very time when resources appeared to become available for the more decorative side of urban improvement. A distinctive phase in urban evolution was thus emerging.

The city beautiful idea helped urban reformers make the vital breakthrough to regarding the whole city rather than any individual structure as the fundamental unit of design. The quest became the 'gleam of a common ideal'.[21] City critiques grew more sophisticated. Bringing 19th century dissatisfactions together in a kind of city beautiful blueprint for Melbourne was the architect William Campbell.[22] The grid plan bestowed 'a monotonous and uninteresting appearance'. Approaches to the city fell short of the noble gateways required. The boulevards failed to pierce the centre proper and the railway stations provided initial impressions of 'crowd, noise, and dirt' rather than 'spaciousness and dignity'. With too many 'abnormal structures', 'lofty erections', and unattractive advertisements disfiguring city blocks, the city's architecture as a whole lacked 'sufficient corps d'esprit'. Public spaces were lacking, and many public buildings found themselves at the corners of streets in positions which did not lend themselves 'to a broad and monumental treatment'. The cutting of new diagonal streets would provide more direct communication, opportunities for architectural treatment, and 'unobstructed sites for special buildings and statuary'. The major inspirations for all of this were overseas cities such as Washington ('planned like a wheel') and Paris ('a constellation of stars').

A lightning rod for civic design and related questions of town improvement was the federal capital project. The idea of a new city arose out of the constitutional debates of the 1890s. This project was vital in focusing professional attention on issues of integrated design.

The 1901 Congress of Engineers, Architects, and Surveyors, held in Melbourne to consider the planning of the projected federal capital, was a landmark event. It was very much a home-grown occasion. International inspiration only lightly dusted proceedings, with Australian aspirations and expertise the order of the day. There were passing references to Athens, Edinburgh, London and Chicago, but more was to come.

The force of overseas example

Progressive ideas for an artistically-inclined planning of the modern city filtered into Australia from Europe and America from the 1890s. Many architects had ties to England and imported a British sensibility. John Sulman was among them, but he also brought a worldly cosmopolitanism when he emigrated in 1885 on a mission to clean up both the cities and the architectural profession. Architects and government officials who had the opportunity to travel overseas experienced first-hand the civic beauty of cities such as Paris, Vienna, and Washington. The European 'grand tour' was de rigueur for many leading citizens and solidified the broadly accepted linkages between neo-classical design and the culture of advanced western civilisation. Architectural and building journals from the 1890s also carried frequent references to the new world, and, increasingly from 1900, reproduced the views of city beautiful identities such as Charles Mulford Robinson and Daniel Burnham.

Although having the greatest impact in North America, the World's Columbian Exposition made an indelible impression on Australian observers able to see it firsthand. Sir Arthur Renwick, the New South Wales government's chief representative, reported enthusiastically on every aspect of exhibition – 'a glorious sight; with its domes, its white palaces, statuary fountains, and electric fountains.[23] New South Wales even had a pavilion, known as Australia House, a 'small but tasteful' classical building fitting the overall architectural style by local luminaries Holabird and Roche, and said to have been inspired by the old General Post Office in Sydney.[24]

The architectural splendour of the Chicago Exposition did not go unnoticed through the 1890s. But its wider planning significance was not appreciated until the early 20th century. Sydney architect John Barlow captured this shift in criticising the classical inspiration of the architecture but praising the overall ensemble: 'the most splendid group of buildings that the Christian era has produced'.[25] By the 1900s, and with the federal capital project in the air, Washington was also an influential icon, surfacing in secondary sources as well as being an obligatory stop on overseas fact-finding missions. Such study tours, a significant conduit for the importation of planning ideas, took in other North American cities and frequently also covered Britain and continental Europe.

For artistic inspiration, Australians still looked to Europe as much as the United States. Brisbane architect Lange Powell gushed with his impressions of Paris: 'unsurpassed dignity' and 'stupendous magnificence'. By contrast, London was a let-down where 'the good is looked for among mediocrity'.[26] The strong European influence extended into the 1920s. In a lecture on 'Civic Architecture' to the Institute of Architects of New South Wales, the planner Norman Weekes showed lantern slides of almost exclusively European subjects – Place de la Concorde, Greenwich Hospital, Marble Arch, Champs Élysées, Rue de Rivoli, and other continental squares and building groups. Professor of architecture Leslie Wilkinson provided a similar coverage a few years later.[27]

The American connotations of the city beautiful were diluted by their absorption into an architecturally inspired planning heavily informed by British ties. British hegemony meant that Australian designers were less under the spell of the strict École des Beaux Arts tradition that had such a stranglehold on American civic architecture and planning. While a general eurocentricity can be read into the three-dimensional design imagery of many early Australian experiments in civic planning, this did not embrace Camillo Sitte's picturesque tradition, which was generally deemed unsuitable for modern Australian cities. In effect, Australian planning largely drew from American and British influences, which thus made for a rather eclectic city beautiful ethos. Sulman's authoritative 1921 textbook *An Introduction to the Study of Town Planning in Australia* was fairly even-handedly informed by both the historic capitals of Europe and exciting new developments in the United States.

No. 67 **EXAMPLE OF NEW SUBURBAN ROAD, ADELAIDE** (60 feet wide),
After completion by local authority, and showing need for improved methods.

No. 68 **EXAMPLE OF NEW SUBURBAN ROAD IN UNITED STATES,**
Showing design suited to residential conditions and amenity.   The roadways are laid down in concrete and surfaced with asphalt.

An Adelaide street versus a planned American street. *Proceedings, First Australian Town Planning Conference, 1917*

Hallmarks of the artistically planned city

The ideal modern city which began to crystallise in speeches and articles in the early 1900s was a dreamy concoction of grand public buildings and squares, homogeneous townscapes, distinguished residences, noble boulevards, parks and parkways. The hallmarks were order, harmony, formality, and symmetry. Major streets would be wide, straight, even colonnaded, with their vistas terminated by symmetrically placed objects. The preferred architectural styles reflected establishment tastes, with a penchant for the neo-classical. Major civic buildings were preferably showcased on open sites surrounded by parkland, public squares, or wide streets. Where several related government buildings were involved, their grouping in a centre was considered desirable. Other institutional complexes, such as universities and hospitals, could be treated similarly. The

'Elizabeth Street — chaotic'. *Architecture, July 1924*

principal entrances to a city – railways and waterways – were accorded conspicuous importance as landmark elements.

Many distracting features in existing commercial zones had to be eliminated. Features contributing to urban ugliness included bare sides and backs of high buildings, iron fire escapes, shop awnings, undisguised service facilities on rooftops, such as water tanks, and the 'multitudinous tramway, telegraph and telephone posts and wires that cobweb the sky, and obstruct the view in any busy street'.[28] Advertising billboards affronted professional taste as streets were 'disfigured by condemnable inventions of hucksters and tradesmen, in typical offence … against the amenity of the community … every wall, tower, tree and building by outrageous placard and written advertisement'.[29] Even fruit vendors' stalls were seen as a problem. Skyscrapers were questioned on 'humanitarian, artistic, and precautionary principles'.[30] Greater regulation of the streetscape and the skyline was required.

Delivering the finishing touches to the city as a work of art were appropriately designed and situated fountains, statues, roundabouts, obelisks and other street accessories such as lamp standards. The ideal landscape was self-consciously mannered, but remnant environments along watercourses and foreshores were also valued as natural beauty spots. There were also many left-over 'open places, odd corners, intersections of streets, and waste strips' which might 'be made a delight to the eye and a tonic for the jaded mind'.[31] A peculiarly Australian fear of vacant lots was their exploitation for illegal working class gambling in the form of 'two up' schools.[32]

War memorials became a special concern after 1916. With over 60 000 dead and 152 000 wounded, World War I had an enormous impact on all facets of Australian society in the early 20th century. It was a significant brake on the advance of the town planning movement, but unleashed aspirations and refined planning ideals towards peacetime productivity, progress and efficiency. The war helped prolong the city beautiful cause as Australians erected more memorials than any nation to commemorate the fallen. While most memorials were spontaneous grassroots efforts, the making of major monuments in the capital cities was firmly situated within the broader contours of city improvement. While the cause was an expression of national unity, consensus on many matters was often harder to forge. Questions as to a utilitarian versus a monumental structure, the best site, the ideal form, the precise identification of who was to be honoured, and the eligibility of designers 'were debated for years'.[33]

Promoting the cause

Ways of making cities more beautiful through planning were promoted through several channels. Six are readily identified. The first and most fundamental was community education. The main instruments of communication were public lectures, newspapers and popular periodicals. Other initiatives were seized. In 1921 the Town Planning Association of New South Wales sponsored a 'city beautiful' essay competition for school students. In a similar campaign in Hobart in 1924, hundreds of schoolchildren submitted essays on improving the look of their city as part of an American style 'clean up, paint up' campaign.[34] The key ingredient to be inculcated was civic pride – which cost nothing. Nevertheless, this was considered an uphill battle in Australia in comparison with other parts of the world, especially the United States, where the strength of civic pride was 'almost a bore to visitors', according to the town clerk of Sydney.[35]

Many would have agreed with the architect George Sydney Jones that once citizens began to take pride in their own homes, the city beautiful would be taken to heart.[36] George Taylor characteristically assembled his own narrow version of the city beautiful in which town planners 'must come down out of the clouds' to concentrate on the housing needs of individuals and their immediate urban environment. The key message was that the city beautiful 'begins at home', as urban reform reduced to home ownership:

> Give the worker every chance to own his own home; encourage him to have simple tastes in decoration. Have front garden competitions; give prizes to the prettiest street, and encourage pretty towns as we encourage pretty railway stations; and so the "City Beautiful" will develop, and at the same time develop the individual.[37]

Taylor went beyond rhetoric to develop what was effectively a second promotional strategy by offering active support to communities forming themselves into improvement leagues to pursue local causes such as beautification and tree planting. In 1921–22 he serialised his book *Town Planning with Common-sense* (1915) as 'Town and District Development' in his journal *Property Owner* as a primer for 'encouraging local development and improvement'. Taylor was also involved in the Newcastle 'betterment' board in the 1920s.

A third pathway was through augmentation of council powers, although it was conceded that artistic salvation through regulation would only work when allied to community education and professional edification. Existing powers were circumscribed on aesthetic matters. The *Local Government Act 1906* of New South Wales was typical of early statutes in sanctioning new parks, gardens, street trees, public buildings, and even 're-arrangement and beautification' but not extending to aesthetic mandate over building design. The push for new planning legislation assisted the cause when artistic issues were flagged. The standard town planning bill promoted by planning pioneer Charles Reade in several states between 1915 and 1919 aimed at comprehensive new powers to secure better health, amenity and convenience of local areas, and its schedule listed a number of matters with which local planning instruments could deal. These included parks and open spaces, public squares, monuments, 'conservation of the natural beauties of the area', and for buildings generally:

> the prevention of the erection of ugly buildings which may destroy local amenities, the placing of new public buildings, harmony in the exterior designs of buildings, uniformity or variation in height of buildings in particular roads, determining character, location, purpose, and dimensions of buildings, or the height to which buildings may be erected … the prohibition or regulation of the placing of advertisements, advertising hoardings, illuminated signs and other advertising devices, and other disfigurements.[38]

Fourth, the ultimate planning document at local or state level was a general development plan inclusive of aesthetic content. A string of early efforts to secure this were unsuccessful. The 1908 Royal Commission for the Improvement of the City of Sydney and Its Suburbs was the first major city investigation to flag aesthetic questions but declare influentially that their importance lay more as a by-product of good planning.

Fifth, short of securing statutory backing, building and, in particular, architectural journals became enthusiastic about constituting advisory bodies to help government adjudicate on the aesthetic merits of new development. These were variously styled 'art commissions', 'courts of design', and 'councils of taste'. Beauty could not be secured until society was trained to recognise it, argued Sydney economics professor RF Irvine, and only an educated cadre of expert architects and planners could offer 'the right kind of guidance'.[39]

Finally, government was looked to for leadership. Perth identity JS Battye contended that the typical Australian attitude of 'expecting the Government or some other authority to do everything for him is not conducive to even the elementary stages of developing the City Beautiful'.[40] Others disagreed. Irvine, one of the most intellectual planning advocates, saw public sector leadership as necessary to rise above the conservatism of the 'commercial community'.[41] And certainly the survey in this book indicates that many dreams were only kept alive by public sector interest and investment. This ranged from the development of Canberra and other government buildings at federal level to the stimulus of beauty through planning inquiries, advisory bodies, improvement schemes, royal visits and even Depression-era employment relief schemes at the state level, and the provision and maintenance of parks, trees, and paved streets, placement of memorials, and community facilities at the local level.

The main players

Like town planning generally, the cause for better urban aesthetics was essentially a middle class preoccupation and crossed party political lines. There were admittedly conservative, more business-minded advocates who baulked at large-scale state intervention, but the need for parks, foreshore drives, well-sited public buildings, and 'harmonious development' advocated by an extreme right-wing group like the New Guard in New South Wales comfortably found common ground with a more moderate mainstream.[42]

When local progress and improvement associations pursued issues of beautification in the 1900s, their modus operandi was usually disconnected from the wider cause of town planning. Together with the forums opened up by professional bodies and the public discourse

promoted through newspapers, they nevertheless helped build receptiveness to more coordinated action and paved the way for town planning associations from 1913. Of the latter bodies, the short-lived Womens' Section of the Town Planning Association of New South Wales
remains the closest to the American model of an organised beautification movement. It provides a glimpse of the struggle involved in leav-
ening the masculine hold on the planning movement.

The germ of the idea dates back to at least 1909, when Florence
Taylor, the journalist-architect wife of George Taylor, wrote in her
'Home Building' section of their magazine *Building* about her desire
to inaugurate 'Women's Associations for civic improvement'. She was
influenced by the village improvement associations and womens' civic
leagues which formed an important grassroots strand of the American
city beautiful movement. Florence Taylor became even more enthused
after a visit to the United States in 1914 and the following year she
organised the Women's Section in the Town Planning Association of
New South Wales (established by her husband in October 1913). The
agenda was set broadly on the 'human side' of planning, not purely
aesthetics but an eclectic set of causes, including tree planting,
boulevards, banning of ugly hoardings, and general 'city and suburban beautification, removing of unsightly features and other improvements of cities and towns'.[43] The initiative was commended by John
Daniel Fitzgerald, who felt 'civic beautification and sanitation were
merely housekeeping on a broader basis'.[44] The section quickly grew to
100 members but disintegrated within months when Marion Mahony
Griffin challenged the authoritarianism of the Taylors and the inherent
marginalisation of women members.[45]

The theme of improved urban aesthetics as an integral element
of town planning reform was most conspicuously associated with
the built environment experts whose general thoughts, practical
suggestions and debates featured in professional journals and daily
newspapers. They may not have typecast themselves as city beautiful
aficionados, but these prominent architect-planners and local
government reformers sought, like their American contemporaries,
to mitigate 'tensions between civic ideals and commercial pursuits'.[46]
More names will surface in later chapters; here the most prominent
crusaders are briefly introduced.

John Fitzgerald.
*Proceedings, First
Australian Town Planning
Conference, 1917*

William Bold.
Perth City Council

John Sulman.
*Architecture,
May 1919*

Well travelled and high-profile barrister John Daniel Fitzgerald (1862–1922) was the most powerful political figure associated with the early planning movement. Influenced by Bellamy's *Looking Backward* and a NSW commissioner for the Chicago Exposition of 1893, he evolved into a politician in the progressive mould, becoming minister for health and local government in the Labor-breakaway NSW Nationalist government of 1916–1920. Fitzgerald pitched his planning message to the 'citizen who wants to realise the best possibilities of the city beautiful'.[47] Beautification was a key 'section' of town planning for him, encompassing a miscellany of actions including tree planting, preservation of natural beauties, parks, fountains, statues, arches, and 'and the curtailment of everything which may disfigure the city'.[48] The 'securing of harmony in the architectural features of the city; the proper grouping of public buildings, the censorship over matters which may tend to injure the aesthetic side of the city, or destroy beautiful surroundings' formed an additional section.

William Bold (1873–1953) was town clerk of Perth for nearly half a century. Like Fitzgerald, he was an enthusiast of British politician Joseph Chamberlain's style of municipal socialism. Bold was 'anxious to mould Perth into a model city'.[49] A report on 'Perth Improvement' in November 1911 contended that 'it is advisable from many points of view that every effort to attain the ideal of "the City Beautiful" shall be made by the Council of every City'. His *Report on Tour Round the World* (1914) had 'profound consequences for the history of Perth after the World War I, with its central thrust being the need for planning on "City Beautiful lines" '.[50] Installing the city plan as 'the key-stone of the arch of successful municipal effort', Bold imported a suite of best-practice ideas and encouraged the council into large-scale programs of boulevard building, residential development, and beautification.

As cities were composed primarily of buildings, most architects saw town planning in architectural terms. Locally trained architects studied at night at technical colleges and gained experience by day through articled positions. University-level education did not begin until after World War I. Early instruction was stylistically eclectic, but beaux arts precepts of form and composition were taught. They figured prominently in the Melbourne University Architectural Atelier from 1919, which had a predilection for the neo-classical in important public buildings and large-scale design projects from the 'perspective of the City Beautiful movement'.[51] Some of the leading architects from the end of the 19th century had been born and educated abroad and so brought worldliness to their Australian practices. There were several individuals whose writings and works on the artistic side of town planning assumed national prominence. Notable among them were John Sulman, George Sydney Jones, John Smith Murdoch, and Walter Burley Griffin.

Sulman (1849–1934) was the leading planning advocate of his generation. He was an influential teacher, commentator and practitioner who assumed important roles on many advisory committees and competition juries. His writings on the laying out of towns, the design of the federal capital, the improvement of Sydney, and principles of civic design culminated in the seminal *An Introduction to the Study of Town Planning in Australia* (1921). 'No town or city', he wrote, 'can be considered complete without the expression of the ideal in concrete form'. Sulman likened painting to planning: 'the former seeks art in small framed spaces, the latter in wide, prettily and properly planned spaces'.[52] He conceded that picturesqueness might be used to good effect by securing a kind of cumulative beauty from 'minor effects' but ultimately rejected a Sittes-que approach as unrealistic for the requirements of modern cities. Routinely endorsed in Sulman's writings were civic centres, gateways, arcaded streets, park improvements, and smaller artistic embellishments. While often derivative, the accessibility and authority of his ideas effectively moulded Australian thought on the subject. Thriving on the advancement of public architecture, small and large, he remained active to the end.

An early ally of Sulman in his personal intrigues against the Institute of Architects of NSW, George Sydney Jones became one if the institute's stalwarts as a long-serving secretary, three-time president, and its first life member. He had studied in London and was admitted as a member of the Royal Institute of British Architects in 1891. His most famous building was a competition-winning Administration Building in Canberra (now Sir John Gorton House). His opening address at the 1917 national planning conference established town planning and civic art as 'one and the same', meaning the objective was not expensive buildings and magnificent avenues, 'though these may add to the fineness of a city', but rather a five-fold agenda of traffic convenience, zoning, parks and playgrounds, housing, and the 'concentration of civic buildings'.[53] He endorsed a 'homogeneity of spirit in design' and bemoaned 'lost opportunities to appreciate the value of the centre line and the aesthetic effect of the street terminal'.[54]

The self-effacing Scot John Smith Murdoch (1862–1945) was not given to speeches and papers but initiated projects of national significance in several cities. In Scotland he was articled to the firm of Matthews and Mackenzie, later responsible for Australia House in London. Murdoch joined the commonwealth government in 1904 and became director-general of the Department of Works in 1925. His core philosophy was that the 'foundation of all aesthetics in architecture is utility', which David Rowe notes made him rather well suited to the parsimony of government service.[55] Murdoch was a devotee of beaux arts design, his understanding enhanced through friendship with fellow Scottish architect John Burnet. He progressed toward an eclectic, stripped classical style which helped to create a distinctive interwar image for the federal government, especially in Canberra. An official fact-finding tour of Europe and North America in 1912–13 took him to Washington and Chicago, where he first met Walter Burley Griffin.[56]

Charles Coulter.
National Archives of Australia, Series M1535

Walter Burley Griffin (1876–1937) directly imported American influences. He graduated from the University of Illinois in 1899 and practised in Chicago to 1914. He worked for Frank Lloyd Wright from 1901 to 1905 at the architect's Oak Park studio, where he met his partner in life and creativity, Marion Lucy Mahony (1871–1961). The couple married in 1911. The following year came success in the competition to design the new capital of Australia. The win made him a celebrity in America for a short time. One of many public addresses was to the 8th Annual Conference of the American Civic Association in Baltimore in November 1912, in a session chaired by the planner John Nolen, with the Kansas City developer JC Nichols speaking on the Country Club District, and the prominent city beautiful advocate J Horace McFarland.[57] The American architect Cass Gilbert, when asked in 1918 who were the best American city planners, nominated

Griffin alongside FL Olmsted Jr, Edward Bennett, Arnold Brunner, and himself.[58] Griffin was familiar with the Chicago style of planning under Burnham and revealed that 'The Chicago Exhibition gave me my first lesson in town planning'.[59] Yet he did not bring an undigested city beautiful ethic to his Canberra design but rather adapted and in so doing transformed and then transcended its principles in applying them with brilliant originality to the Australian landscape. 'It was hopeless to attempt in the old way to build up a "town beautiful" ', he said, 'with the selected units taken from this, that, or the other style at the will of the architect or the owner'.[60] Griffin's search for homogeneity in design rejected the dominant preference for neo-classical design and instead took all-of-a-piece inspiration from more exotic places such as Latin America, and most importantly from readings of site and situation.

John Barlow and Robert Charles Given Coulter were two Sydney architects conspicuous for their advocacy of the city beautiful. Barlow (1860–1925) was foundation editor of the *Journal of the Institute of Architects of New South Wales* which became a mouthpiece for city beautiful idealism and specific improvement suggestions in the early 1900s. His own musings centred on attempts to reconcile the axiality of the full-blown city beautiful idiom with the informal beauty of natural environments and competing charms of pre-industrial cities. He was a prominent advocate for a board of experts to vet new architecture, but was surprisingly cautious about the wholesale remodelling of Sydney. He valued the charm, picturesqueness and 'unexpected architectural effects' of the central city, advocating improvements which conserved the essential character of places.[61] Barlow designed St Kevins, Paul Keating's former home in Woollahra, and his landing pavilion at Farm Cove, erected for Federation celebrations from late 1900, was later re-assembled at Ashfield Park, where it served as a bandstand for many years.

Many of the enduring images now associated with the city beautiful strand in Australian planning were the work of Coulter (1864–1956), an architectural draftsman in the Department of Public Works of New South Wales. Coulter studied art with Julian Ashton and was an exhibiting member of the Royal Art Society.[62] A compulsive painter and

sketcher, his favourite medium was watercolour, but he was no Jules
Guerin and many of his renderings now look stilted and backward-
looking in their frequent attempts to adapt a modernism encased in
the architecture of neo-classicism to the Australian urban environment. Privately he had success in housing, park and beach improvement competitions. He had close associations with the federal capital
project over a long period, was official artist for the Sydney royal
commission of 1908–09, and visualised most of the Sydney Harbour
Bridge proposals and associated and later projects for JJC Bradfield, a
civil engineer with a taste for urban beautification.

The sphere of influence of other architects was more limited, but
collectively their voices indicate the many early facets of artistically
inclined design. In Sydney they included Norman Weekes (1888–1972),
BJ Waterhouse (1876–1965), and Gordon Keesing (c1889–1966) who studied under the atelier system in Paris and announced plans to launch a
society of beaux arts on his return to Sydney just before World War I.[63]
He later worked with Jack Hennessy, who also returned to Australia
with a beaux arts training from the University of Pennsylvania.

In Melbourne, two names are prominent and interlinked. Both
Harold Desbrowe-Annear (1865–1933) and Frank Stapley (1858–1944)
worked for the architect William Salway. Stapley endorsed a permanent
form of civic commemoration of the kind that Annear had produced in
his Corporation Arch on Princes Bridge, marking the opening of the first
Commonwealth parliament.[64] He also shared Annear's commitment to
town planning. But these men were representative of very different
aesthetic modernisms. For a time Annear alternated between daring
Arts and Crafts architecture and formalistic beaux arts city planning.
An ambitious project for the siting and design of a national war
memorial in Melbourne integrated a fundamental reworking of street
arrangements, park planning, and the location of public institutions.[65]

By contrast, Stapley designed mostly industrial buildings. Elect-
ed a Melbourne city councillor and rising to mayor in 1917–18, he
came to stand for commercial concerns such as zoning, traffic and
infrastructure reforms. He conceded that the artistic was a 'cinderella' to the utilitarian, an imbalance which could be held responsible
for 'much that is drab and unsightly in our cities and towns', and, as
chairman of the Melbourne Metropolitan Town Planning Commission

1923–30, sought to correct this.[66]

In Perth, the most authoritative early voice apart from Bold was George Temple-Poole (1865–1934), principal architect in the state's Department of Public Works between 1891 and 1897 and a four-time president of the Western Australia Institute of Architects. His seminal statement was a 1911 newspaper article headlined 'Perth as it Should be' which tried to redeem the city 'from its present unattractiveness' and rescue it 'from a chaos'.[67] Numerous suggestions for improvement were made, including a new civic centre, parks, green belt, 'magnificent boulevards', and riverfront beautification, but the major proposal and lynchpin of all the remodelling was the relocation northwards of an intrusive east-west railway corridor to create a grand civic place in the heart of the city.

Striving for beautility

The aesthetic improvements these individuals worked towards seemed incontrovertible. But a larger agenda was at work, even when the artistic turn was at its most idealistic. An American editorial entitled 'Beauty a City Asset' reproduced in the *Journal of the Royal Victorian Institute of Architects* in 1913 captured this bigger picture:

> A city with streets convenient for traffic and parks for recreation, with refined and dignified buildings, graceful and inspiring statuary, attractive and well-planted parks, combined in one harmonious composition, becomes a city useful, a city practical, a city attractive, and a city healthful. This combination is an asset which accrues in the culture and refinement of the public and in the enjoyment of the people. At the same time it is a great financial resource.[68]

Each and every element of the ideal city had its own rationale beyond the aesthetic – if only rhetorical. For example, gateway features would send a powerful message of citizenship to newcomers. The colonnaded street was valued 'both for its artistic values and its utilitarian worth in overcoming the pedestrian traffic problem'.[69] Freestanding public buildings had diverse rationales: they minimised the risk of fire, dampened the intrusion of street noise, and secured dignity, sunshine and air.[70]

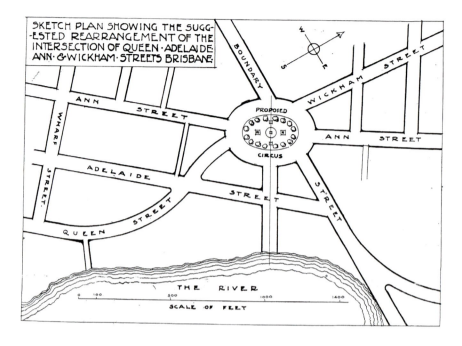

'Town Planning Suggestion' for Brisbane by Robin Dods rationalises
a nightmare intersection while creating a public space for a monument,
views to the river, and new commercial frontages.
The Salon, November 1913

A popular slogan for the doubters of urban reform was 'Town
Planning Pays'. In aesthetic matters, the bottom line was also financial.
'There is nothing that pays so well as beauty' wrote WE Bold, quoting a report of the Philadelphia City Parks Association.[71] Investment
in beauty, it was argued, could be returned several-fold in increased
prestige, rates and other taxes, population growth, wealth retention,
and tourist expenditure. The logic of re-ordering and embellishing
cities was ultimately linked to the promise of economic betterment.
Australian cities in the Federation era were keen to establish their
competitiveness and attractiveness in a new political landscape in
which positive foreign opinion and world city status were also at stake.
Beauty was good business and good for business. Daniel Burnham was
quoted approvingly by the Royal Commission for the Improvement of
the City of Sydney and Its Suburbs in 1909:

The delightfulness of a city is an element of first importance to its prosperity, for those who make fortunes will stay, and others come if the attractions are strong enough; and the money thus kept at home added to that freely spent by visitors, will be enough to ensure continuous good times.[72]

Shifts in the awareness of beauty's benefits, akin to the same evolution in American planning thought, can be traced through the pages of the journal *Building*. In 1909 the notion that beautiful buildings 'add greatly to the happiness of people' is recognised.[73] By 1910 this has matured to an appreciation of the manifold local improvements that could promote prosperity, including clean and well-lit streets, a good hotel, rest rooms for women, drinking fountains, and 'attractive approaches to the railway station'.[74] In 1911 comes full-blown recognition that the 'world-trend of civic planning' points to the importance of civic beauty as an asset and that 'no city can make itself beautiful in a day or without concerted effort'.[75]

If the case for a beautiful city was compelling, its 'other' in the guise of the unabashed utilitarian city was unappealing. 'There is no doubt that a city planned from a utilitarian stand-point alone could be a very undesirable one in which to live', wrote Brisbane planning figure RC Nowland, 'Civic beauty should be a happy combination of the aesthetic with the utilitarian'.[76] Florence Taylor told the story of a fellow passenger on a Sydney ferry ride from Neutral Bay to Circular Quay waving toward the Botanic Gardens and declaring their commercial development 'has got to come'. She saw things differently:

For the greater portion of my life I have been in the commercial swim, as the saying goes, and I appreciate the necessity of cultivating what is designated "the commercial spirit"; but it has not become an obsession with me, because I have never allowed it; because I have always realized that conscience must go with commerce, and the appeal of humanity is greater than the greed of personal ambition. Commercialism has its moral side, and it must be respected quite as much as the mercenary side, if we are to prosper. Clean minds and healthy bodies, cultivated in the blessedness of sunshine and the freedom of open spaces, are just as essential to the conduct of the world's greatest schemes as the capital to float them. The one is dependent on the other.[77]

In these terms, the Botanic Gardens were already a commercial asset in the 'moral uplift' afforded the population. In a presidential address to the Institute of Architects of NSW, AW Anderson acknowledged that architects did not routinely secure commissions for 'the stately cathedral' of the city beautiful but that this should not mean reverting to a purely utilitarian stance for everything else. 'Are we to be merely producers of utilitarian structures speaking of commercialism, money-making and being rent products only?'[78]

The war memorial movement confounded the distinction between the beautiful and the utilitarian in sometimes unpredictable ways. Hence George Sydney Jones in his speech on 'Australia and Civic Art' to the 1917 Town Planning Conference suggested that the best memorials were institutions which would directly improve people physically, mentally and intellectually.[79] On the other side, George and Florence Taylor's journal *Building* took the opposing stance, recognising that there could be things which served no practical purpose 'other than to inspire, uplift and be a perpetual source of delight'.[80] When this debate flared in local communities, the view that national idealism and artistic creativity were the losers in utilitarian memorials often prevailed. But it was not universal, as shown by a roll-call of memorial forms split between obelisks, crosses, arches, allegorical sculpture and the ubiquitous soldier figure versus memorial halls, parks, grandstands, and even hospitals. Hybrid solutions – like clock-tower memorials – spoke of compromise.

Striking the right balance could also prove difficult in more wide-ranging debates and there were often tensions between the professional approaches of surveyors, engineers, and architects. Louis Curtis in his presidential address to the Institution of Surveyors NSW in 1914 acknowledged the conventional wisdom that 'the aesthetic and practical should go hand-in-hand' but maintained that 'the practical must receive first consideration, for the aesthetic is a phase of after treatment which in its result is only limited by the taste of the artist engaged upon its elaboration'.[81] This was contested by John Sulman, who argued that town planning required imagination and artistic skill of the highest order and that sewers were not a first consideration in town design. Rising above professional jealousies, the planners' argument was that urban design and improvement was a collaborative art especially 'with regard to the artistic treatment of all matters of public interest'.[82] In an ideal world, even the design of a light standard on a nondescript street corner was dependant not only upon the architect's aspirations, but also the nature and design of the surrounds, electricity supply, the proximity of other infrastructure, not to mention the availability of funding.

In a public lecture entitled 'Town Planning: What Everyone Should Know' during the 1917 Adelaide Planning Conference, the Victorian architect James Morrell cautioned that 'It must be remembered that idealism that was not practicable was not ideal'.[83] This was a sweet summation of a broad consensus uniting the built environment professions and the community. But what did it actually mean in practice? How was the best balance struck? Ultimately it would be contingent on circumstances but inexorably into the 1920s came an underselling of aesthetics as a primary goal plus a more precise specification of a range of collateral benefits attached to specific projects with some artistic content. This trend and the nuances involved can be picked up in numerous commentaries and articles. The views of John Fitzgerald, George Taylor and Frank Stapley are representative of both the diversity and trend of opinion.

From the 1900s, Fitzgerald was the master rhetorician, capturing the essence of the planning mission in its early days in speeches and articles for a general audience. His central proposition was that 'the advancement of commercial activity and of physical adornment and beautification may be pursued simultaneously, and the greatness and the beauty of a city advanced with equal foot'.[84] Hence, the town planner was not only 'a beautifier of cities – a mere aesthete. He is that – but he is much more'.[85] Following the edicts of planners would lead to 'a nobler type of citizenship in Australia, and raise the living conditions of our people to heights of utility and beauty undreamed of now'. Sceptics abounded, as Fitzgerald conceded that 'the hardest task … was to convince a doubting public that we were not a mere brand of dreamers and enthusiasts aiming at impractical aesthetic futilities but … could stand the severest tests of a Chamber of Commerce'.[86]

George Taylor grew restless with such oratory and attacked Fitzgerald as 'that incurable dreamer'.[87] In the 1910s he rounded on artistic planning and its proponents and placed himself in the vanguard of advocates shifting planning from a seeming cult of do-good missionaries to a profession of sobre practitioners. He visited the United States on the eve of World War I. Having left Australia with high expectations, he returned with a rather jaundiced view recorded in his book *There! A Pilgrimage of Pleasure* (1915). The greatest disappointment was the city he most looked forward to visiting: Chicago. He was immediately struck by a gulf between the gilded city of Burnham's imagination and the realities of the metropolis. He was shocked that 'the human element has not been given much consideration'. As long as there were swathes of substandard housing, so would 'Chicago's aristocratic city plans, remain on the walls of her Art Institute as unrealized ideals'. Back home he adopted an uncompromising stance and became an arch-critic of 'the spectacular aspect of town planning'. He told a Victorian royal commission on housing that North American city planning which strove for 'the pretty appearance' generally neglected a basic principle of town planning, namely utility.[88] In his revealingly titled book *Town Planning with Common-Sense* (1918), Taylor scolds the 'useless passengers' of the planning movement:

> It is the town-planning extremists who desire to drive wide "tree-lined boulevards" through cities, pushing back the houses into sky-reaching tenements ... The town-planning extremist agitates for driving fine avenues and widening streets regardless of expense ... Finance is the basis of every successful movement designed for permanency, and every town-planning venture should be based upon a firm financial basis and not upon 'spoonfed philanthropy'.[89]

In the 1920s things settled down under the leadership of people like Frank Stapley, although he could be similarly intolerant of impractical aesthetic schemes. A Melbourne proposal to demolish valuable market buildings for a central city square was lambasted as 'another of the hastily-considered and amateurish suggestions which divert the citizens' attention from far more important proposals in connection with the future development of the metropolis'.[90] Stapley defined planning as a business proposition attending to primary goals of transport, water supply and sewerage. Pleasant boulevards and public spaces had their place but their economic value had always to be scrutinised and defended. Like John Nolen, he maintained that beauty would come from order. Even land-use zoning recommendations could be artistic: 'although they are purely utilitarian proposals they must lead to the orderly growth of our cities with aesthetic gain'.[91] In short, 'the best results' occurred when the utilitarian was combined with the artistic.[92]

The battle for acceptance

There were always formidable obstacles to the realisation of city beautiful dreams. The constraints were cultural, economic, political, and ideological. In a 1921 address to the Town Planning Association of NSW, Fitzgerald cynically captured the hurdles which he and other planning advocates faced:

> the universal maxims have prevailed ... which govern most things in Australia – (a) Never look ahead – you are a dreamer; (b) never advocate a big thing – you are impractical and dilettante; (c) always turn down a big project, not because it is unsound, but because it is big; (d) always assume that Australians are incapable of doing the big things which other nations do easily.[93]

At the heart of the problem was a seeming lack of civic pride, hence the effort given to community education. Sulman described the problem as 'the dull inert mass of civic indifference'.[94] John Barlow linked 'the extraordinary apathy evinced by our people with regard to artistic matters' to commercialism.[95] RF Irvine felt that Australians were just 'too satisfied with ourselves' to really care about suggestions for improvement.[96] The architect James Peddle saw the nub of the problem in Australian individualism compared to the Americans, who 'will do anything to make their city beautiful, and each owner of a lot or house thinks of it as a unit in the larger whole, and delights in sharing its charm and beauty with his fellows.[97]

The architect and town planner Alfred John Brown attributed this individualism to the British way of life 'where we don't look too much for the big stick to be waved'.[98] Fitzgerald had expressed a similar view in more despairing tones many years earlier: 'Must we accept it as incontrovertible that the British people cannot accept great schemes of city improvement, symmetrical in design, artistic in plan?'[99]

More fundamentally, the political economy of early 20th century Australian cities called for a planning attuned to business development and growth. What was said of 19th century Melbourne remained true there and elsewhere: 'grand schemes of municipal improvement stood little chance of realization amidst the more insistent demands … for better roads, street lighting, dock facilities and policing'.[100] The bargaining power of private capital seriously frustrated any far-reaching improvement schemes for freehold property holdings. Even more modest interventions, such as controls on advertising, could run foul of private interests. Both state and capital easily baulked at the perceived costs of aesthetic initiatives. In Australia, lamented *Building*, 'there is a tendency to consider cost to such an extent that all other considerations for beauty and refinement are overshadowed'.[101] Civic beautification was invariably seen as a public function, and the costs of implementing major proposals were usually regarded as prohibitive by politicians already nervous about the state's direct involvement in urban development matters. The public often shared this sentiment. Perth librarian JS Battye in his 1934 talk on 'The City Beautiful' noted the grand image conjured up by this phrase was soon 'overpowered by the fact that to do these things requires expenditure which we are in no position to afford'.

Financial solutions did exist, for example through the recouping of outlays from increased property values, but legal and administrative complexities limited the application of this model and the powers of most local authorities were circumscribed in any case. When the interests of local, state and even federal government were inter-linked, seeking a unity of purpose and action could be nightmar-ish, as it often remains today. Even commonsense cooperation over street widenings and landscaped roundabouts could break down at municipal boundaries.

Where city beautiful thought sat within contemporary planning ideology was also important. Civic art in its various forms not only had to compete with other planning priorities, usually judged more important, but also faced hostility from some practitioners. Overseas icons were not always accepted at face value. William Earle, when acting government town planner of South Australia, regarded the Fairmount Parkway in Philadelphia as a costly example of the 'lack of foresight in the early design of the city'.[102] The landscape architect Thomas Mawson's proposals for Bolton raised the question of just 'how much comfort has been sacrificed for appearances' in such a 'symmetrical scheme'.[103] The ever-sceptical George Taylor damned the work of the 'academical designers' who had produced the Cleveland Civic Centre.[104] Taylor contracted American writer FW Fitzpatrick (1864–1931) to share his often dyspeptic views with the readers of *Building*. Uncontroversially, Fitzpatrick saw art not as embellishment but 'the function of doing things well' with a collateral payoff for business. But not at any cost. His 1915 paper 'The Thrall of the Axis' was critical of city beautiful plans that sacrificed commonsense for balance and symmetry, as well as the planners who conceived them 'just to satisfy [their] senseless, purely theoretic longing for a pretty paper arrangement'.[105]

Aesthetics in the evolving planning agenda

It might be asked: with friends like this, who needed enemies? But the city beautiful as the touchstone of city planning was never more than a fleeting episode, confined primarily to the years immediately post-Federation when the idea of a new federal city was at its most beguiling and an organised planning movement had yet to crystallise. Thereafter, it survived as part of a more comprehensive philosophy of planning and was embodied as an aesthetic element in specific development projects.

The notion that aesthetic uplift alone was what town planning was all about was dissipating even as the Sydney royal commissioners got down to business in 1908. The challenges of actually building a federal city during World War I also expunged much if not all the earlier idealism. By 1916, when the last of the state town planning associations was formed in Perth, art was a bit part in a much larger agenda. Charles Reade, who was a catalyst in the formation of most of these groups following his extensive lecture tours, strongly backed the legislative rather than aesthetic pathway to real reform. Had Thomas Mawson toured at this time, as was mooted, perhaps the mantle of civic art may have flickered brighter. Few of the association mission statements even mention let alone emphasise issues of civic aesthetics although the work on sub-committees and special projects could address opportunities for streetscape improvement, preservation of natural scenery, and general beautification. The agenda of the Victorian Town Planning Association, for example, was driven by a raft of other social and environmental concerns: slum eradication and better housing, garden suburbs, conservation, national parks, green belts, and playgrounds. Although allied to the city square campaign and beautification causes from the mid 1920s, the association's patriarch Sir James Barrett laid down the ruling idea that city planning was always more than the city beautiful – this was 'incidental, the real motive is community living'.[106]

Charles Reade saw the inaugural national planning conference which he instigated in 1917 in Adelaide as confirming the need for the planning movement to move beyond beautification to practical planning, consideration of economic and technical matters, and effective action. He felt that 'the beautification motive' preceded town planning proper but had no direct bearing upon it, and (perhaps with Adelaide in mind) could even engender 'a certain pride of city which tended more to confuse than encourage clear understanding of Town Planning aims'.[107] Despite this, the cause of civic art was prominent in several conference presentations, notably those of the architects John Sulman, GS Jones, George Temple-Poole, and Albert Conrad. Rhetorical flourishes continued into the plenary sessions at the second national conference, held in Brisbane in 1918. The reformist Labor premier, TJ Ryan, felt that Washington was 'the most beautiful city' he had ever visited, making 'an impression that will never fade'.[108] But here was the more emphatic turning point comparable to the first 1909 American conference of planners, with discussion dominated by issues of repatriation and soldier settlement, legislation, roads, housing, open space, zoning, and financing. WG Layton (the deputy town clerk of Sydney) sought to maintain some beautilitarian balance: 'The aesthetic is just as necessary as the material. If we are to have good citizens, we must appeal to the finer senses of our people, and teach our children to understand and value the beautiful things in a city, as well as the material things'.[109]

Urban aesthetics survived as one minor component of wider strategies into the 1920s, when interest in comprehensive planning came to define the central concern of mainstream planning. Just as garden city ideals were relegated under the heading of 'housing and land subdivision', the city beautiful was usually dealt with under 'civic art and amenities'. By the 1930s the Depression had largely extinguished the flame of artistic planning as a core planning goal. But there was one last major battle of ideological correctness to be fought to confirm this declining status.

Another of George Taylor's colleagues who shared his robust views about practical versus idealistic planning was David Davidson, a similarly rambunctious character who thrived on controversy. In the late 1920s Davidson followed John Sulman as both president of the Town Planning Association of NSW and Vernon Memorial Lecturer in town planning at the University of Sydney. His functionalist stance was unequivocal: 'We are often called idealists and visionaries, and rightly so, but we insist that modern town planning is fundamentally and all the time a "business proposition", a modern concept born of democratic ideals. We stress that the basic principle of town planning is to increase the working efficiency of the town'.[110] When appointed inaugural town planning commissioner by the Western Australian government in the late 1920s, he transplanted this stance to Perth and collided headlong with the city beautiful aspirations of William Bold. Bold's ambitions for Perth as the city beautiful par excellence drew early criticism from *The Sunday Times* newspaper, which dismissed him as a 'municipal globetrotter'. Davidson became a sterner critic. He claimed that Bold's grandstanding was missing more pressing social issues, such as poor housing conditions and imperfect building controls. Criticism mounted to eventually justify a royal commission in 1938 into his civic administration. Bold was vindicated as an efficient and conscientious manager, but problems in the administration of housing by-laws and fire-risk buildings were acknowledged. Essentially, the commission 'recognised that in pursuing "City Beautiful" ideals he had become a little careless in the administration of the central city area'.[111] Thereafter, Bold reverted to being 'a more effective supervisor of council operations' without the wholesale delegation which had freed him to pursue his planning activities.[112]

Conclusion

The power of the city beautiful as an inspirational catchphrase began to progressively lose influence and meaning even before 1914. By the end of World War I, the term was used mainly 'in terms of levity, or sarcasm'.[113] Most professional planners distanced themselves from a term which conveyed the erroneous impression that planning was solely about 'production of a picturesque appearance.'[114] Nevertheless, for the first three decades of the 20th century the need to 'solve practical needs artistically', as Sulman put it in 1921, denoted a coherent era of interconnected ideas, personalities and projects that can be united under the city beautiful banner.

There was no shortage of city beautiful-type proposals. The problem was implementation and, with the exception of Canberra, the legacy on the ground was diffuse. Ameliorating the local environment was a concern everywhere, but the character of city beautiful thought assumed noticeable local variations in different Australian cities. In Sydney, it was invoked where appropriate to aid modernisation but there were constant collisions with commerce. Less imbued with natural environmental advantages, Melbourne's long-running obsession was for a civic square, centre, or landmark. Perth and Brisbane had similar aspirations toward central public squares, largely ignored by the first surveyors. In Perth, major concerns were the provision of parkland and parkways plus the saga of dealing with the city railway corridor. In Hobart, beautification of the city waterfront as a tourist destination emerged as the major concern. Canberra as an urbanistic expression of nationalism provided the most distinctive strand at the federal level.

CHAPTER 4

The federal capital

To think of the city beautiful in Australia has been to think almost exclusively of Canberra, the biggest planning story of the early 20th century. Canberra and its designer have attracted a formidable literature covering the 'battle of the sites' (site selection), the 'battle of the plans' (the international competition), the 'battle of wills' during Walter Burley Griffin's tenure as Federal Capital Director of Design and Construction, and the 'battle of ideas' (post-competition evolution of design and development).[1] This chapter takes a fresh route through these events, focusing on aesthetic content in the idea of a federal capital, city beautiful connections in the Griffin plan, the ways in which the project's detractors forced a new trajectory for the federal capital based on more utilitarian principles, and the surviving traces of the aesthetic imagination into the 1920s.

Even the harshest professional critics conceded that the national capital could not be designed and developed purely on utilitarian lines. George Taylor conceded that the city could not be designed solely by, say, an engineer:

> He will consider the lay-out of a city simply as the planning of a factory plant, and, just as in a factory he will provide for quick transmission from one machine to another, so in a city he will provide for ready means

Beaux arts in the bush:
Dalgety as a federal
capital, by Lionel Lindsay.
The Lone Hand, April 1908

Imaginative sketch for
Mahkoolma, by Charles
Coulter, 1906. *National
Archives of Australia, Series
M1537*

of communication with each part, and he will cut out the aesthetic and 'come down to potatoes'. He will allow for sunlight and pure air like the giving of a dose of physic. He will only consider the material and its cost. Therefore, as a town planner, he will fail, because he will be soulless; he will lack the greatest of all forces – imagination.[2]

At the same time, imagination had to be always reined in by practical considerations. Striking the right balance proved a long and bruising story.

Pre-competition ideas

The evolution of generalised notions of a federal city beautiful into more specific planning concepts for a 'practical twentieth century town' saw a maturation of thinking which helped prepare the ground for the international competition of 1911–12. Formal interaction between political and professional discourses was limited. Architects, surveyors and engineers generally steered clear of heady debates about social reform, nationalism, and federalism. Their more earnest endeavours were directed towards working slowly through siting and design principles in ways that helped progress the emergence of the town planning profession in Australia.

Amid broader economic, political and cultural implications, the question of a seat of government was not the major issue in the federation of the Australian colonies in 1901. But it was an inescapable detail which needed to be addressed. There were rival camps. Some observers favoured the 'rotatory principle' of a travelling Commonwealth parliament moving between existing capital cities. There was also the idea of grafting federal capital functions onto an existing city. Another camp preferred a more permanent home, although penny-wise critics inside and outside parliament felt a spartan township would suffice. The architects of federation were eventually swayed by the American constitutional precedent of Washington, DC.

A locational compromise between the competing claims of the two largest colonial cities, Sydney and Melbourne, was embodied in Section 125 of the Constitution Act 1900, requiring the federal capital to be in New South Wales but at least 100 miles from Sydney. This was the catalyst for intensive and sustained lobbying of the federal government by various rural interests in NSW eager to secure the prestige and economic advantages of the new city. Various 'federal capital leagues' touted the physical qualities of competing sites in terms of criteria such as available land, water supply, suitable building materials, accessibility, and climatic conditions. A succession of experts was appointed to gather information and scrutinise rival bids. The site issue was finally resolved in December 1908 when the Commonwealth settled upon the Yass-Canberra district.

The dominant flavour of the federal capital debate in the first decade of federation is captured in the remarks of an unknown member of parliament quoted by the architect John Sulman: 'Very few ideas respecting the actual laying out of the capital were ever put before politicians. All the interest and controversy have so far centred upon the locality'.[3] In addition to this narrow focus, some professionals seemed reticent about discussing actual design issues, possibly reflecting the limited state of local knowledge (one reason for holding an international competition) and a conservative reluctance to move beyond generalities before a specific site was chosen. As stated by a group of government experts in 1900: 'The whole question of the general form of the city design is so dependent upon the topographical features, including the grades, etc of the selected site, that it is impracticable to further discuss anything so problematical'.[4]

Nevertheless, the federal city envisioned by most informed commentators was the antithesis of 'happy-go-lucky' Australian cities. As the illustrator DH Souter put it, 'Nothing that is mean or trivial should be permitted in its design; nothing that is shoddy or sham should be allowed in its construction ... we are building not for to-day or to-morrow, but for all time'.[5] An editorial in *Art and Architecture* was more grandiloquent:

> The Federal Capital of Australia! Who among our young men has not seen visions and, among our old men, dreamed dreams of what the city may be! Her domes and towers rising into the azure, the sheen of still gliding water, the dark woods and, beyond the purple hills and distant highlands; a fair setting for a fair city, say you. A fair setting indeed for a city that, if her people wish it, need be second to none in the world for beauty, health and convenience.[6]

The recurring epithets were pure city beautiful: 'stately', 'artistic', 'commodious', 'sanitary', 'picturesque', 'regal', and 'beauty'. The architect George Sydney Jones encapsulated the nation's task: to create a city which would be 'the most beautiful of the modern world'.[7]

The apotheosis of these sorts of ideals was the artist Charles Coulter's 1901 watercolour depiction of a grand city on the shores of Lake George, near Goulburn. Lake George – despite its alarming tendency to completely dry up through times of drought – was a serious contender as a federal capital site in the early years. It had its share of dispassionate advocates, including the engineer Frederick Gipps, who saw it as a site 'of picturesque beauty' for a city 'worthy of the aspirations of this Commonwealth in the cause of art, culture, and humanity'.[8] Coulter's mix of neo-classical and rococo structures littering hillsides and the lakefront with ersatz grandeur has been described, remarkably politely, as a 'fanciful architectural confection'.[9]

This generalised notion of 'a new Eden' prevailed in official discourse during the site selection process in the 1900s. Investigators dispatched to reconnoitre prospective sites had to bear in mind, among other criteria, 'the object of beautification'. Stomping through the bush in southern New South Wales, the government architect, WL Vernon's, mind was on a future city that 'like all European Capitals and Cities

... [could] rightly lay claim to beauty of situation and appropriateness of combination, of city and surroundings'.[10] He was assisted in this mission by Charles Coulter and another artist, JW Tristam, who transformed places like Tumut and Mahkoolma into beaux arts cities of spired buildings, arched bridges, and civic squares.

Many practical suggestions surfaced from the turn of the century, but often as mere fragments decontextualised from any larger plan. Typical were contributions on the subjects of 'aspect' and street orientation submitted to two technical journals, *The Australian Technical Journal of Science, Art and Technology* and *The Surveyor*. A focus of early discussions was the tilting of street layouts away from north-south east-west alignments to maximise sunlight. Sanitary arrangements were uppermost in the mind of the president of the Royal Society of New South Wales in calling for 'an enlightened state policy' to realise a 'new and perfect City of Hygeia'.[11] A prominent Sydney builder, John Young, supplied an extensive list of ideas, including a central park, detached houses, tree-lined streets, good water supply,

'A Waterside Federal Capital' illustrated by Charles Coulter, 1901.
The Governor-General's residence (at right) was modelled on Chateau
Azay-le-Rideau in France. *National Library of Australia PIC R134 LOC2596*

Some desirable features in an ideal federal city expressed at the Congress of Engineers, Architects and Surveyors, Melbourne, May 1901

FEATURE	RATIONALE	AUTHOR
Building design		
Uniformity of design	'Varied magnificence' rather than a 'magnificent variety' should be the aim (Jones)	Anderson, Jones
Limitation of building height	To prevent skyscrapers interfering with other buildings	Inskip, Jones
Grouping of public buildings	Stateliness and the architectural effect of a 'citadel'	Anderson, Inskip
Harmonious colour schemes	Visual harmony	Inskip, Jones
Infrastructure		
Underground services	To avoid 'a continuous state of upheaval'	Broadhurst, Inskip
Moving platforms, elevated sidewalks	Avoiding traffic congestion; boost commercial frontage	Anderson, Henderson
Land use		
Residential and general land use zoning	To preserve amenity and prevent lowering of property values	Anderson, Blacket, Inskip
Control of advertising signs	'This modern barbarism' (Jones)	Jones, Inskip
Fountains and drinking fountains	A climatic-relevant street decoration 'for man and beast' (Inskip)	Broadhurst, Hall, Inskip, McDowall
Landscaping		
Lake or riverfront location	'Healthful and lend more picturesqueness' (Evans)	Evans, Inskip, Luffmann
Open space and gardens	Health, beauty and showcasing buildings	Inskip, Jones, Luffmann, Broadhurst
Wide and tree-planted streets	For traffic and views of architectural features; planting for shade and beauty	Broadhurst, Inskip, Jones

Source papers: JT Noble Anderson, 'A Twentieth Century City'; Cyril Blacket, 'Some Conditions to be Inserted in any Federal City Building Covenants'; A Evans, 'A Waterside Federal Capital'; R Henson Broadhurst, 'Suggestions concerning the Laying Out of the Commonwealth Capital'; JA Henderson, 'Notes Re Improved Facilities for Locomotion in Cities'; GC Inskip, 'The Federal City'; G Sydney Jones, 'Some Thoughts concerning the Federal City'; C Bogue Luffmann, 'The Agricultural, Horticultural and Sylvan Features of a Federal Capital'; A McDowall, 'Notes on Standard Marks of Reference for the Direction of Building Line of Streets in Cities'.

an efficient sewerage system, frequent garbage removals, common service trenches, and even the utilisation of 'rainwater from roofs of houses ... in watering trees or gardens'.[12] Through various federal and state government reports produced during the site selection process runs an undercurrent of ideas with physical planning implications, such as the need for topographic variety, the desirability of a river location, and the possibility of 'ornamental waters'. A recurrent notion was securing 'rising knolls for public edifices' – a desired attribute well represented at the site eventually chosen.[13]

The periods of most intense activity in translating these rather generalised notions of a city beautiful into more concrete planning statements were in 1901 and 1909–10. The first comes at the moment of federation, when the idea of a federal city animated nationalistic fervour within the design professions; the second after a definite site had finally been chosen.

The 'Congress of Engineers, Architects, Surveyors, And Members of Allied Professions, to discuss Questions relating to the Laying Out and Building of the Federal Capital, and matters of professional interest generally, held in Melbourne during the Commonwealth Celebrations, May 1901, at the Institute Rooms, 175 Collins Street', to give the occasion its formal title, was the first significant opportunity for interested professionals to intensively discuss the federal capital project. Also the first conference on town planning in Australia, it was held to coincide with the first sitting of the federal parliament. The importance of the 1901 congress was in beginning to pull disparate threads toward a common goal: the planning of a total urban environment that could be beautiful.

Across 12 papers which varied widely in scope, intellectual rigour, and technicality, an extraordinary array of issues was canvassed, including traffic flows, public transport, water supply and waste management, provision of parks and public gardens, controls on residential densities, building covenants, fire-proofing, and air-conditioning. Many of these issues had been inherited from the milieu of 19th century urban reform, and their relevance in the restructuring of established cities would also not have been lost on delegates. The significance attached to aesthetic elements such as the location of public buildings, 'picturesque features', and 'schemes for architectural adornment' was evident.

Beautification of utilitarian features was also canvassed, and two papers suggested the treatment of humble surveyors' marks as either ornamental drinking fountains or street gardens. The most individualistic position was that of Bernard Hall, director of Melbourne's National Gallery, who wished 'for the sake of picturesqueness, that the new city will be built in the usual miscellaneous way'. The position was not shared by fellow delegates who would have agreed with GS Jones's call for 'some uniformity of spirit of design.' Jones was even brave enough to attempt an early summation of the ideal city:

> We are probably all agreed on general principles as to what the plan should be – for instance – that the streets should be wide and tree-planted, that the circus, the square and the boulevard, straight and curved lines, park lands, gardens, and the like should find their proper places; that the public, semi-public and private building blocks should be disposed in due relation one to the other on sites best adapted for each, and with due regard to the future expansion of the City.[14]

Some delegates were anxious that the congress produce definitive outcomes in terms of technical principles, professional opportunities and government commitment, but the full gamut of issues proved impossible for delegates to assimilate. The question of city design was restricted to a general resolution:

> That in the opinion of this Congress it is important that the Federal Capital should be laid out in the most perfect manner possible, and that, to avoid the mistakes made in many cities of spoiling the plan by utilizing existing buildings, it is desirable that in any site obtained, all obstructions be removed that would in any way prevent the adoption of the most perfect design.[15]

Through the latter part of 1901, local understanding of just what the 'most perfect design' might entail was advanced through further debate, primarily in the eastern states; Western Australia was always antipathetic to the federation ideal. In September 1901 several joint meetings were held between members of the institutes of architects and surveyors of NSW in Sydney to discuss major papers by their respective presidents, John Barlow and George Knibbs. In some ways, Barlow's vision was unremarkable for the time: a predominantly radial-concentric city with 'triple avenues about 150 feet in width', circuses at

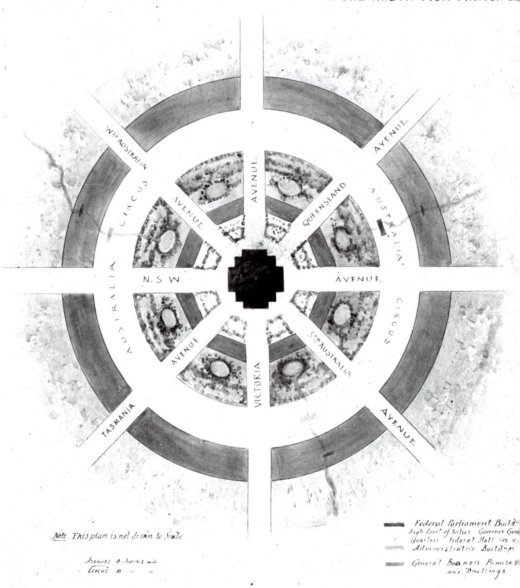

Radial plan for the federal capital: Vic Mann's 'rough suggestion'
of Alexander Oliver's ideas, 1901. *National Library of Australia, Map RM2479*

major street intersections 'marked by a great fountain or monument', and 'trees everywhere'. More eccentrically, influenced by his views on the picturesqueness of old Sydney, with a touch of Camillo Sitte, he dismissed the idea of a grand master plan and envisaged the new city core 'as complete and self-contained as the town of medieval days surrounded by its wall'.[16]

Knibbs's paper was an abbreviated version of an elaborate statement presented a few weeks earlier to the Royal Society of NSW.[17] 'The Theory of City Design' stands as a seminal contribution to early planning theory, certainly the most substantive modernist treatment since John Sulman's 'The Laying Out of Towns' in 1890. Knibbs explicitly engaged

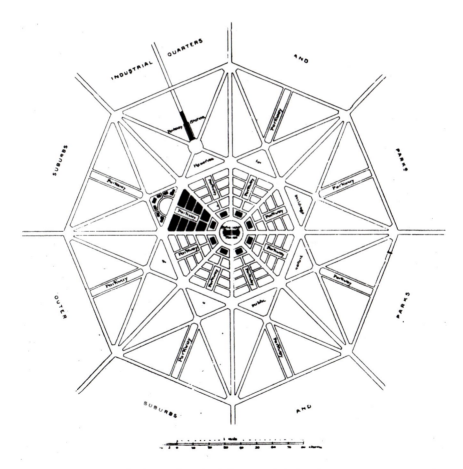

'Spider's web': John Sulman's radial planning.
J Sulman, The Federal Capital, 1909

the combination of the utilitarian and the artistic in his treatise. He portrayed the creation of a capital city as a synthesis of sound 'technical preparation' and 'aesthetic consciousness'. The former embraced general laws of city design regarding radial street systems, land use zoning, and building controls. The latter was based on symmetrical but not excessive grouping. 'The possibility of beauty' was further enhanced by other considerations such as the provision of parks and gardens, tree-planting, 'foliage-squares' and other public spaces and embellishments which could also function as 'a desirable corrective' in breaking up the 'wearisome regularity' of long straight streets. Amplifying the need for the 'spatial provision necessary for the proper viewing of all features of interest', Knibbs characteristically devised a scientific rule that around every monument 'the unobstructed space should be between a distance equal to the height and that equal to at least three times its height' to enable it to be seen with maximum advantage.[18]

Knibbs credited Alexander Oliver with sparking his own interest in the federal capital project. In November 1899, Oliver, president of the NSW Land Appeal Court, was appointed a royal commissioner by the last colonial government of the state. He was charged with investigating the competing claims of the federal capital leagues and providing the first analysis of the suitability of places suggested for the seat of government. Although beyond his initial brief, Oliver was known to advocate 'the advisability of having a sketch design' to develop specific layout ideas.[19] After submitting his report, he made such a sketch, which was then translated into a 'larger plan' by the Sydney artist-architect Vic Mann.[20] Oliver's plan was based on 'the radiation principle', drawing on Renaissance concepts, with grand avenues named for the states focussed on a citadel of central parliamentary buildings. Open space was plentiful, but Oliver also had one eye on utility: his parks could initially be commercial tree plantations, to be harvested in stages with the income assisting 'the more elaborate development' of the resultant parkland.[21]

Individuals with an interest in the actual design of the projected city used the press or submitted their ideas for consideration direct to the commonwealth government. The most complete statement came from John Sulman. His paper on 'The Federal Capital', written after the Canberra site was confirmed, emerged first as a series of articles in the Sydney *Daily Telegraph* (of which he was a director). It was later reprinted as a pamphlet and reproduced in the *Journal of the Royal Institute of British Architects* (RIBA). A shorter version was included in the *Transactions* of the 1910 RIBA Town Planning Conference in London. Sulman played no role in the deliberations of 1901, probably because he was still estranged from the New South Wales Institute of Architects after years of bitter professional disputes. His schematic plan embodied the radial 'spider's web' planning ideas which he first advocated in 1890. His federal capital was 'primarily ... an official city', with the main parliament building standing out 'against the sky' on an elevated site at the hub of an octagonal-shaped city, criss-crossed by wide radial and diagonal avenues. The insertion of parkways was direct testimony to American city beautiful influence, while the avoidance of east-west and north-south streets revisited local concerns for house and street aspect. The parliamentary citadel was surrounded by major government buildings 'on fine sites' in an artistic arrangement. The intersection of radial avenues and ring roads created sites for roundabouts and other features contributing 'artistic value'.

In the decade after federation, then, several key planning ideas emerged through political debates, government reports, professional exchanges, and scientific papers. Beyond the obligatory references to banning slums and insisting on technical up-to-dateness, the recurring values were the importance of radial city planning, multiple centres, ample parkland, a waterside but flood-free city, dominant public buildings notably a parliament house, provision for expansion, and reservation of elevated sites for major public buildings and monuments. A strong theme was the notion of securing an amphitheatre-like location to best 'present the artistic features essential for the development of a really beautiful city'.[22] Moreover, the underlying notion of fusing the artistic and the utilitarian had been established at the 1901 Melbourne congress. Sulman's schematic plan fused these ideas into a complete graphical statement. By 1911 even the president of the Local Government Association of New South Wales was advocating preservation of 'the natural beauty of the land', convergence of radial avenues on suitably grouped public buildings, ample provision of parkland, and the extension of main avenues from two or three main radial points with avenues between them on a rectangular system.[23]

The design competition

While the international design competition for the federal capital in 1911–12 is a crucial event in the Canberra chronology, 'it was also a culmination … of thinking about the way Australia could create the ideal city.[24] Early professional discussions indicate that Australians were still quite removed from global advances in planning theory and practice. Consideration was thus 'often limited to identifying what qualities a Federal Capital should have rather than debating these qualities in a comparative sense'.[25] Home-grown inspiration was frequently mixed in with populist images of stately cities, Renaissance and colonial models, historical documents such as Wren's 1666 scheme for London, and relatively obscure writings such as Horace Bushnell on 'City Plans' in his *Work and Play* (1864). The one contemporary name to surface in early debates was Joseph Stubben, the German advocate of extension planning.

The appointment of Joseph Davis to an overseas fact-finding mission marked the beginning of a more concerted official effort to keep in touch with foreign developments. In 1906 the prime minister, Alfred Deakin, instructed Davis, under-secretary of the NSW Department of Public Works, to 'obtain such particulars, plans and documents as in your opinion will be of assistance in connection with the founding of the Federal City'. Davis – who had attended the joint institute meetings in Sydney in 1901 – returned 'with much useful information' from Paris, London, Washington and Ottawa.[26]

In 1909, Sulman pronounced that planning was 'comparatively new in Australia' and that 'local effort' because of this 'lack of experience' would likely not produce 'the best result'.[27] He suggested that men of the calibre of architects Aston Webb and Daniel Burnham might ride to the rescue as technical advisers. Other observers felt that only a small number of individuals would have the practical experience capable of preparing a capital city plan from scratch. One Canadian journal ventured to mention just five names: Burnham, New York architects Cass Gilbert and Arnold Brunner, Canadian expatriate architect-critic FW Fitzpatrick, and Frank Miles Day, a former president of the American Institute of Architects.[28]

The idea of an international city design competition to attract the best plan from the best in the world was mooted as early as 1901 and garnered support as the safest strategy. While the competition announced by the commonwealth government in April 1911 was not a surprise, almost every aspect of its staging and management was controversial, from the amount of prize money through the adjudication process to the result. The RIBA protested an arrangement giving a government minister the final say and prohibited its members from participating. This boycott could not be ignored by sister institutes in America and the Australian states. The mess made of the jury process and the measly prize money on offer to entice the top professionals perhaps combined to deprive the competition of names like John Nolen, Raymond Unwin, and EH Bennett (his former partner Burnham was diagnosed with cancer in 1909 and died a fortnight after the Australian jury gave its verdict).

Detailed descriptive information on the Canberra site for prospective competitors was made available through government offices in all the state capitals, the Australian High Commission in London, public works departments, and British embassies or consulates in nine other world cities: Berlin, Cape Town, Chicago, Ottawa, Paris, Pretoria, New York, Washington, and Wellington. The data included two cycloramas of the site prepared by Charles Coulter. Competition conditions were not prescriptive. The 'panoramic value of the city surroundings' and prospects for 'ornamental water' were mentioned, but the only specific directive was that the parliamentary building 'should be so placed as to become a dominating feature of the city'. Reference was made to the proceedings of the 1910 RIBA town planning conference as necessarily having 'a marked influence upon city design from the utilitarian, the architectural, the scientific, and the artistic standpoints'.

The compromise jury appointed by the Commonwealth comprised Melbourne surveyor JM Coane as chairman, Melbourne engineer James Alexander Smith, and Sydney architect John Kirkpatrick. Six major evaluation criteria were agreed: general convenience, hygiene, expansion, economy, architectural and general effect, and miscellaneous. The latter included 'aboreal treatment' but aesthetic treatment – including prospect, architectural possibilities, ornamental waters, parks, and allocation of public buildings – was flagged under the penultimate category.

American dream: Harold Magonigle competition entry.
The Salon, July–August 1912

The chill of authoritarian axiality: Eliel Saarinen competition entry.
The Salon, July–August 1912

The total of 137 plans submitted for judging by early 1912 provide a kaleidoscopic overview of the state of town planning on the eve of World War I. It was a collection of the weird and wonderful, amateur and professional. Some plans were highly mannered and theoretical, while others had no convincing sense of order. The diversity of global planning cultures was on display, from tightly-knit schemes organised around networks of public squares inspired by traditional European cities to very stern and formal geometric solutions.

The timing of the competition meant that city beautiful ideas would surface in many submitted entries. Groupings of public buildings, adaptations of the Washington mall, and park systems and residential parkways were common, particularly in the American entries. New York architect Harold Van Buren Magonigle (1867–1935) promoted a grand axis linking what is now Parliament House and Civic Centre. Magonigle had worked for Calvert Vaux, was an alumnus of beaux arts giants McKim Mead and White, enjoyed success in architectural competitions, and specialised in memorials. A major work of Magonigle's was the Liberty Memorial in Kansas City (1921). Bernard Maybeck (1862–1957) submitted a more complex plan inspired by Parisian boulevards. San Francisco-based Maybeck designed the Palace of Fine Arts for the Panama-Pacific International Exposition of 1913. He had studied at the École des Beaux Arts and was a former employee of the New York architects Carrère and Hastings. He later shared the idea with the prime minister, WM Hughes, of building Canberra as a temporary international exposition to ensure that it would develop 'rationally and beautifully'.[29]

The three judges were split on the merit of the entries. Coane awarded his first prize to the Sydney team of Charles Caswell, Charles Coulter and Walter Scott Griffiths. Like Coulter, Caswell had prior knowledge of the Canberra site in his day job as a public works engineer. Walter Scott Griffiths was a draftsman who succeeded Charles Reade as government town planner of South Australia in the early 1920s. In collaboration, they were able to strike a rapprochement between the engineering and artistic viewpoints through a policy of 'Give and Take'.[30] But they later squabbled as to principal authorship, although Coulter's unequivocal role was to visualise their federal city in three dimensions, the task he had done for others since 1901, with

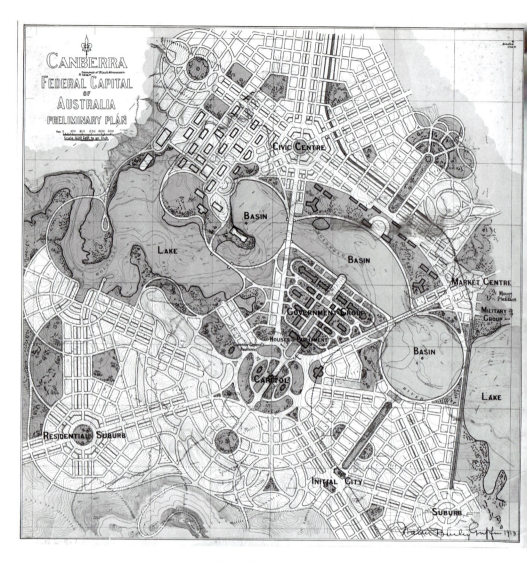

Walter Burley Griffin Preliminary Plan, 1912.
National Library of Australia, MAP8984.C351

the same riot of classical styles perpetuated.[31] JD Fitzgerald felt the plan lacked symmetry and was 'too scattered'. The pragmatic surveyor Louis Curtis concluded that it would make 'a beautiful city from the aesthetic point of view, while its practicability is far and away above any of its competitors'.[32] This was not something he would say of the entry preferred by the other two judges and accepted also by the home affairs minister, King O'Malley: Design No. 29 by Walter Burley Griffin.

The Griffin plan

The prize-winning entry by Walter Burley Griffin in partnership with Marion Mahony Griffin bore the undeniable hallmarks of a classic city beautiful plan. It was extravagant, formal, geometric, and artistically produced. The plan conveyed a monumental city dominated by grand axes and vistas, ensembles of monolithic buildings, terminal landmarks, citadels and cumulative massing. Magnificently visualised on large drawings on silk by Marion, it was a work of art in itself.

The Griffin Plan embodied values and design elements connecting it to the emerging vocabulary of mainstream modernist planning: the holistic, organic approach to urban form and function; the pre-dilection for specialisation of land use functions; the penchant for segregated residential spaces; the idea of road hierarchies. The feature that really distinguished the scheme from most of the other entries was its metropolitan scale. Griffin's vision was of lateral rather than vertical extension. Few other entries anticipated long-term growth needs, although second-prize winner Eliel Saarinen submitted a remarkable satellite town plan in the image of Ebenezer Howard.[33] The critical Griffin diagram is the 'City and Environs' plan, which shows a suburban metropolis structured around a triangulated series of specialised sub-centres, three times as large as a town for 25 000 required for the competition.

In this and other respects, the Griffin plan brought together many of the ideas which had already become defined as theoretically desirable in Australian professional circles: the representation of the site as a stage setting, the specialised centres, the radial avenues, the ornamental waters, even attention to the micro aspects of beautility in designing and siting complexes such as the gasworks both 'for economy and to avoid ugly tanks so conspicuous usually'.[34] This integration of desirable features goes some way to explaining why it appealed to members of the Federal Capital Designs Board.

Griffin saw himself as an original and was notoriously guarded about his influences. As James Weirick, has noted, the brilliantly executed plan arrived on the scene fully developed and workable but with nothing in Griffin's previous track record remotely of the same scale and sophistication.[35] Griffin told *The New York Times* in June 1912

Walter Burley Griffin,
c1921. *National Library of
Australia*

Model of federal
government group in
the Griffin Plan. *P Reid,
Canberra Following Griffin,
National Archives, 2002*

that 'I have planned a city not like any other city in the world. I have planned it not in a way that I expected any governmental authorities in the world would accept. I have planned an ideal city – a city that meets my ideal of the city of the future'.[36]

The sources and symbolism built into the plan still challenge scholars. There is an obvious coalescence with the more suburban trappings of the garden city, the morphological influence of other city plans such as the polygons featured in Wren's plan for rebuilding London after the Great Fire, and German-style extension planning. Like most American entries, the winning scheme reflected the underlying influence of beaux arts lines in envisaging a monumental city dominated by grand axes, vistas, and landmarks. All major avenues, 200 feet wide, were channelised into specialist traffic corridors divided into 'at least quadruple rows and supplemental shrubbery parkways for shade and shelter, wind and dust arresting', also commanding views of 'terminal objectives, either natural or artificial'.[37]

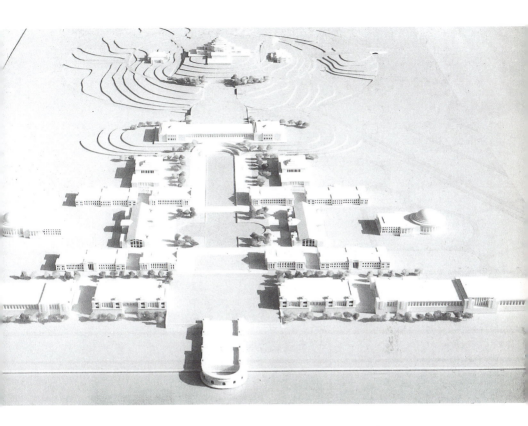

In a metropolis of sub-centres, one of the apexes of the triangle defining the core functions of the central area was an 'urban administration centre'. Here, across the ornamental lake from the federal centre, Griffin envisaged a mix of functions serving the everyday administrative needs of residents. The centre was to have been spatially independent from a 'retail-wholesale centre' but linked to it via a 'municipal axis' along the base of the triangle. Renamed simply 'Civic Centre' in Griffin's revised 1913 preliminary plan, in line with US city beautiful usage, its planning was to have afforded 'further opportunity for ex-tending the harmonious public grouping of the parallel-set system of the Federal Groups'. Griffin initially schemed a 'pyramid' treatment with post office, criminal and local courts, banks, and allied institutions grouped around a central 'City Hall or Administration Block' on the site's highest point. This civic centre recalled a host of American plans as did other elements. Nearby, great importance was attached to a rectilinear campus plan, an indirect reflection of the growing importance and prestige of campus designs in the USA in the early 1900s. There were also parkways and large-lot suburbs within a gently geometric contour-controlled street plan.

The influences of the World's Columbian Exposition, Washington, DC, and the Plan of Chicago are evident singly or in combination in the plan. The 'White City' had a major impact on Griffin, not in terms of specific architectural styles, but in its power of ensemble. His original 1912 text explained:

> Possibly the fullest scope for this tendency has been given designers in the numerous exposition projects, typical and best of which may have been the Columbian Exposition at Chicago, where the restriction to one colossal scale and single type of design around a rigidly formal enclosed court produced an impression outliving those of all subsequent experiments, or of perhaps any architectural ensemble of modern times.[38]

He later elaborated:

> The Columbian Exposition was our great example of a scheme or system. It is not only an example for our time, but perhaps for all time ... the thing that appealed to everybody, the thing that made that exhibition last for twenty years in the minds of all people, was that it provided a place for everything and had everything in its place. It was the first great effort that I know of on a large scale to make such a success, and simplicity is what we have got to strive for to get out of our complexities. Without this we cannot expect a homogeneity.[39]

The memory of the 1893 exposition was invoked by specific structures, such as a casino and a watergate feature, the latter along with other city portals was a particular preoccupation of the city beautiful. But most revealing is the configuration of space at the core of his plan, with a formal grouping of uniformly-scaled federal government buildings set around a water court. Another possible design influence was the layout of the 1904 World's Fair in St Louis, where Griffin's brother Ralph lived. Griffin described the major structures in this group of government buildings as having a 'connected park or garden frontage ... as in the case of the Mall at Washington'.[40] The ensemble presented the opportunity for 'cumulative massing' rising to the 'dominating architectural feature' of the Capitol building, which was reminiscent of Burnham's towering city hall in the Chicago Plan completed two years earlier, albeit with a ziggurat rather than a dome.

Reminiscent of Burnham's 1909 concept was the proposed cultural zone on the northern shore of the lake, with the same congregation of museums, sporting facilities and public parkland close to commerce as in Chicago's lakefront Grant Park. Griffin's lake was similarly a focus for water-based recreation, with a shoreline lending itself to the same 'boulevardisation' treatment. The dramatic artistic presentation by Marion Mahony recalls the renderings of Jules Guerin for the Chicago exposition and amplifies the intellectual connections between the two plans. Both stressed the importance of unity and the organic nature of city form and function; in Griffin's words: 'Unity essential to the city requires for so complex a problem a simple organism'.[41]

There are also similarities to John Nolen's plan for Madison, Wisconsin (1911), which similarly addressed the city's needs on several levels: as state capital, educational centre, and place of residence. Its centrepiece was a mall–axis, flanked by symmetrically placed public buildings, linking a dominant state capitol at the apex of radiating avenues to a landscaped waterfront devoted to public uses. Elsewhere, Nolen, trained as a landscape architect, was alive to the conservation of natural beauty and there was the same overall commitment to beauty as something immanent in the plan itself rather than affixed afterwards.

While these multifarious elements connect the Griffin plan to international influences, there were significant departures from conventional city beautiful thought. Its inspiration was a rich collage of diverse artistic, sociological and philosophical underpinnings derived from a whole raft of antecedents: Patrick Geddes, anthroposophy, German expressionism, and ancient and oriental cultures, to name a few. The Griffins were not speaking exactly the same language as a Daniel Burnham, Cass Gilbert, or even CM Robinson.

The winning plan was skilfully adapted to the 'irregular amphitheatre' of the site rather than arbitrarily imposed upon the landscape. As Peter Harrison later observed, the 'buildings are made important not so much by their size, height or architectural significance, but by their setting … it is not an architectural composition, but a landscape composition'.[42] There are in fact few direct references to architecture and what there was broke from conventional neo-classical inspiration. Like his early mentor Frank Lloyd Wright, Griffin had no interest in 'rehashing the completed Roman expression':

> For the essential uniformity in style it is hardly advisable to recommend, however, an adaptation of any historical style which different requirements will inevitably render a caricature instead of a reminiscence of its own proper grandeur. Thus are Greek temples rendered boxes with glass windows instead of masses of masonry, and colonnades are applied in front of windowed walls to the detriment of light and comfort, and thus are noble features like columns, capitals and consoles mutilated and distorted, distributed for every sort of function except their inherent one of support. That sort of treatment may be well enough in some scene painting and even exposition buildings, but can by no means be considered dignified, as permanently standing for the life and government of a great modern commonwealth.[43]

The plan overall represents a deep-seated integration of buildings into the landscape, with its two main axes – land and water – revealing defining natural elements.

The Griffin plan lacked the pompousness and predictability of many monument-focused city beautiful plans. It was very different from other imperial capitals, such as Pretoria and New Delhi, planned at the same time. It was far less overblown and unresolved than Ernest Hébrard and Henrik Anderson's pure beaux arts world city of peace project, also creating international attention at the time, and which George Taylor sought to attract to Australia. The Griffin plan eschewed the sombre heroism and ceremony of these plans in favour of a more 'open and festive' response 'in the manner of the American world's fair complexes at Chicago and St Louis'.[44] The centrepiece was in fact not the parliamentary building, the conventional locus of power in a federal city, but a 'Capitol' conceived as a space 'for popular assembly and festivity'.[45] The plan was arguably closer in spirit to the original L'Enfant plan than the Senate Park Commission makeover with its axial alignments informed by the wider natural setting rather than memorials.[46] Griffin wrote in his competition report that 'the mountains retained in their natural state [were] treated as the termini of the principal axes of as many important vistas as possible'. Orientating vistas to distant mountains rather than man-made objects also drew on eastern influences. Overall, the plan was imbued with a more complex geometry and mysterious symbolism than was typical of the city beautiful genre; it may have recalled the Burnham plan but was animated 'by quite a different spirit'.[47]

If the Griffin plan appealed as the plan that Australia had to have, connected compellingly into state-of-the-art city beautiful ideas and at the same time more subtly revealing numerous other sources, then Marion's brilliant perspectives sealed the deal. Immediate reaction to its announcement as the winning plan in May 1912 was generally positive. Even George Taylor, who led a campaign to have Griffin brought to Australia to develop his plan, declared that 'there is no question that the first prize plans were the best sent in … The view from the Capitol with its magnificent tree-lined streets each ending in a fine centre should, if constructed, prove one of the finest city vistas in the world'.[48] But its innovative mix also proved an unsettling gumbo, with what Paul Reid called 'Australian pragmatism and Chicago idealism' on a collision course.[49]

Problems with the Griffin plan

The major problem Griffin faced was a small cabal of senior public servants who had their own ideas about how to build a federal city and had indeed set about doing that even before the international competition. Their machinations anticipated broader concerns that surfaced about the impracticability of the plan, quite apart from the dawning recognition of the expense of building 'the city beautiful of our dreams'. Contemporary issues of most concern included the extensive cut-and-fill earthworks required in places to make the site conform to the plan and the lack of detail regarding important engineering matters. Griffin conceded that 'matters of street equipment, drainage, engineering and construction, in almost infinite variety and extent' needed to be addressed in due course.[50] But critics attacked his failure to incorporate these elements from the start.

The disgruntlement of some fellow competitors was probably un-derstandable, but not atypical. The Australian team behind the so-called 'merino' entry No. 10 was most put out. Walter Scott Griffiths felt the Griffin drawings 'would be more appropriately hung in a young maid's bedroom' and proved 'total ignorance of the subject of Town Planning'.[51] Charles Caswell was appalled to learn from Griffin first-hand that he had devoted barely six weeks to preparing his design and gave no serious thought to engineering problems, 'believing that they were mere matters of detail'.[52] An issue for Caswell was that jury member JA Smith was a mechanical rather than civil engineer and chairman JM Coane confided that he had great difficulty convincing Smith and Kirkpatrick of the importance of practical engineering matters as 'quite beyond their comprehension'.[53]

Local consternation was fuelled by expert criticism from abroad. The British town planner Patrick Abercrombie's review actually misread the Griffin plan, criticising the lake as separating the city into two halves, the land axis as 'an unpardonable error' for focusing on 'a natural impasse', and the 'somewhat eccentric method of presentment'.[54] British and European critics aligned to the garden city movement saw only an endless repetition of star-points and gridiron streets. WR Davidge criticised a geometric design seemingly based on the site fitting the plan rather than vice versa, the absence of a greenbelt, and large swathes of unpicturesque gridiron streets.[55] In view of Griffin's obvious effort to address landform and demonstrable skills in community planning, the contemporary concern that the Canberra plan ignored the dictates of topography is puzzling but nevertheless hit home and persisted. With Canberra in mind, FW Fitzpatrick was critical of the 'paper attractiveness of our projects, the unyielding insistence we place upon an imaginary, a drawn "balance" that in reality generally means absolutely nothing'.[56] Werner Hegemann, the German-American planner and architectural critic, was similarly but more politely critical in *The American Vitruvius* (1922).

Less than a month after the public announcement of the Griffin win, commonwealth bureaucrats were plotting to adapt the winning plan to their long-standing ideas, which revolved around a more compact city, less expensive to develop, and adjacent to the main parliamentary zone on the southern side of the Molonglo River. The infamous departmental board, headed by Percy Owen, the Director-General of Works, reviewed all major and minor prize winners in the competition to concoct a synthetic design which it saw as providing for 'creation of a City which will be practical as well as beautiful'.[57] Similarities with the

Impression of the departmental board plan by London artist G Bron. *The Sphere, March 1913.*

Caswell, Coulter and Griffiths plan were evident. John Smith Murdoch, as a member of the board, was troubled by the artificiality of Griffin's plan, including its contours, lake basins, placement of buildings and 'system of hygiene'. Apparently never a fan of the federal capital project, he supported the move to a more 'economical' city beautiful planning while still respecting natural contours.[58]

Initial reactions to the departmental board plan were not all unfavourable. GS Jones felt some details could be improved, notably the locating of military barracks on the land axis, but overall felt that such particulars did not 'greatly mar a plan which is practically and aesthetically good'.[59] JM Coane felt that it was 'unquestionable' that the board had succeeded in devising a scheme 'worthy of the occasion, from the aesthetic as well as from the utilitarian standpoint'.[60] Tellingly, the home affairs minister, O'Malley, concurred: a city laid out on these lines 'should be both practical and beautiful'.[61] A major implication here is that a misaligned balance of beauty and utility had been corrected and the basis for a better compromise had been reached. Others disagreed. In the *Town Planning Review*, Patrick Abercrombie made a devastating critique of an amateurish plan resembling 'a third rate Luna Park or the Christmas production of a toy factory'. These comments were echoed without acknowledgement in the Australian architectural journal, *The Salon*. WL Vernon described 'an inferiority of conception'.[62]

Incredibly the hodgepodge departmental creation was the official city plan when Canberra was officially named in March 1913. The governor-general, Lord Denman, looked forward to a city inspiring 'in its noble buildings, its broad avenues, its shaded parks, and sheltered gardens – a city bearing perhaps some resemblance to the city beautiful of our dreams'.[63] But the balance of opinion doubted the plan's abilities to deliver these outcomes and professional and political lobbying saw some justice done when the departmental board plan was dropped. Griffin was invited to Australia in August 1913 and was subsequently appointed Federal Capital Director of Design and Construction, formally taking up this position in May 1914, two years after winning the competition.

Griffin had been briefed on the departmental board's concerns by Murdoch in Chicago in 1912. He subsequently made adjustments to appease its criticisms but his basic design remained intact. Opposition and resistance to his authority within the public service would prove so dysfunctional that in 1916–17 a royal commission into the administration of Canberra was convened. It documented in appalling detail the hostility and uncooperativeness shown towards the American. Griffin's problems were sometimes self-inflicted: he was not the smartest political operator and proved a mediocre administrator. But the cards were stacked against him, indeed they were against the federal capital project itself, particularly during wartime when resources were scarce and national priorities lay elsewhere. Many in the planning movement shared a view aired in the broader community that the development of Canberra should not proceed during these years and resolutions to press on with the project were actually lost at both the 1917 and 1918 national planning conferences. But Griffin seemed to attract real personal venom, particularly from George and Florence Taylor, who had a spectacular falling out with him and Marion. Initially one of his greatest supporters, George turned on Griffin as 'an idealist who cannot get down to facts':[64] This was a typical rant:

> Canberra is too great a national problem for it to be entirely trusted to the whims and fancies of an aesthete and idealist. There is no doubt as to his ability as a landscape architect and town-planner, but he is not practical and business-like enough to conduct the constructional and developmental part of the scheme; he requires sound level-headed business men to keep him within reasonable expenditure, and expert engineers, architects, builders and real-estate experts to keep him down to earth and restrain his artistic flights.[65]

Post-Griffin Canberra

In 1921 the commonwealth government instituted a new governance regime to accelerate the relocation of the national parliament from its temporary quarters in Melbourne. Griffin protested dilution of his role within a committee structure and declined to join the new Federal Capital Advisory Committee (FCAC), his place being taken by Sydney architect HE Ross, with the chairmanship going to John Sulman. The FCAC got down to business in its first general report. Acknowledging and endorsing early aspirations towards 'a beautiful City', it nonetheless recommended that the task of building a monumental city with its ornamental lakes, boulevards, bridges and grand public buildings should be deferred for decades, perhaps generations on the grounds of cost. The accent for the foreseeable future was to be on 'utilitarian development and economy'.[66]

A quite different planning context for Canberra was constituted,

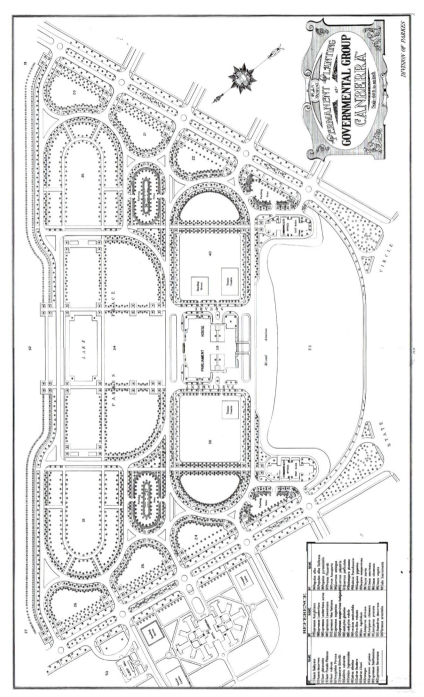

Perfect landscape symmetry for the Governmental Group, Federal Capital
Commission 1928. *National Capital Authority, The Griffin Legacy, 2004*

one that stressed garden suburbs, tree planting, unpretentious construction, and 'provisional' public buildings. Government parsimony and public apathy had aligned with a new planning ideology stressing cost-effectiveness, efficiency, and functionality. The city beautiful was put on hold. Even while the FCAC was required to adhere to Griffin's geometric street plan, decisions were made that departed from both the letter and spirit of the Griffin plan. The 'garden town' trajectory effectively destroyed the urbanity inherent in Griffin's vision. Specific siting, aesthetic and land use planning judgments for retail centres, public buildings and residential development contrary to the original plan had long-term consequences.

Nevertheless, apart from the greening of the city area through extensive plantings, there were three sites where city beautiful connotations were prominently maintained. One was the development of the Civic Centre, a task initially guided by Sulman. He wrote to the responsible government minister in 1922 to advocate 'a self-contained shopping centre surrounded by a continuous colonnade to give that shelter from sun and rain which retail traders find essential and usually provide by ugly verandahs'.[67] Sulman's colleague HE Ross would have given strong support, having urged better forms of weather protection than the 'hideously excrescent' street awning in the federal capital debates back in 1901.[68] The Sydney and Melbourne buildings with their distinctive Mediterranean-style loggia verandahs were completed by other architects in the late 1920s. They are the most complete realisation of Sulman's views, outlined in *An Introduction to the Study of Town Planning in Australia* (1921), on the value of island sites for major buildings and the need for proper planning of central retail facilities to ensure maximum feasible exposure to sunshine and fresh air.

A second outcome was the agreed design of the central parliamentary zone with its provisional parliamentary building (1927) and flanking office buildings (West and East blocks) set within an almost perfectly symmetrical geometric pattern of streets, paths, gardens and formal tree plantings. John Smith Murdoch was the key player in carrying out this 'City Beautiful landscape composition', with West Block even needing an additional storey to maintain the balance between the buildings when 'viewed between trees'.[69]

The national war memorial was a third development which

brought together many city beautiful themes in a very Australian context. The idea was conceived in London by Australian military officers, including the honorary Captain Charles Bean, and realisation owed more to Bean 'than to anybody else'.[70] He was the official war historian in World War I, a former *Sydney Morning Herald* journalist, and an early supporter of town planning reform, active in Sydney's parks and playgrounds movement. From the beginning there was a fusion of monumental and utilitarian aspects which elsewhere frequently broke apart. The memorial was to be an economical combination of museum and shrine. An official memo by the acting minister for home and territories in 1922 noted that 'no piles of sculpture or other artificial monument can ever rival this assemblage of war material and war memories'.[71] The Australian War Museum Committee was comfortable with this direction and the *Australian War Memorial Act* 1925 provided for a memorial to include war relics and documentary records.

Griffin's plan had identified the slopes of Mount Ainslie as a 'commanding' situation suitable for a commemorative or purely monumental structure, but placed a recreational casino on the most prominent site, astride his land axis. Selection of this location for the memorial is variously attributed to Percy Owen, the surveyor-general Colonel JTH Goodwin and FCAC secretary Charles Daley.[72] Regardless, the choice ruffled few feathers. The building would face Parliament House just as the All-India War Memorial Arch looked towards the Viceroy's Palace down a ceremonial avenue in New Delhi. The War Museum Committee conceived a stand-alone edifice that:

> ... should ... have gardens around it [and] should be in a pure Greek style of architecture with as much simplicity as possible ... of white Australian marble or brilliant white stone ... set in heavy formal native trees ... in front will be a memorial group of statuary with a simple inscription.[73]

As a federal government initiative in the distant bush capital, the project was relatively free of the controversy that attended many state and local memorials – until the 1927 design competition, which identified no winner within the stipulated £250 000 budget from 70

More garden town than city beautiful: Anzac Parade to Parliament House, Canberra in the 1950s. *Noel Freestone*

Australian War Memorial in the 1950s. *Noel Freestone*

entries. The assessors were Sydney architects Leslie Wilkinson and Charles Rosenthal, and John Smith Murdoch. The journal *Building* was predictably critical of the entire competition process and conditions, describing the panel as architecturally unrepresentative and biased toward Sydney and Melbourne competitors. Murdoch was singled out for particular vitriol as an architect 'whose tastes have been formed by years of operation in a government office, where cheeseparing is more in evidence than beautiful art'.[74] Subsequently two Sydney architects, Emil Sodersteen and John Crust, were invited to collaborate and submit a joint hybrid design, which broke from the pure neo-classical tradition for major public buildings and was well received.

At a 1928 Parliamentary Standing Committee on Public Works inquiry, Griffin resurfaced to concur that the memorial was sited in 'a suitable place'. William Blackett, president of the Royal Victorian Institute of Architects, praised the dignified design as 'a monument of memory rather than of war'. John Sulman urged that the architects be consulted on the layout of the extensive grounds: 'I should not leave it entirely to gardeners, who very often make a mess of such things. They have no ideas of vistas'.[75] Griffin's 'Prospect Parkway' had been transformed into Anzac Parade when the foundation stone was laid on Anzac Day 1929, but the building was not officially opened until Armistice Day 1941. While the combination of memorial and museum was unusual for such a major monument, in Canberra they were 'fused with great architectural skill into a most harmonious whole'.[76]

Conclusion

The Federal Capital Commission both completed the FCAC's task of opening parliament and continued 'the denigration of Griffin's plan'.[77] From the late 1920s, the significance of Canberra as a planning achievement waned. From the early 1930s the sprawling garden town was to attract damning criticism from leading world planners such as Thomas Adams. Beyond the axial geometry of the central 'parliamentary triangle', the Griffin scheme in the larger sense as a three-dimensional urban environment was abandoned. Resuscitation of development after World War II acknowledged the specialness of the place as a national capital but was driven by a strong modernist aesthetic.

Perspective from the Caswell, Coulter and Griffiths federal city plan, 1912.
National Archives of Australia, Series A170, item 20

The federal capital competition was arguably the highpoint of the city beautiful dream, and, according to JD Fitzgerald, with Griffin's scheme Australia had by far its best chance 'of building the much-talked-of City Beautiful'.[78] Thereafter, this opportunity slipped away, with disagreements between Griffin and just about every other stakeholder in the project during his stormy seven years in control. In large measure the problems turned upon just how to make artistic planning practicable. There was little that was not controversial about the national capital but the perceived impracticality of Griffin's design was the critical sticking point for Australian bureaucrats and politicians over a protracted period.

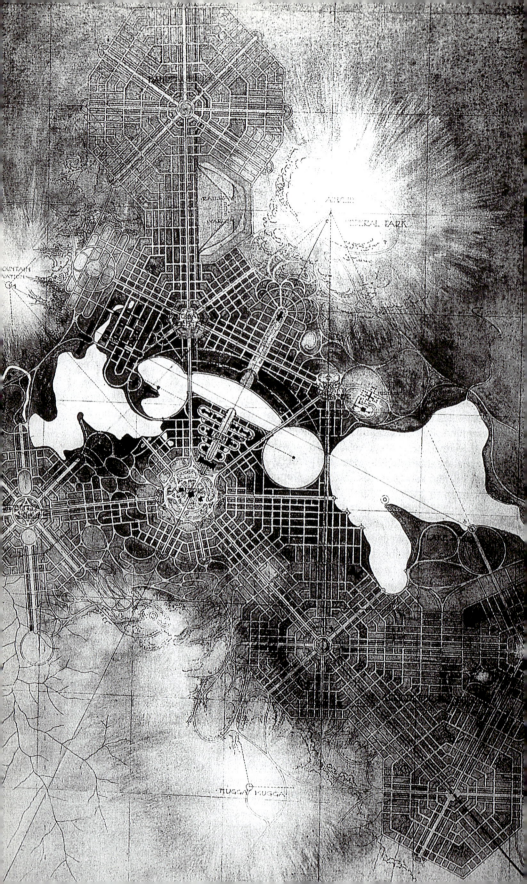

For all its uniqueness, Canberra is a representative story of the city beautiful elsewhere: early excitement over the artistic city, rapprochement with more pragmatic goals, and the working out of a resolution which sought a 'better' balance between them that was acceptable to proponents and the wider community through incremental 'commonsense' planning shaped by politics and financial constraints. But Canberra, with its unique system of leasehold land tenure, was less typical of the aesthetic tensions between culture and commerce in other Australian cities.

Walter Burley Griffin's City and Environs plan for the federal capital, 1912.
National Archives of Australia, Series A170, item 38

CHAPTER 5

City
plans

In the years leading up to World War I, the federal capital project was an enormous catalyst for the emergence of an organised planning movement. New towns generally were the ultimate laboratory for application of planning ideas, and other opportunities would open up as part of resource development and closer settlement schemes. Walter Burley Griffin himself designed the irrigation area capital of Griffith in NSW as a virtual mini-Canberra. The most systematic policy was implemented in the last hurrah of the settlement frontier, in 1920s South Australia under the office of the government town planner. A design template influenced by the garden city movement was laid down by Charles Reade in 1919 but it did have boulevards, a civic centre 'where future public buildings are to be located', and paid attention to 'architectural terminals to principal streets'.[1] The actual designs were a mix of the mundane and the grandiose, with the latter reflecting the enduring impact of the city beautiful. Cape Thevenard, planned by Walter Scott Griffiths, successfully combined 'a "City Beautiful" design with a workable pattern of functions'.[2]

The relevance of city beautiful principles to the design of new cities was readily apparent. How they might be systematically adapted to regional visions of existing metropolises was less certain. The first major project to at least consider an overall plan incorporating aesthetic values was the 1908–09 Royal Commission for the Improvement of the City of Sydney and Its Suburbs. This chapter concentrates on the origins, nature and outcomes of aesthetic issues at the Sydney inquiry, which represented an unprecedentedly wide-ranging investigation of urban conditions. Of interest is the way in which the commission was aware of, and responded to, international precedent. While subscribing to the notion that practical physical reforms could also look good, the commission ultimately gave precedence to concerns of utility. The lead was followed by the first generation of comprehensive metropolitan plans in the 1920s. The Melbourne and Perth plans are surveyed. Both assembled major projects in train that are examined in greater detail in later chapters.

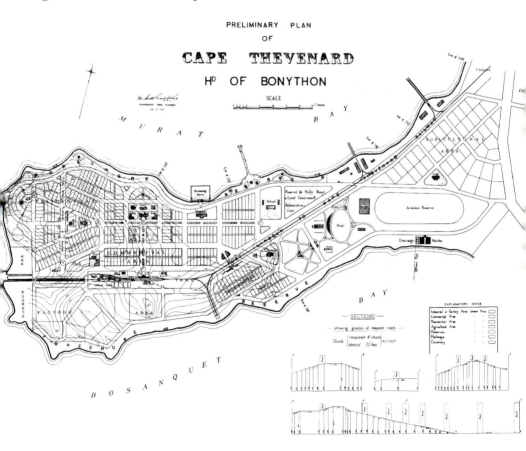

Plan for Cape Thevenard by Walter Scott Griffith. *Government Town Planner of South Australia Annual Report, 1922–23*

The Sydney royal commission 1908–09

The Royal Commission for the Improvement of the City of Sydney and Its Suburbs came at a time when the city was seeking to position itself – regionally, imperially and globally – as a major economic player and maritime metropolis. The final 1909 report represented a watershed in Sydney's planning history, integrating incremental, ad hoc moves toward city improvement into a general stock-take of recommendations which established a foundation for successive rounds of public investment and reformist endeavour.

Recognition of the 'physical deficiencies' of inner and metropolitan Sydney made for an 'environment conducive to planning'.[3] The bleakest but ultimately most stirring summation of this situation was by JD Fitzgerald. He decried the 'civic anarchy' and 'planlessness' of a city:

> ... flung down in a crazy mass, formless, inorganic, a maze of slums ... cul-de-sacs; a tangle of competing and incompetent civic, governmental, and private authorities; its commercial centre crowded and embarrassed and choked by the narrowness of its planless thoroughfares; its outer suburbs reproducing the defects and the mistakes of the inner core of the city.[4]

Through the 1900s there were many ideas being advanced to improve the efficiency and dignity of the city – schemes for 'rearrangement and space-making', as *The Sydney Morning Herald* described them.[5] These involved an inventive array of suggestions for new roads and bridges, railways and subways, improved wharfage, the remodelling of slum districts, and public plazas. It was said that 'every second individual in Sydney appears to possess a scheme for city improvement based more or less upon the ideas of Mr John Barlow FRIBA whose claims deserve better recognition'.[6] The engineer Norman Selfe and the architect John Sulman – whose influential compendium of architectural, street and traffic modifications, *The Improvement of Sydney* (1907), was published in the lead-up to the commission – were especially prominent. Statutory authorities, notably the Sydney Harbour Trust, had independently embarked on their own projects, leaving their mark on city streets. The city council was also restless. The visit of the US fleet in 1908 sparked a variety of suggestions for how the occasion could be remembered permanently. The lord mayor, Thomas Hughes, canvassed numerous possibilities – fountains, street gardens, roadside tree plantings and park improvements – as part of his vision for 'permanently beautifying the city'.[7]

In October 1906, EW O'Sullivan, a former minister for public works, moved in the state parliament for a select committee to report upon 'the best suggestion for the improvement and ornamentation of Sydney, the suburbs and environs.' In the 'federation euphoria' of 1901, O'Sullivan had proposed to redevelop Fort Denison with a 250-foot-high memorial, yet another 'Australia Facing the Dawn', as Port Jackson's answer to the Statue of Liberty.[8] It was precisely this kind of project which convinced commentators that development 'in a becoming manner' required some form of coordination.[9] O'Sullivan's idea lapsed, but Sydney City Council continued to pressure the government into preparing a kind of regional plan beyond its own limited jurisdiction.

On 29 October 1907, Sir Thomas Hughes – both Sydney's lord mayor and a member of the legislative council – formally moved that the state government be 'invited' to appoint a royal commission. The government was watching and waiting, and the idea of an investigatory royal commission had several advantages over rival bureaucratic models. Time-proven for complex inquiries and with an established imperial imprimatur, royal commissions had the connotations of reformist government yet could delay precipitate action. They were state-controlled but constituted at one remove from the political hurly-burly.

On 14 May 1908, the governor of New South Wales issued a warrant for a royal commission which was authorised:

> to diligently examine and investigate all proposals that may come before [it] for the Improvement of the City of Sydney and its Suburbs, and to fully inquire into the whole subject of the remodelling of Sydney ... that [this] inquiry be made, primarily, in view of the present circumstances of the State, and the present requirements of the city and suburban population; and secondly, and independently, in view of the progress of the country, the extension of the Metropolis and its Suburbs, and the increase of population and traffic within the next twenty-five years ... [that it be authorised] to consider the expediency of constructing such lines of railway and tramway as may

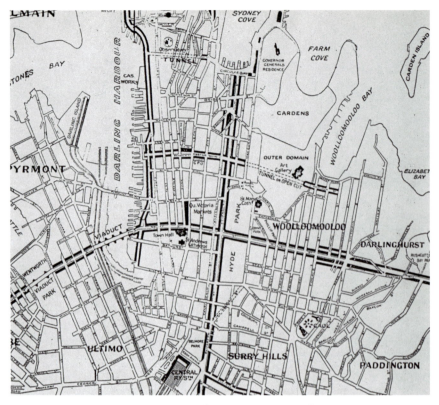

An early 'broad general scheme' of street improvements for central Sydney.
John Sulman, The Improvement of Sydney *1907*

be necessary to meet the increasing demands of traffic, of widening existing streets, and of opening up fresh avenues of communication; and generally to make such suggestions as to ornamentation and improvements as will tend to add to the attraction and beauty of the City and adjoining Suburbs.[10]

The commission was made up of 11 members under the presidency of Hughes. The all-male membership represented state and local government, business interests, and the professions of architecture, engineering and building. Politicians dominated and connections with the city council were evidently highly valued. The commissioners had just six months to report, but were unable to complete the job and sought an extension. There was a short Interim Report, issued in December 1908, and the Final Report was dated 25 June 1909. Comprising 50 pages of description, analysis and recommendations, it was complemented by several short appendices, minutes of evidence totalling 253 pages, and 56 plans, maps and sketches. Typical of other royal commissions, information-gathering proceeded mainly by the interviewing of witnesses, the evaluation and comparison of their evidence, and the compilation of findings. A total of 40 witnesses was interviewed in 90 meetings held between June 1908 and May 1909. They ranged from built environment professionals to senior and junior public servants, local government representatives, sundry business people, trade unionists, and church leaders.

Recommendations

The commission organised its report into four core topic areas: traffic considerations, slum areas and housing reform, future growth of the city, and beautification, augmented by a discussion of specific improvement schemes. The latter is especially revealing of its modus operandi in adopting and amplifying proposals put forward by witnesses or other ideas that had been in the air for some time. A total of 40 specific recommendations was made. But the discursive report made numerous suggestions and endorsements at various points – and by another count made some 60 recommendations, ranging across transport and accessibility, physical improvement, and the social environment. The spatial focus was clearly on the central city, rather than the suburbs, and the functional emphasis was emphatically on improvements to the city's circulation systems.

Major transportation recommendations were the introduction of underground electric railways for the city centre, electrification of the entire suburban network, and a tunnel under the harbour to the north shore. These effectively rubber-stamped proposals by the Chief Commissioner for the Railways. In addition came 16 site-specific recommendations involving new street openings, widening, re-gradings, and extensions. The major preoccupations were relieving general traffic congestion; facilitating better access to and from port areas and the central railway; improving flows into, out of and across the city; and better differentiation of civic, commuting and freight traffic flows. Recommendations on slum clearing and housing reform embodied a strong ideological preference for low-density suburban living. New powers for all local authorities were endorsed to compulsorily acquire and remodel slum areas, develop new housing, and prevent the growth of further slums. As for longer term growth considerations, additional powers for local authorities to prevent replication of 'straggling suburbs' and ensure orderly new development including provision of open spaces were recommended.

The aesthetic agenda

Proposals aimed solely at materially beautifying the city were of secondary importance. The commission made this clear: 'the works designed to meet the necessities of our growing traffic should have precedence over those of a purely aesthetic character'. With only one architect member, the beautification impulse was kept in check. Nevertheless, 'improvements designed to add to [Sydney's] beauty and attractiveness' were said to be given 'the fullest consideration'. The commissioners were well aware of Burnham's dictum that a physically attractive city aided regional and international competitiveness. As the 'second richest city in the British Empire', and potentially 'the richest city in the world', Sydney was now 'expected to dress for the occasion'.[11] A central concern was for beautification to pay its way by being combined with more hard-nosed improvements. This sought-after synthesis of convenience and stateliness was central to the commission's thinking. As one of the commissioners put it, the inquiry was Sydney's best chance to be 'what she ought to be – a combination of business utility and city and suburban beauty'.[12]

The royal commission's report remains one of the most internationally-informed of all modern planning reports for Sydney. Australians traditionally looked abroad for lessons and inspirations because of their colonial consciousness, so-called cultural cringe and geographic isolation. The early 1900s were marked by innovations abroad in civic improvement and planning that could not be ignored. Under the premise that the infant metropolis was equivalent to European cities 50 years before, looking overseas was effectively looking into the future. Three different relationships to foreign knowledge thread through the report and minutes of evidence. One is the notion of foreign precedent as a positive model – something inspirational to emulate. The second is the negative model – an example to be avoided. The third was more rhetorical – an acknowledgment of foreign initiative but a conviction that Sydney could do better.

The minutes of evidence are littered with references to Parisian boulevards, American parkways, European arcaded streets, union stations, park systems, art commissions, and improvement associations. References are made to specific places such as the Kingsway/Aldwych improvement and Thames Embankment in London, Liverpool's Queen's Drive, the Vienna Ringstrasse, and public spaces such as Trafalgar Square and Place de la Bastille. The commissioners sought information on many matters, including 'the general beautification and adornment of cities', with a rather motley coverage of plans and reports being obtained. Two of the most intriguing documents were Daniel Burnham's 1905 plan for San Francisco and the New York City Improvement Commission Plan (1907), an ambitious, multi-borough plan firmly in the city beautiful tradition. Of the international names mentioned in the evidence, Burnham's was the most frequently cited, even though the commission was unable to draw upon his greatest work, the Chicago plan, then in course of preparation.

Generally, the positive influence of overseas schemes seemed more inspirational than explicit, with everything needing to be adapted to the specific circumstances of Sydney. The major impact of the international connection was the discovery that many other cities around the world were organising and re-making themselves as places to live and do business in, and that Sydney had to emulate their drive or fall behind.

Global examples cascaded out of some witnesses, notably JD Fitzgerald and Joseph Maiden, director of Sydney's Botanic Gardens and officer-in-charge of Centennial Park. In promoting the international diffusion of planning knowledge, such advocates fall into Sutcliffe's category of 'intermediaries alive to foreign developments'.[13] Not coincidentally, both were also prominent in promoting aesthetic considerations. Fitzgerald's evidence stressed improvement from the decorative standpoint and drew on his articles in *The Sydney Mail* in May and June 1908. A major theme was a system of radial centres delivering both convenience and attractiveness. He suggested the removal of Darlinghurst Gaol at Taylor Square for a 'splendid city improvement' on one of 'the finest elevated site for public buildings in Australasia'. The cosmopolitan Fitzgerald demonstrated his worldliness with references to authorities such as Charles Mulford Robinson, and bombarded the commissioners with plans and images from around the world. Joseph Maiden gave similarly wide-ranging and internationally-informed views. Targeting parks, he made extensive references to examples in Europe and the United States, quoted Frederick Law Olmsted on the societal payoff from open space, and provided an array of illustrative examples from the fountains of Versailles to the park statuary of the Berlin Tiergarten.

While John Barlow took the opportunity to reiterate his idiosyncratic view about the artistic value of crooked streets, John Sulman put aside his disappointment at not being appointed a commissioner to submit breathtaking but unconvincing proposals. These related to improving approaches to the city from its two main gateways: Central railway station south of the CBD and the northern ferry terminus at Circular Quay. The former cloaked Belmore Park with a magnificent semi-circular terrace to improve the outlook to the city. The latter was a symmetrical scheme with a grand 270-foot-wide boulevard leading south from the quay, watergate features, memorial arch and a new Customs House to balance the bulk of a remodelled Goldsbrough, Mort & Co. wool store.

Sulman's artist was Charles Coulter who had also been appointed chief artist to the commission. His classically-tinged images are its main legacy. The commissioners appear to have been more than satisfied with his efforts, awarding him a bonus of £35.[14] But the international reception was devastating. The *Journal of the Royal Institute of British Architects* referred to an 'architectural treatment' which was 'inadequate' while the *Town Planning Review* found it 'pitiful in the extreme'.[15] Coulter stepped outside his assigned role on one occasion to present a personal scheme for the beautification of East Circular Quay with a new naval college and band rotunda. It was rejected for being 'designed entirely from a decorative standpoint'.[16]

In deliberations on aesthetic matters, a consensus emerged around certain concepts and desired outcomes. The key design and streetscape principles were homogeneity without monotony, unity, harmony, symmetry, and spaciousness. Historic preservation did not register, apart from the need to protect St James Church in any remodelling of the southern end of Macquarie Street. Natural scenery should be conserved,

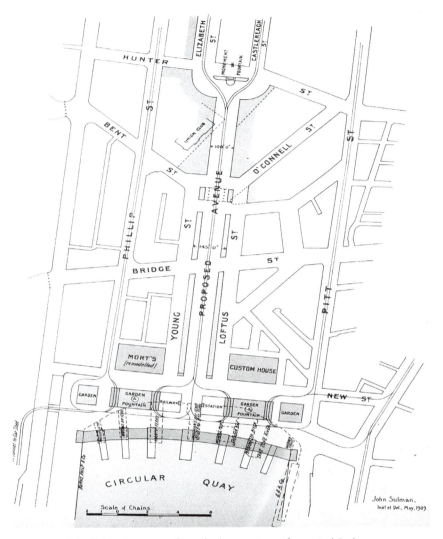

ROYAL COMMISSION ON SYDNEY IMPROVEMENT.

PLAN ILLUSTRATING MR. JOHN SULMAN'S PROPOSED CENTRAL AVENUE AND REMODELLING OF CIRCULAR QUAY.

John Sulman's proposed new harbour gateway for central Sydney.
Royal Commission on Sydney Improvement, 1909

particularly around the harbour foreshores. The pivotal recommendation was a new Building Act 'to check the anomalies in architecture, disfiguring awnings, unsightly commercial signs, in short, everything that tends to mar the appearance of streets'. This would enable council powers to regulate the height, style and character of buildings and could be supplemented by broader town planning controls. It was supported by 13 mainly site-specific recommendations:

1   The improvement of the approaches to Central Railway Station by carrying raised roads to the platform level.

2   The extension of Moore Street to Macquarie Street.

3   The widening and regrading of Macquarie Street.

4   The remodelling of the Rocks area and the extension of George Street in a straight line to Dawes' Point.

5   The realignment of Circular Quay and the resumption of the woolstores and warehouses on its eastern side with a view to remodelling the area on artistic lines.

6   The continuation of King Street to the Domain.

7   The opening of a public thoroughfare in the Domain from St.Mary's Gates to Palace Gardens, giving new frontages to the site now occupied by the Royal Mint, Sydney Hospital, and Parliament House.

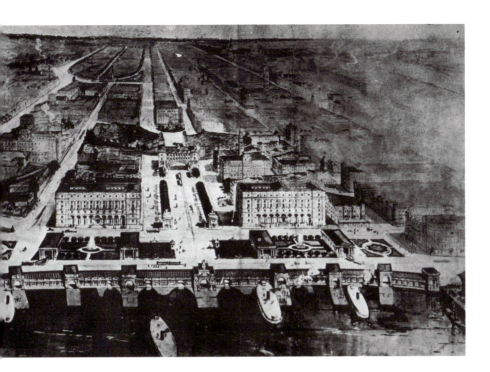

A new approach to central Sydney suggested by John Sulman. *Royal Commission on Sydney Improvement, 1909*

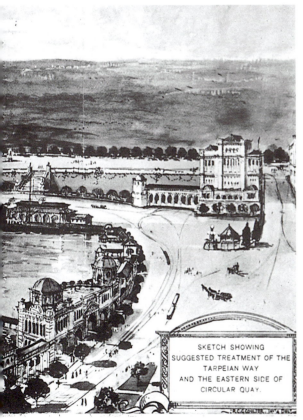

SKETCH SHOWING
SUGGESTED TREATMENT OF THE
TARPEIAN WAY
AND THE EASTERN SIDE OF
CIRCULAR QUAY.

Suggested remodelling of East Circular Quay featuring a Naval College by Charles Coulter. *Royal Commission on Sydney Improvement, 1909*

8 The removal of the King Street Law Courts and the Land Titles Offices.

9 The widening of College Street.

10 The formation of a circus at the junction of College, Oxford, New Wexford, and Liverpool Streets.

11 The removal of Darlinghurst Gaol.

12 The ultimate widening of Flinders Street and Randwick Road.

13 The planting of trees in our principal streets and avenues.

Several observations can be made about these recommendations. Four main aesthetic hot spots were evident: Circular Quay, Central railway station, Macquarie Street and the Darlinghurst Gaol site. Most contentious was Circular Quay and the issue of an overhead station as part of the city underground rail loop. The commission recommended that any station 'should be designed on ornamental lines, in harmony with the general scheme for the improvement of the water-front'. Despite the opposition of witnesses such as Sulman and two dissenting commissioners, it was a fatal official endorsement that helped to pave the way for the monolithic station erected in the 1950s. The boldest suggestions were for a new north–south road into the Domain and the demolition of Darlinghurst Gaol 'for a public building of an ornamental character … or for a park, or for both'. Overall the aesthetic recommendations were restrained. Most had an almost seamless overlap with general road improvements in that they involved widenings, extensions, realignment, and new frontages for public buildings. Planting of trees along road corridors was endorsed, but a strict caveat applied – only 'where they would least interfere with business and traffic'.

PROPOSED REMODELLING
OF
QUEEN'S SQUARE.

Widened Elizabeth-street.

St.
Entrance to

BIRD'S-EYE VIEW OF CIT
MOORE-STREET EXT

Recommended remodelling of state government quarter at northern end of
Hyde Park. *Royal Commission on Sydney Improvement, 1909*

Coulter's artwork may suggest otherwise, but criticism from Charles
Reade onward that this was a plan to 'haussmannise' a city 'engulphed
in the maelstrom of modern economic developments' seem wide of the
mark.[17] The commissioners were adamant that 'an ideal plan of city reconstruction … could not be carried out except at unreasonable and
unjustifiable cost'. And the witnesses agreed. Sulman was asked by
Hughes, the commission's president: 'You do not think we could go as
far as Baron Haussmann?' 'No', Sulman replied.[18]

Impact of the royal commission

The Sydney royal commission presented to the state government 'a scheme of improvement which will not only meet the increasing demands of traffic for many years to come, but will also contribute greatly to the attractiveness of the city, while at the same time preparing the way for more general improvements in the future'.[19] Its report was deeply pragmatic, and while it conceded a place for the city beautiful – along with the city healthful and the city social – its preoccupation with economic growth, economy, and functional efficiency was unswerving and anticipated city functional planning in the interwar years. The whole exercise was primarily a means for an urban growth machine mobilised by elites to influence government policy towards removing impediments to efficiency and facilitating greater business opportunities.[20]

The planning strategy endorsed by the commission was an inventory of important projects, but with neither implementation schedule nor a budget. The commission opted out of preparing a comprehensive, integrated plan – what it called 'a symmetrical scheme'. There were several reasons, foreshadowed in the interim report in late 1908. A significant constraint was that this approach was simply too complex and beyond its expertise and resources. Sydney's topographically challenging site and its advanced stage of development combined to complicate application of theoretical planning ideas. And ultimately, reasoned the commission, such a scheme would simply have been too costly anyway.

The values which underlay the commission's recommendations were unambiguously archetypal expressions of early modernist planning: the importance of spaciousness, order, development on 'harmonious lines', public regulation and control. What was undeveloped at this time, however, was a master-planning consciousness. The Sydney report lacked the holism of the best contemporary American reports. Officially completed just ten days before publication of Burnham and Bennett's seminal 1909 strategy, the Sydney report was no antipodean *Plan of Chicago*. The journal *Building* described the exercise as the 'editing' of the city.[21] CEW Bean saw it as a great opportunity lost.[22] Observing from afar, Patrick Abercrombie saw the scheme as 'merely

Widened Oxford Street 'beautified' in 1910–14 into revenue-producing
commercial premises by Sydney City Council. *Author, 1992*

a patching'.[23] British architect Arthur Jemmett similarly bemoaned
the 'lack of any ruling idea or coherence'.[24]

Yet for an advisory report, many fragments of the plan came
true. This was almost inevitable given that the commission not only
represented a timely stock-take of projected public works but codified
many projects already publicly mooted or even underway. Professor
Denis Winston's summation was that 'nearly every subsequent
improvement to the central area of Sydney ... was suggested and clearly
explained in the [1909] report'.[25] Sydney City Council commenced road
improvement works almost immediately, including the widening of
Liverpool, Oxford, Elizabeth, Macquarie, and George streets, and the
creation of Wentworth Avenue (New Wexford Street) to give better

access to Central station. Implementation of some of these proposals would have dramatic consequences. The widening of Macquarie Street North in 1913 was especially controversial because it meant the destruction of a venerable row of fig trees. Several groups, including the Australian Historical Society and the NSW Forestry League, made representations, and a petition with over 800 signatures was lodged with the city council. Fitzgerald and Maiden took opposing positions. Claiming culpability for the proposal, Coulter suggested a compromise to split vehicular and pedestrian traffic which might save the trees.[26] Thorny issues raised in implementing improvement strategies clearly complicated cosy theoretical endorsements. The widening of William Street from 1916 was more socially traumatic, entailing 'the near destruction of a highly specific, relatively integrated local community'.[27]

The direct artistic outcomes were predictably modest. GS Jones in his 1912 presidential address to the Institute of Architects of New South Wales acknowledged the importance of improvements of 'a utilitarian nature' but complained that 'nothing has been done to dignify and beautify the street view' except for small garden lots in Bridge Street.[28] The same year John Barlow was equally critical that new work carried out under the lord mayorship of Sir Allen Taylor was 'quite devoid of architectural distinction'.[29] In the medium term came the making of Martin Place as the city's major ceremonial space, while the widening of Flinders Street and Randwick Road en route to Centennial Park was also a significant aesthetic outcome; these projects are discussed in later chapters.

All improvements were within the Sydney City Council boundary. Contiguous municipalities were less enthused. The inherent problem with the commission's metropolitan vision was political fragmentation. Initiatives such as widened and tree-planted avenues would stop dead at municipal boundaries. The failure to address the need for a greater metropolitan authority was recognised early:

Sydney's first official city plan.
Royal Commission on Sydney Improvement, 1909

PLAN OF THE CITY.

SHOWING CITY RAILWAY, NEW STREETS,
GENERAL IMPROVEMENTS RECOMMENDED
BY THE ROYAL COMMISSION.

REFERENCE.

NEW STREETS
STREETS TO BE WIDENED
STREETS TO BE REGRADED
VIADUCTS
TUNNELS
RAILWAYS
EXISTING TRAMWAYS
RESERVES

SCALE

25th June 1909
PRESIDENT

> The remarkable feature of the report is that it stops short as to what authority should carry out the work. The Government can hardly do it ... it would not dare to face the country with such a programme ... The City Council cannot take action, inasmuch as its jurisdiction stops short at the city boundary, and to give proper effect to any improvement, the same must be carried to the outer suburbs.[30]

The 1909 royal commission recognised that if Sydney was to become a truly imperial maritime city then improvements were necessary to bring it into line with other up-to-date world cities. City beautiful ideas were integral but not the touchstone. In the end the hopes held by *The Bulletin* seemed realistic: 'In the end, Sydney will be only a patchwork metropolis, but there is no reason why it shouldn't be a very beautiful patchwork.'[31]

Comprehensive planning in the 1920s

As significant a fillip as the royal commission was to the emergence of an organised town planning movement, the exercise also cruelly exposed some deficiencies in professional vision and expertise. The commissioners and the structure of their inquiry cannot be blamed. Even the professionals were cautious. Sulman, in his very first appearance before the commission, made reference to Burnham's San Francisco plan: 'it is a very fine one, but far more comprehensive than anything I have dared to suggest, although San Francisco is only about the same size as Sydney'.[32] The concept of comprehensive master planning as it developed through the 1910s into the early 1920s provided a methodology to avoid the atomistic approach of the Sydney royal commission and, while the heyday of the city beautiful had passed, to reserve at least a residual slot for the artistic side of city planning.

The 1920s in Australia was a decade of rising living standards, shifting cultural fashions and technological change. Home and particularly motor vehicle ownership were on the rise. It was a time of rapid urbanisation, with the state capitals consolidating their primacy. Metropolitan dominance was matched by sprawling, low-density urban forms. Local government regulations covering building and subdivision standards injected some semblance of order into the development process, but the all-of-city synoptic approach had not been seriously pursued anywhere since Sydney in 1909 and then Canberra in 1912.

The synoptic approach was firmly in the mould of the American city practical with its detailed surveys leading to a comprehensive master plan. The city was conceived as a living organism. City planning's mission was to ensure the smooth functioning of the primary organs and arteries. The street system, the main means of circulation, and zoning – ensuring a place for everything and everything in its place – were the critical elements. Beauty in itself was placed at the bottom of the list; housing was often excluded. The accent was on efficiency, functionality, comfort and prosperity. Informed planning commentators actively promoted Australian and American cities as comparable 'new world' environments and introduced new terminology into local discourse: zoning, master plans, and planning commissions. In his 1921 textbook, John Sulman endorsed these innovations and went further to commend city-manager governments as a desirable alternative to traditional Australian local government.

Appointment of the Melbourne Metropolitan Town Planning Commission by the Victorian government in 1922 was a decisive blow against 'hotch-potch' city development. Frank Stapley led the lobbying and was rewarded with the chairmanship. The brief was to 'inquire into and report upon the present conditions and tendencies of urban development in the metropolitan area' and devise a costed general plan for 'the better guidance and control of such development'. Fred Cook, a qualified surveyor-engineer with Canberra experience, became the key technical person and 'the originator of almost every aspect of the technical work of the Commission'.[33]

The commission's final *Plan of General Development* report in December 1929 was Australia's first truly comprehensive metropolitan regional plan, with a vision encompassing an urban area of about 250 square miles and comprising nearly 40 separate municipalities, whose combined population was expected to double to 2 million within 20 years. It was an advisory plan, and while some specific recommendations proved influential the onset of the Depression prevented comprehensive implementation. The Melbourne plan adapted the American urban planner Harland Bartholomew's city planning formula into a voluminous tome divided, effectively in order of importance, into 11 major parts: surveys and studies; communications; the execution of improvement schemes (a program of urgent works); zoning; public recreation; public utilities; housing and land subdivision; civic art and amenities; miscellaneous, legislation; and conclusion.

Civic art was accorded a low priority, but one of the terms of reference under the *Metropolitan Town Planning Commission Act 1922* was the need to consider 'open spaces around public buildings and monuments and along water fronts'. Frank Stapley's priorities were simple: 'We must combine utility with beautification'.[34] The surveyor Saxil Tuxen, one of his fellow commissioners, returned from a visit to the United States in 1925 with a blunter view of the main object of planning: 'to make the city efficient, and the least consideration is beauty'.[35] The commission ultimately exemplified the conventional wisdom that beauty was the natural product of rational, scientific planning. Hence, although mono-functional land use zoning was primarily a utilitarian control, it would also prevent the sort of 'mixed' development which 'renders unattractive many of the main roads'. Similarly, disentangling some problematical street intersections at conspicuous locations could also consolidate property that might be suitable for attractive new buildings.

The commission made a series of more direct recommendations for the preservation of scenic amenity in city and suburbs, including greater street plantings and upkeep of nature strips, elimination of cantilevered verandahs, greater controls on unsightly and unsafe hoardings, continuation of building height limits, beautification of the banks of the Yarra in the city, and the appointment of an advisory board of architectural control. It shared its views on 'the suitable location and grouping of prominent buildings', stopping well short of a full-blown civic centre. The more far-reaching recommendations were for various American-inspired parkways which would be first and foremost useful 'from a traffic circulating point of view'.

Perth's Metropolitan Town Planning Commission, with architect Harold Boas as chairman and surveyor and former civil servant William Saw as his deputy, closely followed the Melbourne model in origins, composition, modus operandi, methodology, and ideology but it only

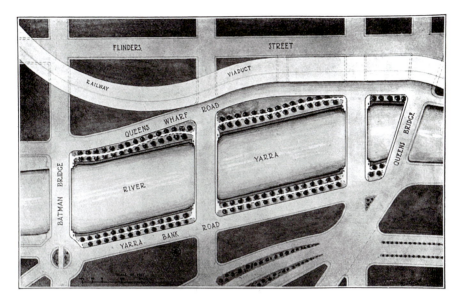

Efficient beauty to encourage 'a higher type of development' on the Yarra,
Melbourne. Plan of General Development, Melbourne, 1929

enjoyed a three-year term and lacked the same resources. Its basic
task remained the same, in attempting 'to visualise possible future
development of the metropolitan area', but the commissioners retreated
from a fully comprehensive statement to redefine their contribution as
'a basis for the preparation of [an] ultimate developmental plan'.

The submitted report, dated 1 January 1931, had a greater number
of general planning homilies and statements of general principles. It
drew on four major themes: consolidation, coordination, economy,
and efficiency. Transportation, traffic and roads were exhaustively
examined. The overall thrust was towards the rearrangement of
government service delivery within a greater metropolitan authority,
leaving local authorities autonomy in 'purely local and domestic affairs'.
The CBD was envisaged as the hub of a radial and circumferential
road network based on the upgrading and infilling of the existing
system. It would undergo a major restructuring, based around the
longstanding idea of relocating the main trunk railway line. Major
regional centres would be linked by a 'parallel railway road system'
while parkways would interconnect reserves and lakes to form a new
outer 'park belt'.

The lingering impact of the city beautiful surfaced in sections dealing with open space and waterfront improvements, and was mainly confined to a chapter on 'amenities', defined as 'those things having agreeableness of situation or character'. The commission defended its examination of these planning issues by noting that 'the cultural or aesthetic side ... is still vital to necessary development, and perhaps more so than ever, seeing that the exacting needs of the times are inclined to make us neglect those things essential for the welfare of man's soul'. Tacitly revealing of Boas's involvement with the conservative Argonauts Civic and Political Club, it expanded this sentiment into the kind of ideological argument more characteristic of the earliest days of the planning movement by quoting a leading American realtor:

> The effect of beautiful surroundings has indeed a very good influence on the lives and outlook of the people. Beauty is effective insurance discontent ... Unrest finds its readiest recruits among men whose lives have been denuded of beauty, whose work has never meant joy to them, whose surroundings have always been drab. Men do not revolt against a civilisation that makes their lives beautiful.

Even the outcome of good planning was expressed using the old catchphrase: 'Given an almost ideal setting, Perth and its suburbs give hopes for a great city in the future – the true City Beautiful – providing we are wise in our generation and lay the foundations on sound lines'.[36]

The major discussion in the 'amenities' chapter was given to 'civic art and architecture'. The central recommendation was an extension of Forrest Place to provide for a new 'governmental and civic centre' (see chapter 7). The commission commended the idea of grouping public buildings for convenience and dignity 'in a lesser degree' to suburban localities. Also endorsed were more statues, fountains and memorials, and the concept of an 'art jury' to police 'the general idea of good taste and harmony'. The discussion tails off into a miscellany of positive actions some intersecting with references in other sections: elimination of advertising hoardings and other discordant 'skyline' elements, introduction of more artistic types of lamp posts, burying of power and telephone cables, street tree planting, opening up of new riverside and ocean drives, and 'the conservation of natural beauties'.

Conclusion

The metropolitan planning reports for Sydney (1909), Melbourne (1930) and Perth (1931) were the three major official planning investigations into the state of Australian cities before World War II. The Sydney royal commission was established at a time of growing but still inchoate interest in urban planning matters, heightened by the approach of the federal capital project. This was the era when the idea of the city beautiful still had power to 'stir men's blood'. The commission took on an explicit brief to investigate 'ornamentation and improvements' across the metropolitan area but Charles Coulter's images belie the business-minded approach adopted. They enumerated a series of desired aesthetic improvements but largely regarded beautification as subsidiary to more pressing utilitarian interventions.

The raw, inductive approach of Sydney evolved into a more sophisticated methodology in the metropolitan plans for Perth and Melbourne. The larger significance of these reports was in introducing the concept of the metropolis into the community imagination and codifying the main physical planning issues of the day. They established an analytical and reporting style which would endure well beyond World War II. Both downplayed but did not ignore the earlier strivings for the city beautiful that had influenced the emergence of a planning consciousness in both cities. By translating the standard American city planning model of the 1920s, they were able to find a place for civic art – and put it in its place. They reached beyond their major preoccupations to assemble hit-lists of actions that would improve urban streetscapes, and sanctioned wider controls on signage, drab buildings, and other unsightly objects. While these aesthetic reforms no longer lay near the cutting edge of planning, they were not inconsequential. As the Melbourne report pointed out: 'All these things, though comparatively trivial when embodied in a report containing so many major recommendations, assist materially in the creation of the proper civic spirit in the community'.[37]

CHAPTER 6

Civic centres

Civic centre schemes were central to city beautiful thinking. In the United States, they were the physical and symbolic pivot of a succession of plans from the early 1900s onwards. 'A city without some kind of civic center', wrote Harvard husband-and-wife team Theodora Kimball and Henry Vincent Hubbard, 'gives to the visitor the kind of impression which would be made by a man without a face. There is nothing to express the soul of the city; it appears to be a jumble of streets and buildings'[1]. Civic centres were envisaged as artistic citadels, capturing higher ideals of civic pride, democracy, and patriotism.

But they also offered solutions to practical problems. They could more than satisfy the need to replace scattered and cramped public buildings that had outlived their usefulness. They could accommodate the expansion and restructuring of urban government. Spacious, park-like settings would minimise the risk of fires, protect citizens from urban dust and noise, and even make central heating plants possible. They could facilitate interdepartmental cooperation, save time and money for citizens, and stimulate turnover for local businesses.

There was no single spatial model of civic centre design. Some civic centres were started from scratch, others capitalised on the strategic location of a single public building. While the first generation of schemes in the 1900s were often associated with dramatic restructuring of gridiron street systems and existing urban spaces, by the 1920s the trend was to respect the existing fabric and not directly challenge or disrupt private property development. The locational preference was on lower value land contiguous to the central business district. Proposals were often linked to broader area redevelopment strategies such as slum clearance and environmental beautification. The penchant was for all-of-a-piece low-rise design, inspired by the World's Columbian Exposition and monumental Washington, DC. Tall buildings were rare, except in the shape of ornamental domes and towers. Public buildings could not compete with the verticality of commercial structures. They were models of decorum contrasted to the chaos of the commercial zone, where motley buildings 'pressed to the lot line'.[2]

The concept had a forceful impact on city planning worldwide and was readily pressed into the service of imperialism. Formal public building groups represented the authority and beneficence of controlling powers. The more city-proud American model was rarely imported completely. Some foreign planners looked askance. Patrick Abercrombie, speaking for many British planners, could appreciate the American civic centre idea but felt there was 'a danger of rather over-emphasising this phase, by a heterogeneous lumping together of big buildings without much spiritual or imaginative content; but at any rate they have stood for a dignified symbol of the civic idea'.[3] This chapter looks at Australian responses. It examines the predisposition to the idea and some of the general principles involved. There were many schemes, with numerous official and unofficial ones undoubtedly buried in local and state government archives. The narratives concentrate on four cities: Melbourne, Perth, Sydney and Geelong. As tortuous and protracted as some of these schemes were, the results on the ground were meagre.

The Australian civic centre

The relentless grid of the colonial town seemed to deny opportunities for civic design. Colonial architects were not devoid of imaginative schemes for treating public institutions and their interrelationships, but the civic realm was usually composed of scattered buildings, and

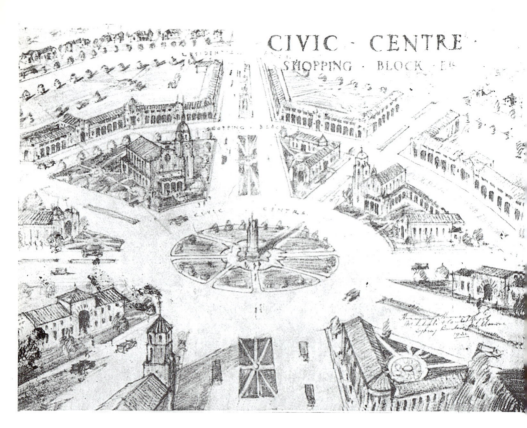

Civic Centre for Austral City project, Sydney, by Jack Hennessy.
Building, January 1931

not always in ideal locations. Nineteenth century interest in the better
design and placement of public buildings carried into the concerns of
the fledgling town planning movement from the early 1900s. Growing
enthusiasm for public building groups partly reflected a view that
their absence was an uncomfortable metaphor for what was lacking in
Australian civic development.

The arguments for civic centres in the local planning literature
revisited overseas themes. Beyond the beautification opportunities
provided, the civic centre was seen as the potential hub of town and
city life. It could encapsulate 'the aspirations of the citizens and pride
of ancestry, love of order'.[4] It should stand for the glorification of
public life and add dignity to local government. It would engender
community spirit and civic pride, and help 'focus the common life of
the community'.[5] In short, the civic centre stood to be 'the harmonious
keynote of the city'.[6] Returning from a study tour abroad, the city
engineer for Melbourne, HE Morton, also stressed their functional

logic: 'appreciable economy in transportation, time and staff can be effected under such conditions'. The grouping of public buildings would assist transactions with government by making them more convenient. Furthermore, it was the 'height of folly and extravagance' to erect an expensive public building to have it 'almost wholly effaced in a crowded business street'.[7] As overseas, the civic centre thus became an enduring synthesis of ideological and practical aspirations. 'Not only motives of civic pride and patriotism go to make the Civic Centre desirable', it was said, 'but also the strongest motives of social and municipal economy and efficiency'.[8]

By the 1910s civic centres had become a favoured element of ideal city, suburban and country town layouts. In 1913 W Scott Griffiths wrote that 'It is desirable in planning a town to have a centre where all our public buildings could be grouped, than to scatter them indiscriminately all over the town, as we usually see them placed in our country. The effect is lost, but if grouped in some centre or square, some totality of effect is obtained'.[9] WE Bold placed 'a spacious civic centre' at the heart of his ideal metropolis. Radiating outward would be radial parks intersecting with a series of ring parkways providing sites for 'minor' civic centres 'where any public buildings necessary for the locality could be located'.[10] Melbourne planning advocate WF Gates foresaw the centre of every municipality having a grouping of public buildings such as a town hall, post office, and library. Even if the architecture were of the 'most modest kind', this spatial clustering would add greatly to the dignity, convenience, public spirit, and beauty of the place.[11] Capturing the importance of World War I as an influence on national identity, a distinctive element was the frequent inclusion of war memorials.

More concrete guidelines were offered by George Sydney Jones and John Sulman in 1921. Jones regarded the concentration of public buildings as one of the five essentials of civic art. In a 1921 'lecturette' to the Town Planning Association of New South Wales, he expanded on the considerations involved. The chief public buildings to be accommodated in a town of 100 000 would be: a town hall, post office, lands office, law courts, churches, schools, public library, art gallery and museum, railway station, public monuments, and places of amusement and instruction. Drawing mainly on European precedent, Jones identified five principles for locating and developing such structures: grouping with the object of creating a centre, traffic conditions, type and patterns of use, homogeneity of design, and 'dignified unity of effect'.[12]

Sulman's was the more authoritative treatment, devoting an entire chapter to the subject in *An Introduction to the Study of Town Planning in Australia*. He linked the modern concept to the ancient agora and town square, reviewing a series of European remodelling projects that lent 'civic dignity' to their cities, such as Trafalgar Square in London and the Victor Emmanuel Monument in Rome. Civic centre projects in several cities, including Cleveland, Milwaukee and Washington, were described. For Australian cities, commanding and convenient sites should be secured, perhaps terminating a noble boulevard, with associated open space treated in an ornamental manner. The assemblage would comprise freestanding sites set within public space to enhance accessibility, sightlines, sunlight, noise control, and fire safety. Sulman was very firm on discouraging any mix of commercial and civic functions. His conclusion reiterated the basic rationale:

> A severely utilitarian citizen may question the need of a civic centre at all, but even such a one must admit that it is more economical in administration to group buildings amongst which there is much inter-communication, than to have them scattered; and as to their inspiring effect in fostering civic pride there can be no question at all, while it cannot be too strongly enforced that civic pride is the basis of all civic progress.

Sulman was enthusiastic about the American civic centre movement:

> To the Americans, conscious of their growth into a world power, and influenced very largely in matters artistic by the French, the dignified self-expression of the city seems to have appealed with irresistible force, and many of the designs are of a high order of merit. [13]

Other observers saw the American approach as a 'fetish', albeit a 'worthy ambition'.[14] The architect John Gawler felt the fashion had 'almost assumed the form of a disease'.[15] In 1920 the president of the Master Builders Association of NSW blamed a rash of civic centre projects in 1920 on two things: the return of Australian soldier-architects from the war inspired by overseas cities and Sulman's Vernon memorial

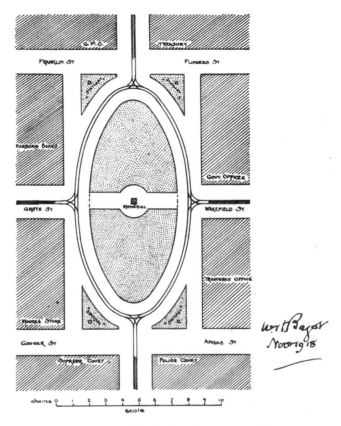

Victoria Square project, Adelaide, by Walter Bagot, 1918.
J Sulman, Town Planning in Australia, 1921

lectures 'setting free many aspiring young town planners'. Their extra-vagant schemes should be withheld until 'other more required matters in connection with city improvement' were addressed.[16] George Taylor wholeheartedly agreed with this conclusion: 'Australia wants less of talk and more of the practical, less of the grandiose and more of the useful, less of the high falutin and more of the common sense'.[17]

A more considered stance was that overseas initiatives were showing up the lack of real civic progress in Australia and that, while every city should not be conceived with unrestrained flamboyance, feasible proposals were welcome. Like many planning terms, 'civic centre' was used loosely to apply to anything from open spaces and single buildings through building groups (for any level or combination of government functions) to an entire city centre (the case of Canberra's 'Civic').

Proposals came and went. For example, on the site of Government House in Adelaide's Parklands, Albert Conrad promoted a civic centre 'adorned with imposing buildings and municipal garden effects'.[18] In Brisbane, architect Arnold Brookes proposed 'an official centre' based around the existing Executive and Treasury buildings with the creation of a new mall, a circus opposite Parliament House, and a new riverfront public place.[19] Treatment of this gateway site was an ongoing concern in the Queensland capital.[20] Aside from Canberra, the federal government demonstrated an early interest in the grouping of public buildings that came to fruition in Perth's Forrest Place and Brisbane's Anzac Square, described in the next chapter. The Commonwealth's more dramatic ventures were actually offshore. There were impressive pavilions within the grounds of the 1915 Panama Pacific Exposition in San Francisco and the 1924 British Empire Exhibition at Wembley, London. The major gesture was Australia House (1917) in the British capital, a cornerstone of the Kingsway redevelopment. It was, said the architect Walter Butler, 'a big building scheme that its predecessors quailed to think of'.[21]

Melbourne

The early 20th century idea of a civic centre for Melbourne was frequently linked to the even longer search for a central square as a focus for civic activities, considered in the next chapter. A typical acknowledgment of the interconnectedness of the issues was the architect William Campbell's 1904 call for a grand square to be 'surrounded by the public buildings of the city' that would make a lasting impression on citizens and the 'passing stranger' alike.[22] A second distinctive factor driving discussion in Melbourne was dissatisfaction with the corner location of the Town Hall, opened in 1870 on a site lacking spatial grandeur or association with other civic

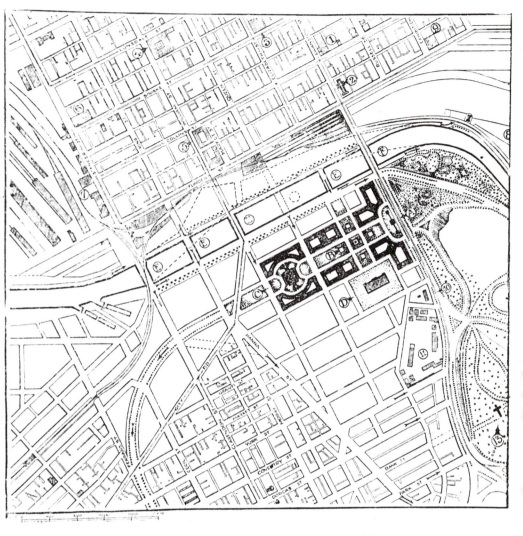

Revised Melbourne project by Alexander Macdonald.
Building, January 1923

functions; it was simply 'stuck on the footpath like a pub'.[23]

In the 1920s, some visionary schemes to tackle the problem once and for all were developed, some in considerable detail. Calls came for relocation of the Town Hall to the northern fringe of the central city, in line with the path of likely commercial development. John Sulman suggested a connection to a new railway loop line and 'the wholesale eradication of slum districts'.[24] The Victorian Town Planning Association suggested a site at the northern end of the Swanston Street axis.[25] The most dramatic decentralisation proposal was FE

Nixon's plan to concentrate the council offices along with 35 federal and 18 state offices at Fishermens Bend in Port Melbourne.[26] Other calls were made to take the idea to the suburbs. The architect Percy Everett devised a scheme for Brunswick comprising a new town tall, mechanics institute and memorial soldiers club.

Visionaries had long looked to the underdeveloped south bank of the Yarra for civic salvation. In 1889 John Keily felt it the natural location for his 'great predominant central feature' in the form of a grouping of major public buildings connected by a high-level viaduct across the river to the Treasury precinct on the northside.[27] One of the most substantive modern schemes was by AJ Macdonald, a federal capital competition entrant who subsequently worked with Walter Burley Griffin in the federal capital director's Melbourne office and served a short time as the first chief technical officer with the Metropolitan Town Planning Commission. He was once described as 'one of Australia's most expert town planners'.[28]

Macdonald's well-publicised idea for redeveloping the south bank of the Yarra used the civic centre idea to integrate a number of contemporary planning and social ideals, evolving through at least two versions after first surfacing in 1920. The allied concerns included rationalisation of the rail yards, additional river crossings, new arterial road links, opening up land for industrial and commercial land use, and a site for a national war memorial. The basis of the original scheme was to effectively extend the city's grid across the river west of St Kilda Road. The central civic zone was a 300-foot-wide mall linking a national war memorial on the site of the present National Gallery to a new town hall. A minor cross-axis on the line of Elizabeth Street terminated at a new war museum (envisaged as a 'facsimile' of Sydney's classically-inspired Art Gallery) near the existing Victoria Barracks. The intersection of the cruciform plan was defined by a series of reflecting pools with a 'Red Cross Memorial to the Sisterhood' arising from the central one.[29] These same elements recur in a revised scheme three years later, which features the opening up of more railway land on the north bank, more efficient bridge and road connections to the south side, and a canalised Yarra. Donald Swanson, brother of the lord mayor and a partner in one of the city's leading building firms, claimed credit for the latter element. Macdonald replied that the idea was 'almost as old as Victorian colonization. No person has a mortgage on the principle'.[30]

Macdonald's proposal was commended by the Royal Victorian Institute of Architects for its novelty and Sulman described it as 'a good plan'.[31] The scheme feasibly applied mostly to public land leased for factory development. The telling factors against it were perceived cost, the scale of dredging required for the Yarra, and the uncertainty of building foundations south of the river. Macdonald's scheme also broke a key design rule in having bridge traffic disgorge directly into the centre.[32] Its ambitiousness was more than matched by another contemporary plan by Harold Desbrowe-Annear, pivoting around a major war memorial, and noted in a later chapter.

The Jolimont rail yards were recognised early as one of Melbourne's most prominent eyesores; 'a black blot on the escutcheon of any view from high positions in Melbourne', according to Walter Butler.[33] Proposals to roof over and redevelop the area became 'a hardy annual'.[34] The most discussed scheme before World War II was the brainchild of James Alexander Smith, sometime president of the Royal Victorian Institute of Engineers and one of the judges of the Federal Capital Competition. The idea was presented at a number of professional and public meetings, with Smith extolling its bigness, simplicity, and practicality.

The inspiration was said to lie partly in the utilisation of railway air-rights in American redevelopment schemes such as the remodelling of Manhattan's Grand Central Station. The 80-acre site was bounded by Swanston Street, Flinders Street, Wellington Parade, and Jolimont Street and its continuation to the river. An existing lower level would remain dedicated largely to railway use, the balance for car parking and cool storage. The new upper level created a platform of public and commercial building sites with more than two miles of new street frontage. Aesthetically, Smith foresaw the chance 'to secure to Melbourne an Architectural river front as noble and as beautiful as any other on this earth'.[35] He was one of Walter Burley Griffin's few professional allies and the American conceived for him a megastructure that stylistically lies midway between the ancient sources that influenced his building ideas for central Canberra and the interwar Chicago school of commercial architecture. An alternative

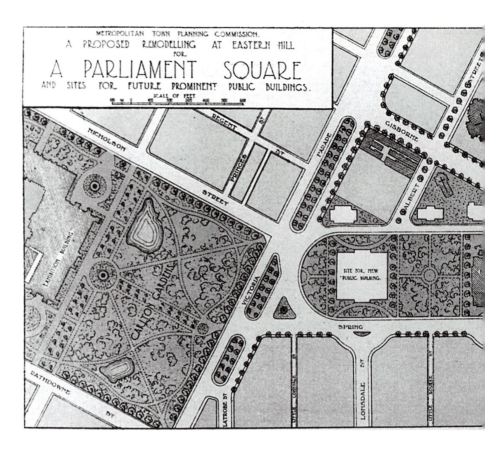

plan by Griffin's colleagues Eric Nicholls and Henry Pynor is similar, but more in the guise of streamlined prairie modernism.

Smith was said to have first advanced his scheme in the 1890s but he felt more confident that its time had come in the 1920s as 'a sound financial proposition'.[36] He felt it offered a more realistic option than the Macdonald-Swanson proposals, which were 'a very expensive undertaking with nothing adequate by way of returns'.[37] Despite Smith's best efforts to sell the scheme as a workable answer to just about everything – beautification, city extension, amelioration of traffic, and more tendentiously a civic centre – it was not well received by those who counted. The architects generally felt that the location was too off-centre to be a centre. The planners at the Metropolitan Town Planning Commission were unable to obtain further details, but regardless felt that a project of this scale would detract from the existing central business district and exacerbate congestion.

The official mood in local and state government circles was generally discouraging. The town planning commission did go some

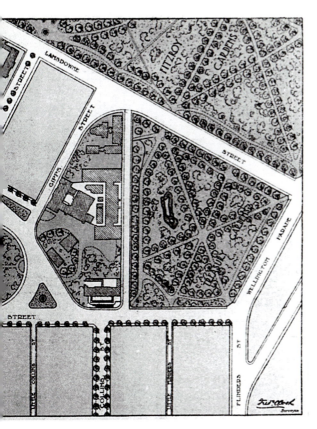

way towards conceding professional interest in the civic centre idea. On the question of 'the suitable location and grouping of prominent buildings', its major recommendation was for a 'parliamentary square' precinct on Eastern Hill, targeting the old Model School (then being used as a high school) for demolition. With a modest remodelling of the existing street pattern 'to harmonise with the park treatment', sites would be created for one major and several smaller public buildings. A virtue of the scheme was that it involved no major compulsory acquisitions and delivered the functional benefit of safer street intersections. The 'parliamentary square' proposal was a typically incremental and cost-effective solution in line with the city practical paradigm and the pragmatic views of the town planning commission's chairman, Frank Stapley, and those of other members. In 1921, even before being appointed to the commission, HE Morton had made his stance clear that 'the interior-remodelling of the city' and the issue of a civic centre should be left aside in favour of suburban planning initiatives.[38] Uncharacteristically, though, the scheme was a hypothetical one. The use of a major new public building in Spring Street was unspecified. The commission was remarkably inexplicit on whether its parliamentary square was to accommodate a relocated town hall, the most obvious candidate, even though it felt that the existing building was on an 'inadequate and unsuitable site' and that its rebuilding after a 1925 fire was an opportunity lost.

Melbourne retreated from its civic centre fetish through the 1930s. Dreams would not entirely dissipate, but for the time being, as Sulman had predicted much earlier, the city would have to be 'content for some time to come with its wide streets and well-displayed buildings'.[39]

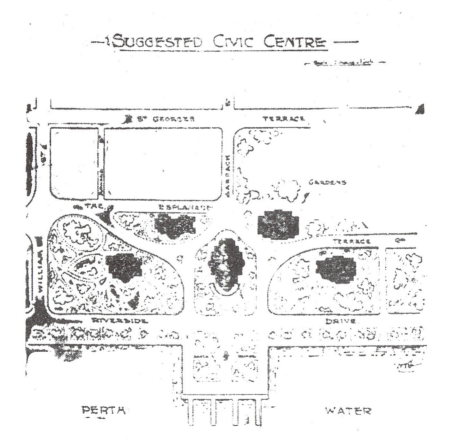

Riverfront project for Perth by Carl Klem, 1933.
The Architect, June 1969

Perth

Early proposals for the West Australian capital were connected with the need for a bigger, better located town hall and the problem of relocating or putting underground the railway tracks that divided the city centre. The rail corridor was a significant constraint to the expansion of the central business district and inhibited easy access to the north, where an art gallery, museum, library and police court were already located.

The mayor's annual report in 1909–10 suggested that a civic centre be considered in connection with site selection for a new town hall. There was ample precedent in the USA, where the idea was popular 'from the Atlantic to the Pacific'. Additional costs would be offset by benefits for the city in improved land values and 'a degree of advertising that was to be had in no other way'.[40]

The key player in Perth municipal circles was not the mayor but the town clerk, William Bold, and the same ideas surface in his report on 'Perth Improvement' (November 1911). This discusses a 'Civic Centre and Public Buildings' along with other pertinent issues such as general beautification, subdivision, streets, railways and tramways. The report laments the crowding of existing public offices and buildings into a small area between Government House and the Town Hall. Bold provides a crude sketch of the Cleveland 'group plan' as a model scheme. A site on the northern side of the railway in the vicinity of the existing library and art gallery is suggested, away from the high-priced property of the main commercial district between Hay Street and St Georges Terrace. 'The effect from an architectural point of view would be good', Bold concluded, 'especially if the various buildings were separated by small gardens'.[41]

The civic centre issue came alive in 1911 as an organised town planning movement began to take shape. The *West Australian* newspaper published a couple of rival schemes. George Temple-Poole advocated complete removal of the railway for the first time, freeing up a significant tract of land for 'civic and public buildings' to help transform Perth into 'a beautiful city' more worthy of the site it occupied. Poole was quite happy for the main Perth railway station, which he had designed, to be sacrificed for this greater good.[42] The assistant government architect,

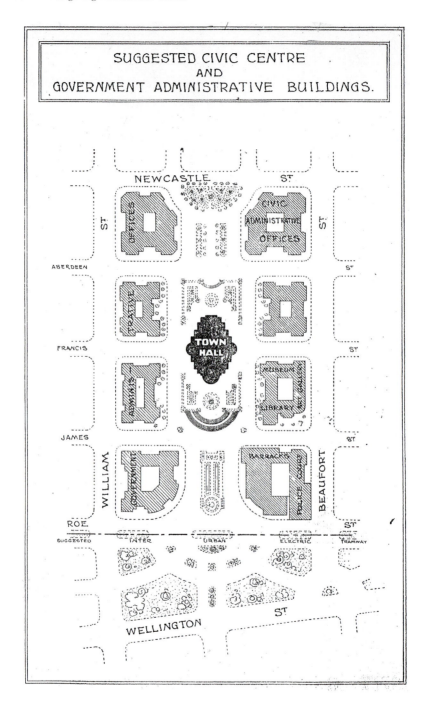

Proposed local and state government building group, Perth. *Report of the Town Planning Commission, Perth, 1930*

William Hardwick, later a successor to Poole as principal architect of the Public Works Department, devised a Washington-like mall for the same corridor. With the railway sunken below street level, he envisaged a 130-foot-wide 'new grand thoroughfare' enabling an 'uninterrupted vista' of some two miles.[43]

Bold's *Report on Tour Round the World* in 1914 carried another general endorsement of civic centres. He returned from the United States with plans and photographs of several centres planned or under construction. He regretted that the search for a new municipal headquarters could not have been linked to the Forrest Place redevelopment to create a truly 'imposing civic or administrative centre in Perth'. MF Cavanagh, president of the West Australian Institute of Architects, continued to back the Hardwick plan: 'what is now an abomination of ugliness would be converted into a thing of beauty and joy forever'.[44] His successor as president, JH Eales, promoted his own scheme for a clump of new municipal buildings that might cleanse forever an area fronting St Georges Terrace of 'dead beats and dossers'.[45]

The late 1920s was a time of 'intense activity and optimism and innumerable proposals were put forward for civic centres located both to the north and to the south of the city core'.[46] Bold reported the suggestion of a new Municipal Building being built over an extension of Forrest Place at Hay Street based on the Manhattan precedent.[47] The surveyor-planner Carl Klem presented a variation on the Poole scheme, with the railway partly removed and terminating at a grand new station, freeing considerable land for development. A public building group north of the former railway right of way was suggested.[48] From the eastern states, Sulman had spotted the potential of the reclaimed land facing Perth Water.[49] A few years later Klem suggested an alternative Swan River site for a new town hall and other public buildings surrounded by open space 'landscaped in a flowing gardenesque style'.[50]

In June 1928 the city council established a special committee to consider the civic centre question, but deferred to the newly appointed government town planning commission. The architect Harold Boas who had moved the motion for the committee was both a councillor and chairman of the commission.[51] Klem was also a commission member, so there was an innate sympathy with civic-aesthetic concerns. The commission's own 'governmental and civic centre' lay north of the railway and was contingent upon removal of the existing railway station and replacement of the heavy rail line with a city electric tramcar service.[52] Arranged in a grid across a 38-acre site were to be eight state and local administrative and cultural buildings grouped around a new town hall ('the pivot of the whole scheme'). The commission recognised not only the public convenience and better interdepartmental cooperation which would accompany such a development, but also its artistic expression of 'the pride of its community, its dignity and honour'. The idea was illustrated with the inspirational plan for the St Louis Civic Centre that had been reproduced a few years earlier in *Building* magazine as 'an object lesson to Australian cities'.[53]

The timing of the release of the commission's report, in the midst of Depression, was hardly conducive to firm government action. The key to the civic centre scheme was elimination of the rail barrier between the main civic and commercial zones of the city, but there was simply no prospect of securing the massive funds needed to relocate the railway. Indeed, the town planning commission had been officially advised of the impracticality of its rail proposals well before its report was submitted to the state government.[54] Bold sought to keep morale up: 'We must not lose sight of the importance of making plans in advance. It would be folly to 'pigeon-hole' the problems now'.[55] It was prescient advice, for many of the same ideas and issues remained prominent in public debate after World War II.

Sydney

'Our Governmental buildings are the queerest hotch-potch in existence. Each is separated from the other; some are half-a-mile apart', complained JD Fitzgerald in 1921.[56] The idea of grouping state and or local government buildings waxed and waned through to the 1930s without any satisfactory resolution.

Somewhat buried in the deliberations of the Royal Commission for the Improvement of the City of Sydney and Its Suburbs was the germ of a proposal associated with the widening of Macquarie Street,

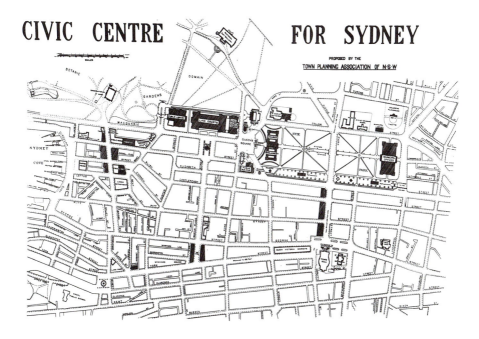

Civic Centre project, Sydney, by Town Planning Association of NSW.
J Sulman, Town Planning in Australia, 1921

Civic Centre project through westward extension of Martin Place,
by Florence Taylor. *Building, July 1929*

where Parliament House was located. The street lacked 'the dignity which should attach to its official character' and an opportunity to group scattered public buildings 'on one imposing site' was identified in the block also bounded by Phillip, Bent and Bridge streets. The idea appeared to have originated with the government architect, WL Vernon, who felt that compulsory purchase of the land not already owned by the state in this block would produce a centre equal to 'the very best parts of Paris'.[57] The commission baulked at a formal recommendation but agreed that 'the grouping on a harmonious plan of public buildings on this block would be strikingly effective'.[58]

The other locality identified in evidence taken by the commissioners as capable of dignified redevelopment for the civic good was Taylor Square, mentioned in the previous chapter. It was the locus of several proposals, including one by JD Fitzgerald and another by DJ Quinn, stepping outside his role of Secretary to the Commission, to advance its claims as 'a good place for the Greater Sydney Civic Centre'.[59] The same idea was resuscitated in the late 1930s by an engineer, Leslie Thornton. His proposal was to constitute a state parliamentary centre there, at the hub of new radiating boulevards. 'Sir John Sulman Avenue' would be linked to Cleveland Street via 'three new gyratory centres developed so as to form sites for statuary or monuments'.[60]

In 1916 the Town Planning Association of New South Wales, led by Sulman, suggested redevelopment of Hyde Park with a new parliamentary building at the northern end and municipal offices to the south. The scheme was exhibited at the First Australian Town Planning Conference and Exhibition in Adelaide. Hyde Park offered attractive parkland building sites, and its longitudinal axis was an extension of Macquarie Street, which was already 'graced' by major public buildings. The key junction of Macquarie Street with Hyde Park north at Queens Square could be made 'the focus of as fine a civic centre as any patriotic citizen could desire'.[61] As well as the innate artistic possibilities, this proposal also responded to the inadequacy of the Victorian-era Town Hall, the need to avoid costly land acquisitions, the possible future location of new underground rail stations, and the supposed declining public use of the park. Sulman declared 'its practical as well as aesthetic value' but the loss of valuable parkland made it an unpopular proposal.[62]

The 1920s saw alternative schemes floated. The architect Sir Charles Rosenthal favoured a civic centre as a means of redeveloping Woolloomooloo.[63] City Commissioner John Garlick suggested a civic complex east of Central railway station, an idea which Sulman seized on to dust off his suggested treatment of the station precinct in 1909.[64] A third proposal from 1927 was a civic precinct in the vicinity of York and Clarence streets formed around a westerly extension of Martin Place. The central features were a new town hall and civic square.[65] This was the brainchild of Florence Taylor, one of the most original if eccentric dreamers of civic improvement schemes in Sydney. She would regularly resuscitate the idea well into the 1950s. Taylor's initial inspiration was the American civic centre idea as reported in her journal *Building*. It was also stimulated by JJC Bradfield's schemes for rebuilding the southern approaches to the Sydney Harbour Bridge. When Martin Place actually broke through to Macquarie Street, there was the further appeal of a direct visual association with the state government quarter.

Geelong

Compared to the protracted ditherings in the state capitals, Geelong devised and pressed ahead with a 'civic centre' strategy during World War I which has resulted in probably the most substantial historic precinct of its type in Australia.

At the same time as schemes for foreshore improvement were being considered, Geelong council wished to create a more effective 'gateway' to the city from the main railway station through Johnstone Park. A proposal developed by Percy Everett in conjunction with local architects Laird and Buchan, and with architect-educator GR King playing a key role behind the scenes, involved extension and interrelating of existing public and administrative buildings plus remodelling of neglected parkland. A town hall and small art gallery (both of classical design) were already standing. The key architectural work was integration of the art gallery into a larger building complex with a 'composite facade' incorporating a war memorial foyer, public library, and new city hall. This would present a more handsome building frontage to the park, which itself would be regularised into a

scalloped combination of discrete lawn and garden
segments separated by narrow radial paths. A new
'boulevard' would define the divide between the
park and building zones, and the centrepiece of the
parkland precinct would be a new band rotunda.
Building hailed the project as 'a commendable step'
towards civic beautification.[66]

While 'the area to be treated' was 'self-contained',
adjacent city blocks contained the post office, court
house, technical college and other public and semi-
public buildings, so that the entire combination
was seen as constituting 'a civic centre worthy of a
progressive city'.[67] The basic scheme has substantially
come true, with the bandstand donated by a mayor
of Geelong, Howard Hitchcock. Neighbouring
institutions. including nearby Gordon Technical
College, undertook extensions and improvements
sympathetic to the classicism of the core area.[68]

The Geelong 'civic centre' showing the classically-styled
art gallery and Peace Memorial Foyer

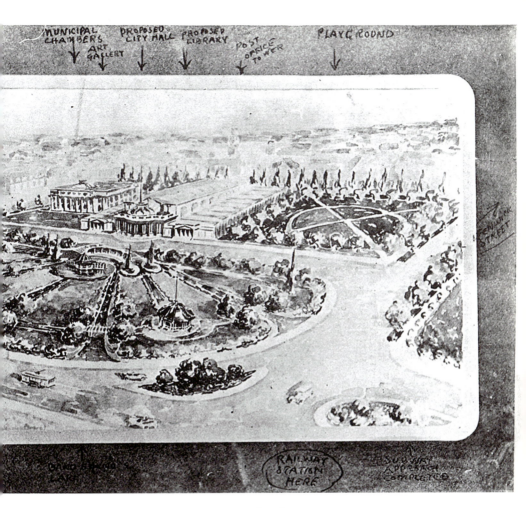

Annotated impression of Geelong civic centre.
Building, September 1917

Conclusion

Few American civic centres were carried out as originally planned. Joan Draper has isolated five critical factors affecting a centre's fortunes: quality of project leadership, available finance and funding methods, appropriate legal powers, the degree of cooperation from potential government tenants, and the design feasibility of the plan. Citing these, Wilson stresses two additional constraints: the large upfront costs of property development and the perceived impracticality of civic centres in securing good government and civic idealism.[69]

Obstacles of expense, property rights, lack of a mandate for development, and question marks over the practicality of designs, kept most Australian schemes on the drawing-board despite the best efforts of advocates to highlight the practical gains from aesthetic improvements. However, the planning movement was not completely united on the feasibility of civic centres. The concept also seemed to lack the constituency enjoyed overseas. State governments, with the greatest powers in the urban development arena, had their own respective parliamentary precincts which had developed in piecemeal manner since the early colonial era but lacked nothing in symbolic power. On the other hand, central city governments lacked the constituency and resources to justify multi-building groupings. These obstacles were greatest in the capital cities. Geelong, a provincial city, had the greatest success, with crucial factors of political leadership, community support, land availability, financing and appropriate design all falling into place. The civic centre label actually attaches to few urban precincts built in the first 30 years of the 20th century. Revealingly, there are at least two freestanding city halls with classical architectural details (Brisbane and Newcastle) from this era which appropriated the label. In a way, these smaller scale, singular civic centre buildings for local authorities demonstrate a populist downsizing of city beautiful ideals.

The civic centre nevertheless remained an enduring ideal into the post-war period, albeit generally moving away from beaux arts inspiration. And stories of some of the contested sites covered in this chapter continued to roll on under the influence of new circumstances. The situation was similar for the idea of the public square, often closely associated with public building groups.

CHAPTER 7

Public
spaces

Colonial town layout privileged the utilitarian over the aesthetic and artistic town planning sought to redress the imbalance. The new generation of modern city improvers lamented the absence of decent city squares coast-to-coast. In Sydney, the architect R Keith Harris bemoaned the want of 'architectural open spaces'.[1] G Temple Poole berated a similar lack of foresight in Perth: 'there are a few open spaces, but no squares or places for assemblage of citizens such as gregarious man requires'.[2] The most significant advances were made where such views engaged with longstanding local aspirations toward particular spaces as conspicuous expressions of civic pride. Indeed, the full stories of such projects are invariably protracted and convoluted, often commencing before a city beautiful aesthetic was even countenanced and extending long after it was forgotten.

Few proposals and projects for public squares attained national recognition, but there were several in the mainland capital cities that could be followed through professional and trade journals. Their prominence derived from their location in central business districts and their status as spaces of metropolitan, state if not national importance. The major case studies in this chapter are drawn from Melbourne, Sydney, Brisbane and Perth. Of most interest are the making of Anzac Square in Brisbane (1930) and Forrest Place in Perth

(1924) and the ways in which the fundamental tension between beauty and utility were negotiated. I begin by introducing the general city beautiful approach to public squares.

The public square

The contribution of public space to civic art is fundamental and time-honoured. The public square in history has been 'a microcosm of urban life'.[3] Early planning and civic design texts such as Inigo Triggs' *Town Planning* (1909), Raymond Unwin's *Town Planning in Practice* (1909), and Thomas Mawson's *Civic Art* (1911) acknowledged historic continuities and paid particular attention to the design of public squares. 'Speaking generally', said Mawson, 'it may be said that the scenic effect of the town as a whole largely depends upon the successful arrangement of its public places, each adequately expressing its purpose and place in the composition'.[4] The spectrum of treatment ranged from the informal and picturesque to the formal and regular. This was a particular focus of debate in European urbanism, with the competing schools represented by Sitte and Wagner. Unwin took the sensible middle ground, eschewing 'a theoretic preference' and instead being guided by 'the circumstances of the site and the requirements of the inhabitants'.[5]

Through the first third of the 20th century under the aegis of the city beautiful movement, public spaces were systematically 're-imagineered' to capture multiple social values: a sense of community and civic pride, a space for commemoration and assembly, a place-making landmark, and an uplifting opportunity for urban beautification. The design treatment naturally veered towards formalism. Public spaces in the *Plan of Chicago* (1909) were invariably spacious forecourts to major public buildings or miniature beaux arts treatments of road intersections in the Haussmann manner.

John Sulman's 1921 book, an otherwise authoritative compendium of architecturally-based planning principles for the Australian scene in this era, is surprisingly unhelpful on the treatment of public spaces. They fall between his other preoccupations of civic centres, traffic intersections, and parks. Inspirational models are nonetheless conveyed in images: Place Stanislaus in Nancy, France, and Place de la Concorde in Paris, for example. The latter received the most mentions of any public space in architectural journals into the 1930s; William Saw for example described it as 'the finest open place in any European city'.[6] An underlying principle does emerge from Sulman's overview and defines the conventional wisdom: 'the shape and character of squares or reserves in any quarter should be as varied as possible, so that each may possess its own individuality'.[7]

There appeared a general understanding that towns needed to have a range of definite 'centres' or 'places'. Thomas Mawson identified six major types, each presenting its 'own unique opportunity': government and administrative centres, traffic, military and imperial, market, religious, and 'professional and residential squares'.[8] An anonymous writer for *Building* identified just three categories – the municipal place, the ornamental place, and the business place – with each interconnected by broad thoroughfares.[9] It was accepted that each type of generic urban space would be governed by different considerations.

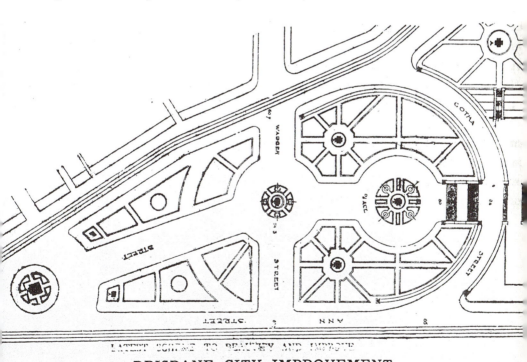

BRISBANE CITY IMPROVEMENT

The model of a formal public square, Centenary Place project, Brisbane.
Building, June 1922

For example, the railway station as the main CBD gateway needed to be complemented by public space sufficient to accommodate crowds. W Scott Griffiths contended that the station should not be located amid the hustle and bustle of office buildings. The pedestrian 'should not, the moment he emerges from the station, be in danger, whichever way he turns, of being run over by road traffic'.[10]

Perhaps the most definitive early statement on the 'value and treatment' of the public square was a 1930 address to the Institute of Architects of New South Wales by W. Hayward Morris. Versions of his paper were reproduced in several professional journals.[11] Morris outlined the three main values of a square as aesthetic, economic, and social. Beautiful forms had to be seen to be admired; there was a crucial reciprocity between buildings and their settings, with a value in grouping elements to achieve a 'desired totality of effect'. Their economic value lay as magnets for the time-saving clustering of activity and in preventing overcrowding of city streets. And they also provided for 'the social welfare of citizens' (even if just outdoor dining).

Melbourne

The longest-running saga in central Melbourne's planning history was the quest for the grand civic space denied the city by its colonial planners. The narrative intersects with the quests for a civic centre and a war memorial, all with the common aim of securing the major landmark needed to make Melbourne more than just another new world gridiron town.

A public square could be the artistic locus of civic life – an outdoor place for pageantry, processions, commemoration, circulation, and orderly public gatherings. As early as 1850, the anonymous author of 'Melbourne as it ought to be' envisaged a mosaic of public squares with one grand central square as 'the focus of commerce and civic activity' at the intersection of Collins and Elizabeth streets. All manner of sites were mooted in the late 19th and early 20th centuries. The aging Robert Hoddle reportedly saw the Queen Victoria Hospital site in Lonsdale Street as the place for 'a very handsome square'.[12] In the 1900s the Commonwealth Public Works Department reportedly proposed a square bounded by Lonsdale, Latrobe, Swanston and

Elizabeth streets, an idea rejected outright because it would cost 'a fabulous amount for resumptions'.[13]

A 1933 report in *Building* by Florence Taylor referred wearily to an enduring issue kept alive by lay observers, architects, and the Town Planning Association of Victoria as 'Melbourne's City Square Obsession'.[14] By that time discussion centered around three possible locations. One was the current City Square site opposite the Town Hall. Before World War II, the south-eastern corner of Collins and Swanston streets was an attractive option because of its prominent location, but the saga really only begins in earnest in the early 1960s.[15] A second was the old Western Market site in Collins Street, suggested by the acting premier, William McPherson, in the early 1920s. This idea was severely hosed down by a blunt-talking Frank Stapley as 'town planning gone mad'.[16] Nevertheless, after the council took possession of the site from the state government in the early 1930s, the Royal Victorian Institute of Architects was invited to comment on its future use and did so 'from the civic point of view, having regard to the matters of finance and aesthetics'. A special committee recommended creation of 'King George Square' sitting above a three-storey 750-car garage, like Union Square in San Francisco.[17] The site was enveloped decades later by the National Mutual Centre redevelopment.

The proposal for a square in front of St Paul's Cathedral, at Princes Bridge at the intersection of Swanston and Flinders streets – representing the main southern gateway to the CBD – emerged as the third hot spot of the interwar period. As early as 1889, John Keily foresaw creation of a space here as akin to London's Trafalgar Square for both 'ornamental effect' and traffic reasons. The politician George Coppin recommended something similar the following year.[18] In the 1920s the architect RB Hamilton examined the problem from the perspective of providing St Kilda Road with 'a much finer climax'.[19] JA Smith – ever ready to accommodate his railway redevelopment dream to community opinion – also tacked on the idea of a city portal at this location. A particular stimulus to debate in the late 1920s was a plan by the Victorian Railway Commissioners for a tourist bureau over a section of railway yards, set back only a short distance from Swanston Street. In 1928 a committee of the Royal Victorian Institute of Architects was invited to consider the proposal and recommended a larger setback to not only offer unobstructed views of the cathedral but create a civic square 'of which Melbourne would justly be proud'.[20] The basic idea proved popular and at various times won the support of bodies such as the Australian Natives Association, Chamber of Commerce, Town Planning Association, and Women Citizens Movement.[21] The matter was considered further by a state government

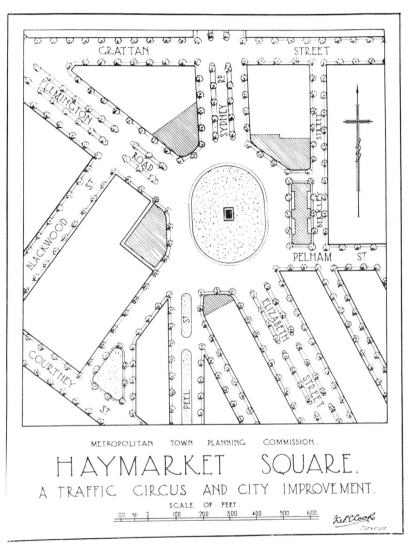

Haymarket Square project, Melbourne. *Plan of General Development, Melbourne, 1929*

committee which ultimately rejected the Royal Victorian Institute of Architects' submission because it was 'almost exclusively aesthetic'.[22]

The Metropolitan Town Planning Commission, which presented its final report in 1930, rounded up such suggestions then in the air under the heading of 'civic art and amenities' and made its own pragmatic pronouncements. The commission's suggested remodelling of Haymarket Junction – the 'most important northern entrance to the City' – into 'Haymarket Square' with a major roundabout was most obviously a traffic-management scheme, but created a more enclosed quarter surrounded by sites for prominent public buildings. The commission was non-committal to negative about suggestions for a city square proper. While it saw such a space as 'desirable', and was adamant about unsuitable locations (notably the site now occupied by Federation Square at Princes Bridge), it provided no guidance as to where one could actually go, despite this being a topic which had been 'the subject of numerous reports, conferences and deputations'.[23] Essentially, it abrogated responsibility for the question to the city council as a local issue, a stance which guaranteed that the question did not go away.

Sydney

Major hot spots in Sydney in the 1920s and 1930s were Circular Quay, Macquarie Street and Martin Place, but little came from a succession of bright and occasionally good ideas, even when injected with some serious government deliberations.

Circular Quay as the northern gateway to the city centre attracted much attention. Walter Burley Griffin on arriving for his second Australian visit in 1914 told a reporter that 'You folk in Sydney have a chance of making a city beautiful that could be easily one of the finest in the world'. Circular Quay in particular 'could easily be transformed into a thing of beauty, and a joy forever'.[24] Of all the influences on the shaping of modern Circular Quay, the decision to complete the underground rail loop across the head of Sydney Cove was the most fateful. From the late 1920s the Institute of Architects of New South Wales tried desperately for design solutions to ameliorate the impact, with Leslie Wilkinson inventing a 'fantastic Venice' proposal in 1930[25] while a comprehensive City Plan Improvement Scheme in 1932 also tackled

the approaches to the Harbour Bridge.[26] In
1937 the NSW government's Circular Quay
Planning Committee, chaired by BJ Waterhouse, recommended 'extensive rebuilding
and beautification' including a new waterfront promenade, symmetrical treatment
of the railway station with flanking pylons
to accommodate ferry offices, colonnading
of new city buildings, and the making of a
'Circular Quay Place' with a central monument marking the 150th anniversary of the
city's founding. But this was an aesthetic
sideshow to the main game: endorsement
of a double-decker road and rail structure across the face of the quay, with the
road continuing in a loop cutting under
the Bradfield Highway for northbound
bridge traffic. The one artistic gain ultimately flowing from these deliberations
was state government agreement to a new
public building in a garden setting on the
western side of the quay. This became the
new offices of the Maritime Services Board
(1952), now the Museum of Contemporary Art.

Various schemes were mooted to improve the dignity and efficiency of the parliamentary and public building precinct fronting
Macquarie Street, Sydney's main governmental strip back to the turn
of the century. The Royal Commission for the Improvement of the
City of Sydney and Its Suburbs in 1908–09 showed some interest (see
chapter 5). More purposeful investigation awaited formation of the
Macquarie Street Replanning Committee in 1936. Its report stated that
'a Public Square should be a feature in the scheme of development',
opting half-heartedly for Queens Square, at the northern end of Hyde
Park. The main design challenge was elsewhere: to better close the
vista to the new Martin Place after it connected directly to Macquarie
Street. A new law courts complex was suggested as the best visual
terminus, with virtually every existing public edifice on Macquarie

The new Venice: Circular Quay project by Institute of Architects of New South Wales. *Architecture, January 1930*

Street, including the parliamentary buildings, being relocated to accommodate the idea. The architect JF Hennessy declared the whole stillborn conception as architecturally unsatisfactory and economically unsound.[27]

The Town Planning Association of New South Wales put forward its own plan for a civic plaza at the eastern end of the new Martin Place. This proposal represented the final hurrah of the pre-World War II case to make Martin Place a true civic heart for Sydney. The sculptor Sir Bertram Mackennal's cenotaph (1929) remains a focus today, within a pedestrianised setting realised only in the 1970s. But the oft-heard complaint over many years was the need to reclaim

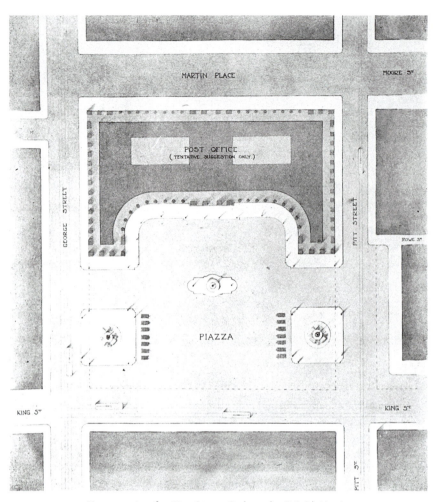

Piazza project for King Street, Sydney, by R Keith Harris.
Architecture, June 1920

and widen the street into a proper square as a more genuine gesture toward the public realm. The Martin Place story is essentially the piecemeal creation between 1870 and 1935 of a new cross-city street.[28] The city beautiful influence from the early 1900s is first marked by recommendations for tree planting.[29] There are also suggestions for the siting of war memorials either astride an eastward extension, as suggested by JH Kirkpatrick, or as a centerpiece of more radical western extensions across George Street, as preferred by JJC Bradfield, Florence Taylor, D Bennet Dobson and CO Harrison[30]. In classic beautilitarian mode, the latter suggestions were all connected with rationalising approaches to the Sydney Harbour Bridge. Eventually, amidst a welter of schemes, all incurring costs additional to road-making, the city council at the height of the Depression decided on the cheapest course of action: to complete a straight extension to Macquarie Street on a 100-foot-wide alignment.

Central Sydney was the site of other grand schemes. One of the most ambitious came from R Keith Harris speaking before the Institute of Architects of New South Wales in May 1920. He criticised Sydney's ad hoc road development and commercial pressures which had resulted in the city being virtually devoid of artistic 'Places, Piazzas, Rond Points, Squares and Crescents [which] form the chief features in a town plan'. [31] Dismissing the potential of the narrow Martin Place, Harris's fanciful 'civic centre' proposed a southern extension of the General Post Office with a new frontage to a King Street piazza, with

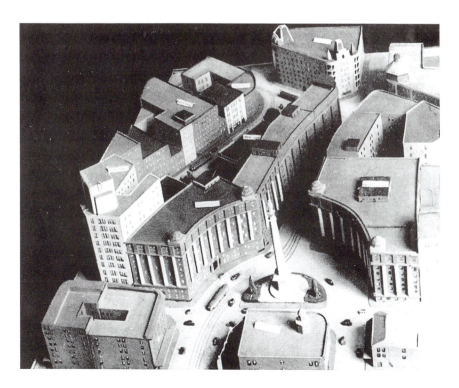

Sydney's Trafalgar Square: Phillip and Hunter streets replanning.
Decoration and Glass, April 1939

a memorial fountain at its centre and two imposing flagpoles around which flower stalls could cluster. Standing more hope of realisation was a late 1930s scheme for the northern extension of Hunter Street. The basic rationale was to improve traffic access to and from Circular Quay, but treatment of the crucial intersection envisaged a semi-circular public space inspired by Trafalgar Square. This proposal is attributed variously to Sydney City Council engineer Alfred Garnsey, the lord mayor, Norman Nock, and the new Town and Country Planning Institute of New South Wales which quickly usurped the Town Planning Association formed by George and Florence Taylor as a source of credible professional advice.[32]

Anzac Square, Brisbane

Many of the trappings of an ideal public square inspired by the city beautiful are captured in the 1922 plan for Cathedral Plaza in Brisbane. This site was once considered a possible site for Brisbane city hall. When the opportunity passed, it was reinvented as a grand forecourt to a new Roman Catholic cathedral to be designed by Jack Hennessy. Foundation stones were laid in 1928 but the building never came. Impressive stone walls in the vicinity are the legacy of Archbishop James Duhig's ambitions but the site lay dormant until redeveloped for an apartment complex in the 1990s. The 1922 public square plan was hailed as a 'fine piece of work' by *Building*.[33] A balanced and symmetrical composition, it would have formed 'an impressive formal landscaped piazza', channeling an axial view from the city centre towards the cathedral.[34] Renamed Centenary Place in 1924 to commemorate 100 years of settlement in Brisbane, the original plan lapsed but the space remains an attractive green island on the fringe of Brisbane's CBD.

Anzac Square was the more important and fully realised public square for Brisbane. In line with the early predilection to prominently group federal office buildings in all capital cities, early Commonwealth governments wished to consolidate various departments scattered in sub-standard rental properties. The chosen site was within a block of some four acres bounded by Ann, Edward, Adelaide and Creek streets, immediately across from the Central railway station. Half of this area was owned by the state government; the Commonwealth split the balance with the Presbyterian Church. The site dropped away from the Ann Street frontage into a motley and underdeveloped collection of buildings, including a school, drill hall, and automotive and other businesses.

It was a drab and unprepossessing gateway to the central city, and more exciting possibilities had already been envisaged. The architect John James Clark realised a suggestion by Brisbane solicitor and politician Thomas Macdonald-Paterson in an ambitious gateway project. John Sulman earmarked the block for 'a fine civic centre'.[35] And before World War I someone had produced a plan for 'new public gardens' in a symmetrical scheme organised around axes and statuary at focal points that also anticipated an extended link through to the main post office in Queen Street. After the war this gardens idea became irrevocably connected to the siting of a national war memorial.

Over nearly a decade, three independent but interlinked narratives required resolution to make Anzac Square: amalgamating and delineating the precise site, arriving at an overall scheme for its treatment, and selecting the best affordable design for its defining war memorial.

An 'Anzac Park' opposite the station was the early frontrunner of all feasible sites for the war memorial. There were some who felt strongly that the entire city block should be secured, but the Commonwealth was not prepared to surrender all its property given its development ambitions and, even more emphatically, neither was the state government. A delegation of citizens and interested organisations who met the state premier, EG Theodore, in October 1923 was left in no doubt. Theodore saw the memorial proposal as 'the revival, in a patriotic guise, of a city garden scheme, which had been turned down in 1912'. He felt that 'the sentimental arguments which have been put forward by the deputation are "All Tosh", and carry no weight'.[36] After extensive negotiations, the site eventually consolidated as open space in 1926 had a 225-foot frontage to Ann and Adelaide streets and was nearly 270 feet deep[37]. The state gave up 178 feet 6 inches of frontage, and while the Commonwealth's dedication of 46 feet 6 inches was more modest, it crucially allowed for the central axis of the square to align with the clock tower of the railway station. Both authorities also gave up land for road widening. Brisbane City Council faced heavy commitments elsewhere in the city with Centenary Square and a new city hall and supported the deal.

On the overall design possibilities, various ideas were floated publicly. The architect James Milne Stewart suggested a podium raised to the Ann Street level with a central cenotaph atop shop frontages and covered parking. The journal *Building* conceded the logic in making the scheme pay for itself 'in our own age' but worried about the lack of soil for trees.[38] The architect James Corrie laid out the square like a Union Jack and similarly incorporated commercial premises as well as an art gallery and lecture hall. *Building* also commented on these inclusions as 'welcome adjuncts by those whose avaricious eyes see in the memorial an opportunity of obtaining something utilitarian'.[39]

The key figure in official thinking was the Commonwealth's

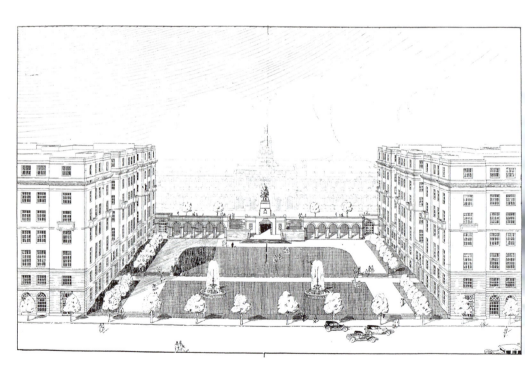

Final scheme for Anzac Square, Brisbane.
Anzac: Lest We Forget, Brisbane 1927

John Smith Murdoch. In 1922 Murdoch was credited with the critical aspects of the eventually agreed design for Anzac Square 'many years ago'.[40] He regarded it as 'a beautiful site'[41] and could not comprehend why railway authorities were not more supportive given the compelling rationale for a major public space at this location in accommodating future larger volumes of pedestrians using the suburban railway system.[42] Murdoch was instrumental in devising an indicative layout showing a central open space suitable for a memorial flanked by new Commonwealth offices on the eastern side and new state government buildings on the western side. The details of this conception evolved primarily through interactions between the Commonwealth and the Queensland Department of Works between 1923 and 1926. The most contentious elements in early plans were vehicular access into the square from Adelaide Street and a pedestrian subway to the station, and their impact on a suitably reverent curtilage for a major memorial. The roadway proposal was strenuously opposed by the Returned Sailors' and Soldiers' Imperial League as 'totally unworthy'. Meetings in 1926 involving Murdoch, James Orwin (State Commonwealth Public Works director), AH Foster, (city architect), and William Earle (city planner) hammered out the key elements: a memorial on the Ann Street level; widening of Ann Street with a new retaining wall required; terracing and balustrading to the lower levels; subway entrance under Ann Street to the station; state offices designed in harmony to avoid an 'incongruous effect'; and no semi-circular drive. Everyday needs were also factored in, with a railway refreshment room, lost property office, and public lavatories. The idea for a small display of historical artefacts came a little later. A sketch by DW Crawford (Murdoch's supervising architect of 1917) illustrates Murdoch's essential vision: 'a well-planned ensemble of stylistically-unified buildings ... separated by an elegantly-landscaped square dotted with shady trees, manicured lawns and featuring a focal memorial structure'[43].

The third critical element completing Anzac Square was the actual design of a memorial. Again, there were numerous suggestions. In 1921 the National Anzac Memorial Committee favoured a replica of Sir Edwin Lutyens' Cenotaph in Whitehall, London and went as far as approaching him for plans but never satisfactorily resolved financial arrangements. The choice of memorial could not move forward until the site was confirmed. That accomplished, Sir Bertram Mackennal agreed to become involved and visited Brisbane in January 1927. He envisaged a memorial over 40 feet high with bronze figures of heroic proportions on a granite pedestal modelled after Lutyens' Cenotaph. In June 1927 William Jolly, mayor of the new Greater Brisbane, and chairman of the Anzac War Memorial Committee, was finally able to launch a public appeal for subscriptions to fund the memorial. His pitch was twofold: while the main objective was to perpetuate the memory of 'those who helped us to Nationhood', an ancillary aim was to stir 'civic pride and aesthetic taste'. The appeal brochure included an artist's impression of Anzac Square based on Crawford's but with Mackennal's massive memorial inserted as the centrepiece.[44] Unfortunately, the target of £25 000 never looked like being reached and Mackennal's proposal was reluctantly set aside.

In 1928 it was decided to invite competitive designs for a memorial to cost not more than £10 000.[45] The competition, launched in July 1928, attracted 50 entries and the £100 first prize was awarded to Sydney architects SH Buchanan and FM Cowper. According to the adjudication committee, the winning concept was a 'very chaste and dignified design and strictly correct from an Architectural point of view'. The committee felt that 'when erected Brisbane would have a memorial (on a smaller scale) quite equal to almost anything in the world'.[46] The memorial was designed as a circular sandstone peristyle consisting of 18 Doric columns (symbolising the year the war ended) enclosing a metal urn of remembrance with a perpetual flame and set back from the street by a paved piazza. The approach from Adelaide Street was by an imposing flight of stairs. The square was beautified by lawns, trees, shrubs and ornamental reflecting pools. The memorial was accentuated as the focal point in the square by three radiating avenues symbolising the defence services.[47] It was dedicated on Armistice (now Remembrance) Day 1930. The total cost of the project was in the order of £19 000. 'Thus has the original idea conceived ... of a park in the centre of the city been fulfilled, and at the same time noble sacrifices, made necessary by subsequent events, been commemorated', stated the *Architectural and Building Journal of Queensland*.[48]

The editor of this journal had documented the saga through the 1920s, with his particular take being a great aesthetic development

Anzac Square, Brisbane

challenged at every step by more base concerns. An early preference was a square covering the entire city block, not a 'pocket handkerchief'[49] or a 'glorified right-of-way'.[50] Within it should be a magnificent monument to the memory of the fallen. While conceding that a memorial hospital would be useful for a generation or two, it would lack the same lasting inspirational impact and in any case the square itself had a utilitarian value 'in providing Brisbane with an open-air space in the heart of the city'.[51] The schematic plan of 1927 caused some alarm at the prospect of 'business buildings' compromising the 'art' of the memorial space.[52] *Building* magazine echoed the same criticism of their 'warehouse exteriors'.[53] The winning design was ultimately seen as another opportunity lost for Brisbane, a good design diminished by compromise:

> There are practical minds with a partiality for utility over beauty
> but art does not subscribe to such tenets. It savours of desecration in
> framing a beautiful site with the cold, dull, presentments of brick and
> mortar or whatever the materials may be ... Art cannot be expected to
> nestle with comfort or throw out its splendid expressive influences at
> the foot of piles of stilled, featureless masonry.[54]

Anzac Square was declared a permanent reserve in 1933 and attracted
other memorials, such as a relocated Boer War memorial (1919) in 1939
and Daphne Mayo's Queensland Women's War Memorial (1932). Two
initial sections of the state office complex were completed by 1933 and
those of the Commonwealth, matching but smaller-scale, a couple
of years later, both in Murdoch's 'stripped inter war classical' style.
The state government building was not completed until the 1950s.
Unfortunately, the third section of the Commonwealth building did
not proceed and the chance to extend the block to Ann Street and
complete the Anzac Square development as planned was lost with
the regrettable decision to build a 15-storey office tower on the site,
completed in 1972.

Forrest Place, Perth

Forrest Place was born of similar circumstances to Anzac Square, but
produced a less complete scheme which less satisfactorily balanced
competing aesthetic values and functional necessities. Problems at
birth were never satisfactorily resolved. The person to blame is probably
the home affairs minister, King O'Malley, who backed the scheme
to develop a group of federal buildings in combination with retail
tenancies as a 'business proposition'. The three-acre site immediately
opposite the main railway station stretched between Wellington and
Murray streets and was acquired in August 1911 at a total cost of
£ 178,376. The prime minister, Andrew Fisher, wrote the mayor of Perth
in December 1911 suggesting that the city council and the Western
Australian government 'may be desirous of making use of this unique
opportunity to inaugurate a scheme for the beautification of the City'
through developing 'a fine approach to the Railway Station, and
giving greater prominence to the new buildings that it is proposed to
erect'.[55] George Temple Poole's 1890s main railway station then opened

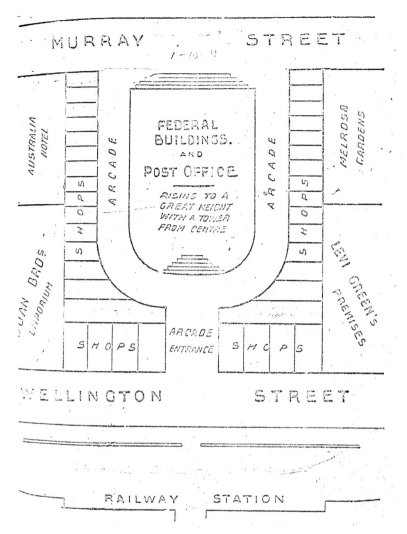

Speculative proposal for new post office and federal buildings in Perth.
Sunday Times, 1 October 1911

up across Wellington Street to a motley collection of retail buildings, an arcade and coffee palaces, framed by the city's two largest retail emporia, Boan's and what became Bairds.

John Smith Murdoch again played a key design role, but with no federal architecture secretariat in the west, day-to-day responsibility devolved to the State Department of Public Works under the supervision of its chief architects Hillson Beasley (1905–1917) and William Hardwick (1917–1927), the latter, noted earlier, also promoting his own schemes for the aesthetic improvement of central Perth.

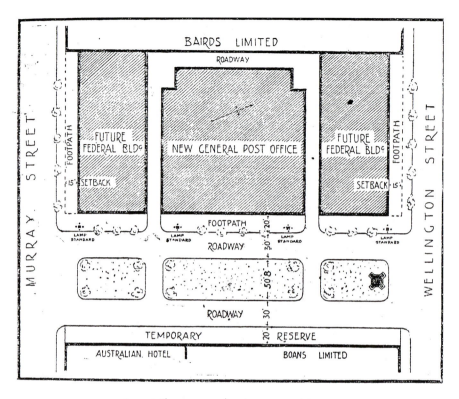

Forrest Place proposal as 'a green oasis', 1923.
West Australian, 6 February 1923

They collaborated with the Melbourne-based Murdoch to produce a first plan in 1913. This connected Wellington and Murray streets by a new 66-foot-wide thoroughfare. On the west side were sites for three major public buildings: nearest the station, a customs house, a Commonwealth Bank at Murray Street, and a central post office in between. On the other side of the street would be a row of new shops and offices. In a city seeking a major public square, the reception to this combination of culture and commerce was not good. A decade of submissions, deputations, correspondence and counter-plans was triggered, the overwhelming preference being for a wider street less directly affronted by a thin strip of retail buildings.

A consensus against the Commonwealth scheme was forged in August 1913 by the city council, chamber of commerce, and professional organisations representing architects, engineers, surveyors, builders and contractors. The mayor wrote the state premier in December 1913 saying it would be 'a calamity' to adopt a scheme conceived on 'narrow lines' that would see 'erection of buildings of a trivial character, and would altogether spoil the effect of the property from a "City beautiful" point of view'. Percy Owen, the director of Commonwealth Works, rejected the criticism and alternative schemes which deleted the shops in favour of open space. Such thinking, he wrote, 'proposes to quite set aside the interests of the Commonwealth in the project, and to regard it largely as one of beautification of Perth. From the economical and Commonwealth standpoint I regard it as impossible'.[56] The prime minister, Joseph Cook, had to defend 'the profit-making scheme of his predecessors' but was more conciliatory.[57] A compromise was reached, with the new street widened to 84 feet and new corner buildings at Wellington and Murray streets set back 15 feet for future street widening. Construction could commence on Murdoch's French Renaissance-style GPO.[58] Progress was slowed by the war, difficulties in securing building materials, and strikes. On opening in 1923, the £400 000, nine-storey, granite and freestone-faced building with its impressive Ionic columns was the largest in Western Australia and housed various government departments.[59]

In the early 1920s with the building's completion in sight and a satisfactory plan for treating the balance of the street yet to be agreed, the Town Planning Association of Western Australia was spurred into action under the leadership of William Saw. The association proposed the preferred option for more expansive treatment as a genuine public square.[60] It perceived an imbalance between the project's aesthetic and financial values: the Commonwealth's thinking was too 'utilitarian – to make as much money out of the ground as possible' and the kind of retail buildings that could be erected could not do justice to the handsome public buildings opposite and would detract from the aesthetics and economics of the overall scheme. The incongruous juxtaposition of small retail shops and palatial public buildings was portrayed as 'ornamenting a super-fine dress coat with lapels of jute from a woolpack'.[61] This line of criticism forced another compromise and in March 1923, following a visit to Perth by Murdoch, the home affairs and territories secretary approved widening the new street to 90 feet.

The problem of the proposed shops on the opposite side of the street remained. However, there were no further concessions from the Commonwealth, despite continued rearguard lobbying by the council. The 60-foot-deep frontage to Boan's western elevation was leased to a wealthy Perth retailer, Padbury, who proceeded to erect a two-storey commercial building, completed in 1924. The Commonwealth Bank opposite arrived in 1933, some years after the street was opened for traffic, and the Customs House site would be occupied by small businesses until the 1980s. The new street was briefly considered a possible location for the state war memorial, but was ruled out because of its narrowness. The development was officially named after Westralian hero Lord John Forrest on 26 September 1923. Padbury's buildings would remain for the term of the half-century Commonwealth lease, an arrangement attributed to Murdoch that at least secured some long-term control over site development. Perth finally had a new street and a couple of fine new public buildings, but not quite the public square which early idealism had envisaged.

Forrest Place – the street, 1935.
JS Battye Library of West Australian History, 816B/B2947

Conclusion

The impress of city beautiful thinking is registered in some of the major public squares, the sites and characters of which were shaped by early 20th century design standards.

Forrest Place and Anzac Square are the most notable. In their day, both were major city gateway sites. Both record the legacy of the Commonwealth's early desire to develop a presence in the state capitals through an interpretation of the American civic centre concept. Such a goal proved more feasible in the smaller cities of Perth and Brisbane than Sydney and Melbourne, where higher land values and other constraints and opportunities presented. Both spaces reveal the neo-classical tendencies of John Smith Murdoch as a central figure in what were complex negotiations involving multiple levels of government. But the histories of both spaces also reflect tensions in the beauty-versus-function debate, a situation ultimately more happily resolved in Brisbane than Perth, where stakeholder balancing of aesthetic and utilitarian was never reconciled, a recurrent theme elsewhere.

CHAPTER 8

The campus beautiful

The civic centre idea of grouping public buildings formally for aesthetic and functional reasons was extended to other kinds of buildings – cultural, educational, recreational, exhibition and general institutional.[1] Three unrealised Australian projects illustrate these wider applications. The architect Howard Joseland's 1918 competition-winning plan for Burnside Homes for orphan boys in Parramatta, western Sydney, was a symmetrical composition, with the homes arranged in a semicircle around a central playing field to capture a communal character.[2] An ambitious redevelopment scheme for the Coast Hospital (later Prince Henry) in Sydney's eastern suburbs in 1914 envisaged a beaux arts composition of single-storey 'ward pavilions' arrayed symmetrically in parallel lines around a central axis comprising administration and reception buildings and nurses' quarters. Set amidst landscaped crescents and gardens, the hospital had a direct tram connection to the city.[3] Finally, Melbourne architect Charles Heath's early 1920s competition-winning plan for the Royal Agricultural Society of South Australia Showgrounds at Wayville in Adelaide was a tightly symmetrical scheme of Romanesque-style permanent halls arranged around a central square linked to peripheral access roads by boulevard-style 'broadways'.[4]

The layout and replanning of university campuses was influenced by similar design trends. Campuses have been laboratories for urban design, even evolving as virtual cities-in-microcosm. They bear the imprint not only of ruling aesthetic tastes at the time of their foundation but successive interventions. Enjoying unified land ownership and control, there are less impediments to the realisation of design intentions than in the 'real world', making them one of the relatively few settings able to express 'a purposeful public order'.[5]

The impact of formal beaux arts principles on American campuses from the 1890s to 1920s is documented by Paul Turner in *Campus* (1984). There were kindred conceptions in other parts of the world over the same period. Australian responses were not as vigorous as in America, but similar aesthetic principles can be read into the development of new or revised site plans for the universities of Sydney, Western Australia, Adelaide, and Queensland.

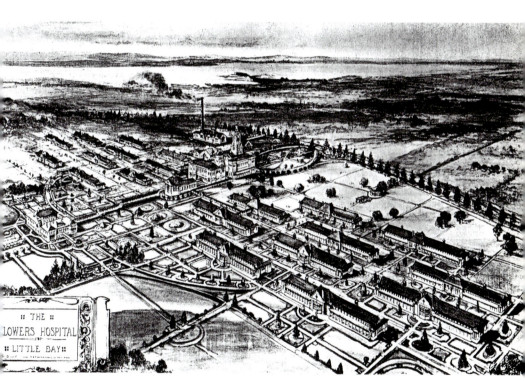

:: THE ::
LOWERS HOSPITAL
:: LITTLE BAY ::

The Flowers Hospital project, Little Bay, Sydney. *Report of the NSW Department of Public Works, 1914*

Wayville showgrounds project by CR Heath.
Building, February 1915

Designing the campus on artistic lines

Many different typologies exist for university layouts. The Oxbridge
model, powerful at the end of the 19th century, derived from the
medieval colleges of Oxford and Cambridge, with their monastery-
like compounds of chapel, library, dining hall and residences grouped
around quadrangles. Usually associated with Gothic architecture,
the accent was on reclusive, compact, space-enclosing arrangements
of linked structures. In European cities, university premises often
intermingled with other buildings in dense town centres. In contrast,
the new world campus tradition descended from Thomas Jefferson's
notion of the 'academical village'. Under the influence of the World's
Columbian Exposition this came to define a more spacious, open
setting, still rigidly controlled, with recurring forms of symmetrically
grouped buildings, axial lines, and focal points. A more informal
style, also with city beautiful connections, was the Romantic campus,
with its park-like settings, curvilinear avenues, and Olmstedian
informality.

But many universities in reality were characterised by a higgledy-
piggledy arrangement of discordant styles and ad hoc development.
Such haphazardness became unacceptable for a tertiary-education

environment from the early 1900s. City planning helped invent the concept of the master-planned campus because the evils and complications of unplanned development were analogous to those of the city proper. Casual, incremental growth would only produce 'a wretched crazy quilt of discordant buildings'.[6] The importance of an overall planning approach was conventional wisdom by the 1920s:

> The key-note of a general development plan is order ... [a] group of buildings ... should be a homogeneous, clearly to be apprehended scheme, in which there is a studied and happy balance of things, of buildings located with regard to their functions, importance and architectural effect, of natural views conserved and topographical advantages skilfully exploited.[7]

The master plan was seen as a vehicle for beauty, although different architectural interpretations were evident. The major design debates through the interwar period posed Gothic in opposition to Classical, formal versus informal, and modern against traditional.

In the United States the city beautiful made a strong impression in this phase of development because of the taste for beaux arts classicism that then held sway among mainstream American architects. An international competition for the University of California at Berkeley, masterminded by Bernard Maybeck and won by the French beaux arts artist Emile Bénard in the late 1890s, produced 'a sweeping victory for formal design'.[8] Charles Mulford Robinson described the project as the 'first permanent conquest' of the movement for comprehensive planning in the United States.[9] A campus had to be not just orderly but also beautiful. Its physical expression had to testify to permanence, cultural commitment, and public order. The outward appearance of the university had to mirror the high values of the institution. But beautiful surroundings had their own instrumentality as a refining and educational influence, a view which reflected the city beautiful movement's belief in beauty as a positive force in ordinary lives. While designing no campuses himself, Daniel Burnham strongly represented the view that 'reciprocal' arrangements and coordination of style, colour and scale were a positive force on students.[10] Acceptance of these ideas by university presidents, regents, patrons, alumni, and benefactors – the real movers and shakers – was critical to any planning beautification program. The president of the University of Washington was a strong supporter of campus replanning on formal axial lines: 'intellectuality and morality are doubled in their efficiency', he maintained, 'when the grace and appreciation of beauty are added'.[11]

Campus beautiful plans were seemingly static set pieces, the products of a slower age, when growth and change seemed more predictable and manageable. They were formal, comprehensive, integrative, and monumental. They sought visual unity and spatial precision, and were not readily able to accommodate whimsy or individualism. Their geometry revolved around symmetry, axiality, and focal points. Groups of buildings were arranged to define a hierarchy of open spaces around major and minor axes. Vistas had a clear purpose: 'It is sound dictum that axes should have their termini upon enduring objects of prominence and not upon any accidental or ephemeral thing'.[12] The favoured foci were key buildings such as libraries and great halls. Gateway structures and ceremonial approaches could form linkages with the city outside. The design parameters were largely variations on the dictums of École des Beaux Arts site planning, even if American interpretations possessed a more open, spatial quality than the French prototypes.[13] The star designers, virtually all with personal École connections, read like a who's who of American fin-de-siecle architects: Charles McKim, John Carrère, Thomas Hastings, Cass Gilbert, Bernard Maybeck, Henry Hornbostel, and so on.

These architects employed a variety of styles, with the classical revival preferred for its appeal to educated tastes, elite learning, progressive education, and visual associations with major public buildings. Many ambitious campus beautiful plans stayed on the drafting board. Those which eventuated were often the product of strategic and enduring partnerships between progressive university officials and talented designers. The main opportunities for fruition came with the relocation of downtown campuses to suburban settings. At their best, like Columbia University, they captured 'in miniature form the urban ideals of the City Beautiful movement'.[14] Schemes to 'city-beautify' existing campuses were more problematical and involved the judicious demolition of old buildings and studied placement of new elements in structured geometric patterns.

The campus beautiful was exported by American architects to countries such as India and China.[15] Some Canadian universities retained Thomas Mawson to inject a somewhat anglicised formality.[16] In Britain itself, 'the classical was not so closely associated with learning'.[17] But symmetrical layouts were evident, the best example being the University of Birmingham, designed by Aston Webb as a monumental semicircle of buildings with a clocktower in 'Edwardian ceremonial' style.[18] Fragments of the same tradition linger in later schemes, such as the British architect Charles Holden's University Garden (1932) at the University of London.[19] The impact of this thinking in the antipodes is captured in the distinctly beaux arts university campus included in the New Zealand architect Reginald Hammond's extravagant 1925 award-winning design for Orakei Garden Suburb, Auckland.[20]

Planning Australian universities

On the eve of World War I there were six universities in Australia: Sydney (established 1850), Melbourne (1853), Adelaide (1874), Tasmania (1890), Queensland (1909), and Western Australia (1910). All were established at critical stages in the cultural, economic and political maturation of their respective states. All were elite cultural institutions, predominantly non-residential, mainly undergraduate, with small enrolments and dependent on meagre government funding and philanthropy.[21] Their early years saw them virtually contained within single buildings. By the early 1900s, three had found permanent homes, best described as university buildings and grounds rather than integrated campuses. The rest made do with makeshift central-city buildings and dreams of noble edifices on splendid sites.

There was a growing awareness of the need to avoid planless building on new sites. The rudimentary state of the older universities was also evident, with Sydney University described in 1919 as distinguished by 'rough bush tracks, hideous tar paving, unworthy lamps, [and] crude posts with their webs of wire'.[22] With master plans in place, both old and new complexes could accommodate growing space needs, avert costly mistakes, conserve and enhance the beauty of their sites, and secure environments conducive to learning and attractive to potential benefactors.

The historical influence of Britain on the organisation of Australian tertiary education meant that the dominant design tradition 'in so far as there was one, was to try to recapture European university traditions through Gothic spires and grass quadrangles, and then allow less expensive and more functional buildings to grow up around the monumental centre'.[23] Professor Leslie Wilkinson established himself as a leading expert on university design soon after his arrival from Britain in 1918. This background, leavened by European travels, was reflected in his prescriptions for campus design.

Outlined by him in an address to a scientific congress in 1926, the site determined the choice of formal or informal aggregation. Enclosed quadrangle and court forms for the 'faculty groups' were preferred, leading up to the most prominent individual buildings (hall, library, etc.) while residential colleges would be 'on the boundaries'. An artistic sensibility could prevail overall:

> The planning for effective vistas, and for composition in which buildings and plantings together produce beautiful effects, need not mar the practicability. In this respect the possibilities of the scheme should be appreciated with the eye of a painter.[24]

Possibilities for more rectilinear and open beaux arts campuses were captured by the federal capital design competition of 1911–12, in which competitors were instructed to accommodate, amongst many other public institutions, a university. Genuine campus beautiful recommendations were, unsurprisingly, American in origin. Harold Van Buren Magonigle placed his campus on the north side of city, in a formal, open U-shaped grouping recalling the academical village idea. The American landscape architect Arthur Comey placed a rectilinear multi-building campus with cross-axes and garden courts on the site now occupied by the Australian National University. The Griffins did likewise.

Walter Burley Griffin possessed experience in campus design.[25] His ideas for a federal capital university were underlain by distinctive philosophical ideas about tertiary education. The theoretical logic of the Griffin campus was concentric circles of knowledge, spiralling outwards from a core of fundamental 'descriptive' sciences through intermediate theoretical sciences to the applied sciences on the perimeter. It was reminiscent of the thematic elliptical rings employed by Frederick Le Play in the Paris Exposition of 1867. Academic schools were orientated to off-campus locations; the medical faculty, for example, would be located near the city hospital, while law and commerce were orientated toward the civic centre. The indicative site plan was (by Australian standards at the time) an extensive formal layout of building footprints, open spaces, and cross-axes. Revised but similar versions appeared in Griffin's 1913 *Report Explanatory* and in his final 1918 plan. In the latter, the buildings are spaced more widely, the university assumes a definitive green heart and the relationship of campus axes to the land and water axes of the city proper is more obvious.[26] George Taylor, when still civil to the Griffins, felt his exotic treatment was the true stamp of Walter 'as a town planner of high ideals and practical purpose'.[27]

Out of this mix of international, domestic, and adapted design influences emerged an eclectic, aesthetic-based planning aligned with the broader 'city beautiful' ethos of the day, and echoing, if distantly, the American beaux arts campus tradition. The common themes as always were the importance of axes, vistas and focal points; geometric clarity; and the ideological importance attached to beauty, albeit always constrained by practical concerns.

University of Sydney

At the very time the town planning movement was making its major impact, the grounds of Sydney University were in dishevelled condition. Edmund Blacket's main quadrangle from the 1850s remained incomplete, huts were scattered around 'like the morning after the fair', and 'the grounds were in an extraordinary state – buildings fenced around with iron railings with horses grazing outside'.[28] Interest in a campus plan was aroused in 1913, the year the first town planning association was formed in Sydney, when the registrar, HE Barff, was involved in abortive negotiations to bring the British landscape architect Thomas Mawson on a national lecturing-consulting tour.

In this climate, the architect John Barr put forward a replanning scheme, published in the *Journal of the Institute of Architects of New South Wales*.[29] Noting the 'awakening of interest in Australia in town-planning ... and a desire that our environment may be made at least a little more beautiful', he proffered a formal plan of the kind 'generally adopted for the lay-out of scholastic or similar groups of buildings'. This involved a regularisation of building sites, proposals for additional and extended buildings, tree-lined avenues, and a new entrance from Newtown Road, with the medical school 'made the chief point of view ... closing the vista'. Also inserted was a new teachers training college,

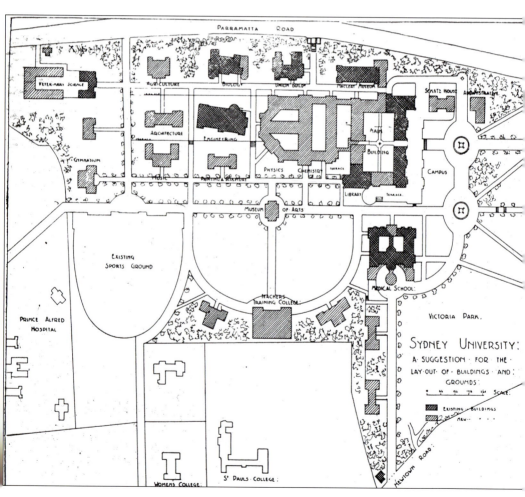

Sydney University project by John Barr.
The Salon, September 1913

symmetrically flanked by two new buildings, and looking out toward a strategically placed 'Arts and Handicrafts Museum'. Barr implied later that such a proposal may have been too visionary for university authorities, their penchant being 'curved roads winding through the grounds'.[30]

In 1914 it was Walter Burley Griffin's turn. The Building, Grounds and Improvement Committee resolved in September to obtain a report from 'a landscape architect on the best method of laying out the University grounds with a view to present and future requirements in regard to sites for buildings for educational purposes, the laying out of roads and areas for playing fields'. Griffin's scheme was submitted in January 1915. It is a good example of his ability to work within the constraints of an existing landscape, and retreats from the bold geometry evident in the *tabula rasa* planning at Canberra. His plan is distinguished by small courts, quadrangles and other open spaces being valued above overall uniformity – the same approach evident in his contemporaneous scheme for the University of New Mexico. It was very much a landscape plan, with a centrally-located 'valley' preserved 'in the form of a "campus" – necessary to secure an adequate spaciousness for the final plan consistent with a full and compact building development'.[31] The building committee acknowledged the plan as 'an admirable harmonious scheme' but sensed 'great expense' and was unhappy with the proposed relocation of the university oval and incursions into the curtilages of several colleges.[32]

After World War I, the university found itself in a better financial position, with the state government agreeing to a £300 000 grant for a six-year building program to address space shortages. The campus was officially the responsibility of the government architect, whose office produced at least two master plans. A 1921 effort was slammed by architectural critic Florence Taylor as characterised by a maze of curved and crooked roads 'that are absolutely contrary to practical utility'.[33] Wilkinson arrived on the scene with clear expectations of assuming a key role in campus design and in July 1919 he was appointed to a committee to advise on general layout. By year's end he was ensconced as the university architect. His plan was completed in January 1920 and officially adopted by the university senate in March 1920.

Wilkinson's scheme has been read as a statement of his ability to marry 'common sense and creative imagination'. Existing buildings, roads and natural features were preserved. It completed the Blacket quadrangle of the main building, and added buildings alongside in prominent positions looking toward the city. It sought to create new open vistas as well as secluded gardens. Like the Griffin plan, it preserved the central 'campus' as a framed, green heart. Overall, Wilkinson's purpose was to introduce 'a sense of unity, order, convenience and, if maybe, eventually beauty, into the University quarters treated as a whole'.[34] The plan stopped short of true beaux arts symmetry, and drew criticism from those who preferred a more emphatic axial replanning:

> Although it is generally recognised (and given a grudging approval by Professor Wilkinson) that axes should be established, in a lay-out of disconnected buildings, this design is singularly lacking in anything of the sort, and the buildings are connected by short roads turning at right angles or merging into other roads. If the creation of a baffling maze was the intention, this has certainly been accomplished, and the unfortunate stranger would probably find himself returning to his starting point without achieving the object of his search; the maze destroys the possibility of forming grand vistas.[35]

On the other hand, John Sulman felt the plan was an exemplary local example of 'civic aesthetics'. As a scheme for new public buildings 'grouped into a well-ordered whole', he bracketed it with American examples such as the Seattle and Cleveland civic centres, and the Senate Park Commission's Washington, DC scheme.[36]

Wilkinson's scheme provided a fillip to orderly planning, and certain buildings were constructed or completed in conformity with its recommendations, including his Physics Building (1926) with its long symmetrical facade and beaux arts circulation planning.[37] However, the plan was not comprehensively implemented. Relations between the university and Wilkinson soured within a few years, the government architect was antagonistic, and university authorities were unwilling or unable to invest significantly in campus landscaping and development. Sydney reverted to its Oxbridge-with-accretions roots and the Wilkinson plan was forgotten in the post-World War II development boom.

University of Western Australia

The University of Western Australia was the last of the state universities to be established under an Act of Parliament in 1911. Three years later the state government made available a 104-acre (42 hectares) site adjacent to Matilda Bay on the Swan River, although most of the university was camped in makeshift premises in the city well into the 1920s. The new site was attractive, and a primary aim of the first chancellor, Sir John Winthrop Hackett, was to respect 'the deep water river front with which this beautiful area is favoured' making it 'one of the rarest attractions offered by any of the Universities of Australia'.[38]

Early in 1914 Hackett was in communication with HE Barff about a visit to Perth by Thomas Mawson to share his landscape planning expertise. Eventually – with Mawson's tour cancelled, unemployment high among architects, a desire to avoid 'costly mistakes' by securing the best plan, and perhaps influenced by the federal capital precedent – Hackett decided to sponsor a design competition. This would be a process to assure conservation of the beauty of the site and its development 'on convenient, wide and spacious lines'.[39] There was inevitable professional criticism about the adjudication arrangements.[40] Twenty-six entries were received from Australia, Britain, the USA, and South Africa. Among the entrants were John Barr and George Sydney Jones. Griffin also submitted a plan, orientated around a main northwest–southwest axis, skilfully exploiting the site with symmetrical, tiered building terraces which recalled the treatment of the central parliamentary area in his Canberra plan. Unlike his Sydney solution, this was a strongly architectonic rather than languid landscape conception. With its far greater density of buildings than Desbrowe-Annear's, perhaps the Board of Adjudicators saw Griffin's plan as an urban conception in excess of realistic requirements.

In June 1915 the adjudicators, who included the chief government architect, Hillson Beasley, met to shortlist the best schemes. The following month the university senate confirmed the winner to be Melbourne-based Harold Desbrowe-Annear. The main formal feature of his plan was a radial ring of avenues with one northwest–southwest avenue constituting the main axis. The unavoidable impression is of a variation on Sulman's radial planning.[41] Its line of sight extended

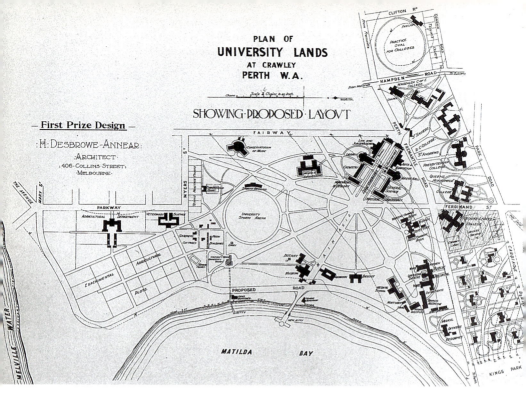

PLAN OF
UNIVERSITY LANDS
AT CRAWLEY
PERTH W.A.

SHOWING·PROPOSED·LAYOUT

— **First Prize Design** —

: H·DESBROWE-ANNEAR:
:ARCHITECT·
·406·COLLINS·STREET·
·MELBOURNE·

MATILDA   BAY

Competition winning entry for University of Western
Australia by Harold Desbrowe-Annear. *University of Western
Australia Archives, Consignment 1092*

across a road intersection marking the main entrance to terminate mid-facade at an Anglican college. The most decisive building aggregations were the gentle arc of the college group and a mini garden suburb of professorial houses on the north side of the road. Overall, it was a rather loose and open plan, with casual building clumps contrasting with the formal axial-semi-concentric template of avenues. Gordon Stephenson was later to describe Desbrowe-Annear's plan as 'in the nature of a geometrical exercise'.[42]

The university senate apparently regarded the competition as a pooling of good ideas rather than the genesis of a single definitive scheme, and in July 1915 requested the building committee to develop its own plan with the assistance of the government architect. Through to the early 1920s, the state's public works department produced several variations of the winning entry, mainly by rotating the main axis to better define a green centre to the site, which was labelled the 'Great Campus'.[43] Regardless, development from 1923 largely ignored Desbrowe-Annear's recommendations, although some open spaces,

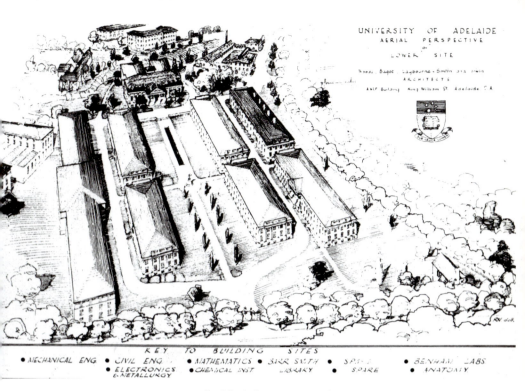

UNIVERSITY OF ADELAIDE
AERIAL PERSPECTIVE
LOWER SITE

Woods Bagot Laybourne-Smith and Irwin
ARCHITECTS
AMP Building King William St Adelaide S.A.

KEY TO BUILDING SITES

● MECHANICAL ENG ● CIVIL ENG ● MATHEMATICS ● BARR SMITH ● SPARE ● BENHAM LABS
● ELECTRONICS ● CHEMICAL INST LIBRARY ● SPARE ● ANATOMY
& METALLURGY

University of Adelaide lower campus plan,
Walter Bagot, dated 1945.
Woods Bagot

lines of avenues, and functional zoning recommendations were to survive. The plan which really established the main north–south spine of the campus and major green spaces and building sites was devised by Leslie Wilkinson in 1927 and embodied his principles of site design, enunciated at the time he was negotiating his involvement with the university.

University of Adelaide

The University of Adelaide was established in the late 1870s on what has remained a constricted site, in parkland on the northern fringe of the central business district. The university developed incrementally, building-by-building, until Walter Hervey Bagot was appointed university architect, a position he held from 1910 to 1945. Bagot had built up an eclectic ecclesiastical, residential, institutional and commercial design practice but the university buildings were his 'mental children' and his persistent battle was 'for uniformity of type'.[44] That building type was a synthesis of Georgian-Mediterranean influences set within a landscaped context. This was in line with the aesthetic tastes of the better known Leslie Wilkinson. But in Adelaide Bagot was the maestro and he remained a regular traveller to Europe, especially to Italy. His preference for 'classical and traditional designs' eschewed the novelty and raw excesses of modernism.[45] His holistic design vision 'established the echo of an Italian hillside village' for the university.[46]

A university expansion scheme from the late 1920s into the former Jubilee Oval of the State Exhibition Grounds conjured an enhanced sense of space on a limited site. The focus of Bagot's 1929 'axial concept' scheme was the new Barr-Smith library, a building opened in 1932 and described as 'more ornate and inspiring inside than outside'.[47] A strong vista led from the library's Classical portico down to formal entrance gates at Frome Road, with pathways marked by poplars and pools and flanked by new accommodation for arts (north) and sciences (south) departments. While Bagot may have been traditionalist, anti-modernist and Europeanist, this landscape was in line with the rectilinear modernism of the city beautiful, albeit leavened through a sensitivity to climate and place. The clear intention was to make an emphatic statement about the status and seriousness of the university's mission. The forecourt approach to the university library defined a major new gateway to the campus for several decades that was simultaneously 'a celebration avenue and ceremonial entry'.[48]

University of Queensland

Like the University of Western Australia, the contemporaneous University of Queensland occupied temporary premises in the state capital for many years before making the move to purpose-built structures on a new site. Early senates were preoccupied with securing more distinguished premises that would avoid 'the shirt-factory style of design'.[49] Several sites were considered. Opposition to suburban St Lucia arose because of its relative remoteness, and a bridge across the Brisbane River offering more direct access to the central city was mooted. The senate finally voted to move to the 100-acre site in 1926. The land title was consolidated and officially handed to the university

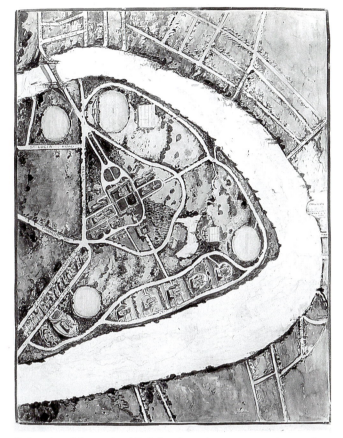

University of Queensland Building Committee concept plan, 1936.
Fryer Library, University of Queensland Library, FW Robinson Papers, UQFL 5

in November 1929 thanks to the generosity of the Mayne family. But it was not until 1935 that the state Labor government of W Forgan Smith committed itself to building there, slotting the development into a series of unemployment-relieving major public works alongside bridges, harbours, highways and dams. Procrastination, building delays and World War II meant that the university did not actually move to St Lucia until 1948.

The near-decade delay between the decision to move to St Lucia and the government's clarification of how it wished to initiate building was a period of active design debate. Suggestions for a design competition were rejected. Instead, a haphazard and ill-directed process unfolded with suggestions brought forth from various quarters. There were several key figures, including Frederick Robinson, a lecturer in modern languages and literature; Andrew Leven, the state government's chief architect; professor of engineering Roger Hawken, a prominent member of the Queensland Town Planning Association; and Sydney planning figure JJC Bradfield, who had been born in Ipswich and was then working on the Story Bridge. The appointment of a joint government–university building committee in September 1935 formalised proceedings to a degree, but committee members advanced their own plans as they edged toward a consensus layout. Bradfield was appointed deputy chairman of the building committee and its final report to the state premier in June 1936 was substantially his work.

There were some common aspects to the various official and unofficial plans devised for St Lucia from the late 1920s. All sought a dignified, beautiful campus. They utilised a central area of higher level ground for the main buildings, a ridge on the southern side for residential colleges, flood-prone land for sporting fields and car parks, and a lagoon on the site was typically targeted as a future ornamental lake. The larger design debate revolved around the degree of formality desired for the main building group and, related to this, whether the campus should be massed compactly or dispersed over the site.

The building committee considered four plans. Two were from outsiders: one by Hawken, originally produced in 1927, the other by Robinson. The Hawken plan was an application of Sulman's spider's web planning at a 'spacious' scale with specialised buildings occupying their own sites. 'The main motive', said Hawken, 'follows the principles of town planning [with] a set of avenues radiating from the central building-pile on the pinnacle of the area, and crossed by subsidiary roads for quick intercommunication. Each avenue would provide a pleasing vista'.[50] Robinson, who had already produced a detailed site-planning report which was virtually 'an unofficial design brief', was quite peeved when his total scheme was rejected but selected features appropriated.[51] His general aim was 'to ensure visible, dignified expression to the University as a living organism'. Oriented towards a new river crossing, a central block of buildings in the Oxbridge manner was the formal 'nucleus' – 'imposing, uplifted, dignified, oriented to command the gaze from all points, impressing on the beholder the "sense" of a University'. 'Individualised and significant space' would be provided in quadrangles, courtyards, and

A proposal for the University of Queensland by JJC Bradfield and RGC
Coulter, 1936. *Fryer Library, University of Queensland Library,
FW Robinson Papers, UQFL 5*

gardens in close proximity to the buildings'. Elsewhere, the natural
beauty of the site prevailed.[52]

There were also two plans by government appointees on the
committee – one by Bradfield, the other evolving through at least two
iterations from Leven. Bradfield's plan, presented at the committee's
second meeting on 23 October 1935, anticipated the form of the built
scheme, with the main buildings occupying the 'central plateau' of the
site and connected by colonnades and cloisters in a semicircular fashion.
The plans attributed to Leven most explicitly suggested city beautiful
formality with their symmetrically arrayed battalions of buildings in
formation. This plan evolved through consultation with staff and was
a creditable attempt 'not only to meet utilitarian requirements but to
invest the Architectural problem with the intrinsic beauty which this
cultural centre demands'.[53]

To all intents and purposes, the committee chose the Leven plan,
only slightly modified to better define a central quadrangle defined
by cloisters and buildings, including a relocated main library. The
committee recommended architecture that would desirably express

'artistry, simplicity, beauty and harmony' with 'a hint of Classical or Gothic [to] add to the charm'. A utilitarian rider was for buildings to be no more than two storeys high to save the expense of installing lifts. The main approach to the campus would be 'a stately avenue' approaching across 'a graceful bridge'. On the periphery would be a riverside road, 'one of the most attractive drives in the environs of Brisbane'.[54]

Characteristically, Bradfield could not resist including some perspective views of this vision in line with the recommended site plan. Though uncredited, the university images were clearly the work of Charles Coulter. His unevenly scaled renderings were not the best examples of his work and to latter-day eyes undercut Bradfield's intention of a 'simple, dignified and harmonious conception' by conveying an almost pre-modern monasticism in a fussy, ornate style.[55] Bradfield, for one, was nonetheless inspired, and, with no apologies to Daniel Burnham, he outlined the dream to university staff on 22 June 1936, two days after his committee's final report was submitted:

> Whoever has the honour to be entrusted with the architecture of St. Lucia should have vision to see where opportunity lies, to aim high in hope and work and dream in terms of the future. He must make no mean Plans, for mean plans have no magic to stir man's blood, or awaken inspiration in anyone, and the University should be an inspiration to her students.[56]

The state government, which controlled the university's purse strings, acted decisively at this point. Rejecting renewed calls for a competition, it appointed Hennessy and Hennessy as university architects in July 1936, an appointment explained by their shared connections to the Roman Catholic Church in Brisbane and its head, Archbishop James Duhig.

Hennessy and Hennessy set about modifying the building committee's site plan, conveying their own proposals to the premier in September 1936.[57] Their aim was to secure a budget-priced 'monumental institution' and to transform all the natural features of the site into 'things of beauty'. They concentrated activity into a D-shaped complex deliberately orientated away from a possible new Brisbane River bridge for traffic reasons. The ends of the long facade of the main building were terminated by a Library and a Great Hall. A series of four smaller buildings were symmetrically placed in a semicircle behind the main building and linked with colonnades to enclose a Great Court. The focal point of the composition was the tower in the centre of the main building. The semicircular-radial form variously recalls the University of Birmingham, the spider's web (Hennessy's father had worked with John Sulman), the Hennessy's Austral City project, and other beaux arts plans with which Jack Hennessy would have been familiar.

The development of the Queensland campus was severely interrupted by World War II, and even before the quadrangle was completed in the 1950s, the main building was overcrowded. While the Great Court precinct would remain the monumental core, a more utilitarian development philosophy descended to produce what foundation planning professor, Lewis Keeble, would describe as a 'hotch-potch of buildings of differing architecture and design'.[58] Stephenson blamed the city beautiful formality of the Hennessy design as a 'monolithic' and anachronistic set piece into which 'substantial new elements' could not be successfully inserted.[59]

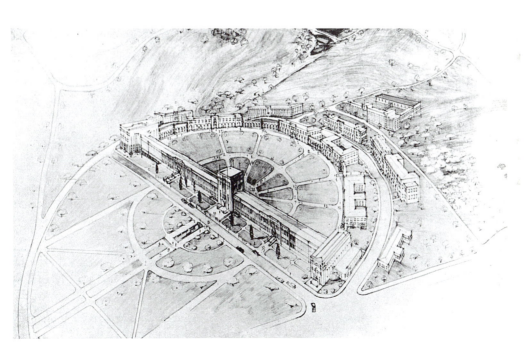

The approved scheme for the University of Queensland
by Hennessy and Hennessy.
Building, October 1936

Conclusion

Like all design fashions, the campus beautiful was eclipsed by later ones. In the United States, it fell from grace as too expensive to implement, unsuited to very irregular sites, and inimical to the preservation of natural beauty. Its stolid buildings were deemed too inflexible to accommodate educational innovations. All-of-a-piece spatial order also came with in-built flaws: 'The stupendous development of modern colleges is apt to break down the frame of a formal scheme however ambitiously it may have been conceived. It is not in the spirit of a great composition to have annexes attached to it which do not stand in close axial relation to the scheme'.[60]

While the American beaux arts campus constitutes a distinctive idiom, there was no such Australian 'school'. The Australian response to grand axiality and neo-classicism was diluted by at least four factors. First, the size of the Australian tertiary education 'system', the scale of universities, and the degree of philanthropic benefaction supporting their development were all modest compared to the United States. Although by the first decade of the 20th century, older universities were in need of surgical replanning and the newest institutions were looking to develop new sites, campuses were far from dynamic cultural environments. In retrospect, it is perhaps not surprising that a systematic discussion of university layouts (when other group building schemes were featured) was missing from Sulman's authoritative 1921 text.

Second, and specifically in terms of design, Australian architects, like the British, were not as seduced by the École des Beaux Arts approach as the Americans and were therefore not as culturally attuned to monumental, *grand ensembles* design. While the neo-classical idiom was realised in individual institutional and commercial buildings on (as off) campus, it was never a candidate for group campus buildings, except in the muted form applied at the University of Queensland.

Third, the whole nature of higher education was still strongly influenced by British models, reflecting the strength of Australia's traditional ties to the 'mother country'. Australian university authorities and architects remained more comfortable with Gothic heritage, and what it connoted, than anything else. This Anglophile tradition extended well into the 1950s, shutting out, among other things, alternative design paradigms. The very word 'campus', which by the early 20th century in the United States had come to apply to the 'green expansiveness' of entire university sites, remained confined to its 18th century meaning of a space in front of or enclosed by buildings.

Finally, the retarded development of landscape architecture as a profession in Australia inhibited the kind of campus plans which so enriched American institutions through the work of HWS Cleveland, Warren Manning, the Olmsteds, and others. When Professor EG Waterhouse, involved in the greening of Sydney University, undertook a 1935 study tour of American colleges and university grounds, he was amazed at the sumptuous treatment of grounds and the demonstrable pride 'the whole community takes in these institutions'.[61]

Nonetheless, paralleling the overseas experience, formal planning ideas in the city beautiful tradition were to resurface in Australian university design post-World War II. The standout example is the original plan for the Australian National University. Robin Boyd described Brian Lewis's stern axial treatment and focal points aligned to Griffin's water axis as a 'dominating little-Versailles'.[62]

Australian National University site plan by Brian Lewis.
Building, July 1950

CHAPTER 9

Parks, parkways and the street beautiful

Charles Mulford Robinson's *The Improvement of Towns and Cities* (1901) provided a definitive statement on the non-architectural components of the city beautiful, with chapters on trees, gardening, parks and drives, and other green spaces. Trees were an 'indispensable phase of urban decoration' in the 'mental picture of a beautiful city or village'. Streets were immeasurably improved by 'parkings', strips of tree-planted lawn. Small squares, circles and triangles formed at the junction of city streets could convey a 'sense of intimate and inseparable connection with the city's life which more ambitious parks too often lack'. Open space could enhance the beauty, dignity and sanctity of public building groups. Parks were the ornaments of the city, the clearest manifestation of a 'mature civilisation'. Park systems with interconnecting 'beauty drives' widened the beneficent influence of parkland.[1]

Complementing showpiece features was a 'little tradition' of vacant lot gardening, clean-up campaigns, tidy towns, street tree planting, school gardens, home garden competitions and other horticultural offshoots. Parkland was as much a cause as an effect of urban beauty since 'a beautiful park may awaken a desire for a lovelier home-garden, and the wish for a beautiful home grows into the wish for a beautiful street'. But vegetation also had a hygienic value. The 'sanitary importance' of trees lay in the process of photosynthesis and in affording cool and shade. 'Urban vegetation makes us happy and does us good, until we hardly know which effect comes first', argued Robinson. At another level, park improvements could benefit property values, engender greater civic pride and patriotism, and attract tourist expenditure. The consultant and lecturer George Burnap attempted to more precisely codify these relationships between beauty and utility. As distinct from the indulgence permitted in private gardens, he regarded public parks as 'apostles' for the city beautiful in necessarily combining these attributes:

> If civic embellishment could be accepted as the only function of parks, their development as beauty spots would be comparatively easy, being simply application of primary principles of pictorial composition … The fact that parks must meet very complex demands of traffic, of wear and tear and public abuse, that they must provide for public utility, convenience and comfort, rest, recreation and enjoyment, imposes a set of conditions which the experienced designer recognizes as more exacting than those encountered in the landscape development of private property. Much as architectural design should express not only good composition but a satisfying of all requisites of construction and use, so a park design must attain pictorial agreeableness without disregard of the practical; service which it must render.[2]

Australian city improvement literature took in the same diversity of elements. 'A Dissertation on their Loveliness and Utility' contributed to *Building* in June 1916 referred to trees as 'Buildings of God'. Parks were equally the centrepiece of a beautiful city. The lord mayor of Adelaide waxed lyrical in 1908:

> Park life is one of the main features of the Cities of the Old World; but we, in Australia, have yet to fully realise it. It should always be our aim to improve our Parks and open spaces, to make, and keep them, beautiful, for no educator of the people is more valuable than the Parks. Their attractiveness is, undoubtedly, one of the causes of that everywhere-increasing desire for a lovelier home garden, and the wish for a beautiful home grows into the wish for a beautiful street. Beautiful streets and picturesque Parks mean the creation of the 'City Beautiful', which is our ideal; with nothing sentimental or effeminate about it, but, on the contrary, it is a vigorous, virile and sane aspiration.[3]

A doctrine of multiple benefits carried over from the 19th century. Parks not only embellished the city; they were its lungs and offered opportunities for physical exercise and recreation. Citizenship, social order, and productive efficiency were enhanced. Utility could not be made 'subservient to artistic and beautiful landscape effects' as it could in private gardens.[4] More satisfactorily combined in the public realm, 'we behold the worthy and scientific treatment of our public services in harmony with the art of the designer'.[5]

This chapter discusses the 'green' aspects of the city beautiful. More 'theoretical' aspects and distinctive Australian themes are examined before briefly surveying some landscapes, including foreshore parks and commemorative roadways, created while town planning aspects of beautification were in vogue. It examines more closely several outcomes, including Hyde Park and Anzac Parade in Sydney, and takes a more synoptic look at Melbourne.

Principles of planning and planting

Like their foreign contemporaries, Australian enthusiasts never specifically defined beauty, instead subscribing to the same sort of 'generalized Ruskinism'.[6] They talked in the same abstract ways about harmony, cooperation, homogeneity and the uniform treatment of landscapes. John Carrère cast the spectrum of green spaces in the city plan as a transect from the primevalism of outer forests through a measured informality in larger metropolitan parks to inner-city squares and manicured gardens where 'nature becomes entirely secondary'.[7] CM Robinson endorsed the same mixing of aesthetics from the geometric formalism of the small city park, perhaps dominated by architectural ornamentation, to the larger reserve, allowing 'natural features ... to be mainly determinate of the style adopted'.[8]

The place of both informal and formal treatments was recognised by Australian planners, along with an admixture appropriate to 'the form of the ground', as Leslie Wilkinson put it.[9] John Sulman codified general guidelines for his fellow planners. In the model artistic city, parkland was preferably treated formally, with tree-lined paths, visual axes, tasteful statuary, fountains and reflecting pools, but with fussy labour-intensive flower-beds kept to a minimum. Site and situation were crucial considerations. There were greater concessions to informality in suburban parks, provided always that the naturalism was functional. Curvilinear paths might be substituted for straight ones if 'the windings have a reason, either of contour or lead to a special attraction or point of view, and are not mere wriggles without an object'.[10] In 1927 in connection with the Hyde Park design competition, Sulman provided an authoritative statement on 'general prin-

PARK DESIGN

BEAUTY

STRENGTH · SINCERITY
UNITY · SCALE · ATTRACTION

UTILITY

CONVENIENCE · COMFORT
RECREATION · EDUCATION

COMPOSITION

LAND ~ LAWNS
DRIVES
WALKS

WATER ~ FOUNTAINS
POOLS
LAKES

FOLIAGE ~ SHADE
ORNAMENTAL

FLORAL
DISPLAY ~ GARDENS
BEDS
PARTERRES

SCULPTURE ~ MOTIFS

ARCHITECTURE~ EMBELLISHMENTS
SETTINGS
BUILDINGS

SERVICE

PARK
REQUIRE~
MENTS
ROADS
WALKS
SEATS
SHELTERS
REST HOUSES

FACILITIES
OF
ENJOYMENT
OBJECTS OF
INTEREST·
GAMES AND
SPORTS

MAINTENANCE~ ADMINISTRATION BLDG·
SERVICE YARDS
& BUILDINGS
PROPAGATING
GARDENS

Copyright 1916 by George Burnap.

Beauty versus utility in park design.
G Burnap, Parks, 1916

ciples which should govern the layout and planting of City Parks' from a planning perspective. Pedestrian traffic should be confined to throughways and short cuts, with one dominant axis becoming 'the main feature of the design'. These 'traffic ways' should be shaded, with tree species restricted 'for unity of effect'. The spaces between them should be grassed and left as open as possible and the overall effect harmonised with the surrounding city through monuments, fountains, sculpture and architectural treatment of entrances, retaining walls and steps.[11]

Charles Coulter's images for the Royal Commission for the Improvement of the City of Sydney and Its Suburbs show the contemporary predilection for the formal treatment of small squares and grassed spaces, planting of trees in linear lines, and systematic perimeter block planting. Even the drift in private garden design in the city beautiful era matched the trend toward classical rectitude, even if in rather relaxed mode. Famous gardens such as Marathon at Mount Eliza on Victoria's Mornington Peninsula, designed by Walter Butler in 1913, featured formal vistas, terraces, ponds and statues. The same ideas surfaced in the work of other leading practitioners, such as Harold Desbrowe-Annear in Melbourne and Walter Bagot in Adelaide. Whatever the precise landscape form, the viewer could be left in no doubt – to quote Joseph Maiden – that the conversion of the 'barren waste into smiling gardens' was by the improver's hand.[12]

Building journals had been quoting foreign reports commending tree planting in towns for both hygienic and 'pictorial effects' from at least the 1880s. Rising nationalistic feelings were expressed by the prominence of native species in emblematic and ornamental plantings.[13] There was growing interest in preservation of native flora and fauna. These concerns filtered into the town planning agenda. One of the original objectives of the Victorian Town Planning and Parks Association was 'to safeguard native animals and plants'. The prominent businessman TH Kelly reminded its New South Wales counterpart of the desirability of Australia's development and beautification 'on the lines of its own personality'.[14] In 1910 Crooke and Blackburne, two Victorian foresters, proclaimed that tree planting was the 'principal feature [of] city planning'. For them, 'the green lustre of trees' made city life 'more endurable, pleasant and healthy', if not proactively 'moulding the character and habits of the population'. Other practical benefits were highlighted in the literature – provision of shade, wind breaks, the absorption of carbonic acid, production of oxygen and minimisation of 'the dust evil'.[15]

Local government and building journals carried articles extolling street tree plantings reproduced from American magazines. By 1910 regional and suburban councils were taking up the question of planting street trees with more enthusiasm. A note in the November 1915 issue of the *Shire and Municipal Record* about shade trees for streets by a 'city forester' in Harrisburg, Pennsylvania (one of the most active city beautiful centres in the United States), produced 'numerous inquiries', with more details having to be supplied in the next issue. Street plantings raised special issues. Species with no 'objectionable character-istics' were important for hardiness, acclimatisation and 'to fit the par-ticular situation … such as … not to be obtrusive or inharmonious with the natural landscape'.[16] Practical problems were also acknowledged. A typical statement was from the mayor of Launceston in 1910:

> The beautifying of the city by planting trees has engaged the attention of the reserves committee, and the annual report of the superintendent indicates where this has been done. The streets, being mostly narrow, the branches of the trees in some instances interfere with the electric and telephone wires, and their roots injure the paths and choke the water and sewerage drains, difficulties which curtail the area for planting. Also, residents enjoying picturesque views complain of the same being obstructed by tree planting, and in many cases have requested the removal and thinning out of existing trees.[17]

The idea of the tree-lined boulevard had crystallised from garden allées and waterside promenades by the mid-19th century. A distinctive contribution of the planning movement worldwide was to provide a scientific analysis and justification for landscaped multi-lane street design. The notion of separating fast from slow traffic, and motor vehicles from trams, by dust-dampening and noise-absorbing street gardens and rows of trees, appealed to both modernist and civic art sensibilities. The uniform lines of trees in city and suburban streets more generally spoke of a unified public domain. The terms 'boulevards' and 'parkways' were often used interchangeably, but these street types assumed different forms. The greatest distinction was between roads that were 'broad, straight, direct' and those 'luxuriously and indolently roundabout sacrificing everything to the one end of beauty'.[18]

The boulevard most obviously connoted a wide, straight, and formal urban thoroughfare with the air of cosmopolitanism. Some reservations were expressed as to their relevance to Australian conditions. While his later writings indicate more comfort with the concept, Sulman's paper on the federal capital to the 1910 RIBA conference cautioned that 'the boulevard, as a public resort, with its numerous cafés, is unknown and would be unappreciated'.[19] John Barlow was also sceptical of the 'noble avenue'. In private hands he saw it as a cynical real estate ploy, but even its finest examples in Chicago and Paris he saw as making for a depressing grandeur.[20]

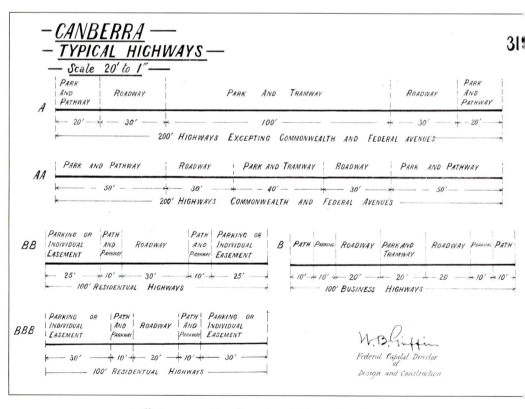

Griffin's cross sections for various Canberra street types, 1917.
National Archives of Australia, Series A192, item FCL1921/490

Parkways attracted less scepticism. They evolved from being park connector and gateway drives towards landscaped corridors for stress-free motoring into suburban and rural settings. The American residential parkway took the park-like street to its apogee. Australian visitors were mightily impressed. In 1914 the town clerk of Perth, William Bold, was taken on an inspection tour of the Kansas City parkway system. He was 'entranced with the beautiful scenes which presented themselves' and returned convinced that not only did the benefits outweigh the costs but that the system was 'adaptable to our own city and would make a wonderful transformation in its appearance'. Twenty years later Denis Winston, who became the foundation professor of town and country planning at Sydney University, felt that 'it would be hard to find a better example of beauty combined with utility' than the American ex-urban parkway; there were 'few finer expressions of engineering and landscape architecture combined in perfect harmony'.[21]

Parks, gardens and the federal capital

City beautiful thought was distinguished by the combination of aesthetic elements. Park and garden planning thus became not just about the particularistic needs of plant selection, footway paving, top-dressing, and ad hoc in situ improvements but an holistic activity linked to a broader scale of civic improvement. Street plantings similarly had to be linked to a bigger vision. The federal capital project encouraged this integration.

Many speakers at the 1901 congress on the federal capital highlighted parks and gardens as integral elements for the ultimate 'twentieth century city'. The engineer George Higgins's opening address identified the importance of 'the arrangement of breathing spaces, and the methods of planting parks and public gardens' as a planning issue. Various statements provide a generalised sense of the ideal landscape envisaged. The thoughts of George Inskip, former president of the Royal Victorian Institute of Architects, were representative:

> Tree-planting in the streets is of great importance in a climate like this, but the trees should not be planted too near the buildings, as they would shut out the light and air. In very wide streets the centre would perhaps be the better position for them. Open spaces should be provided in a

NEW MELBOURNE GENERAL CEMETERY.

PLAN —
proposed allotment
for the
Y.M.C.A —

approved

Portions *now* open for selection.
Lawns and Portions at present reserved from use,
Roadways and Paths.

colored white.
" green
" yellow.

Main Entrance
from
Sydney Road

CHARGES FOR ALLOTME

Exclusive of Interments, in the Portions where new

CHURCH OF ENGLAND PORTION.
Compt. B. ... ... £10 to £50
" A. ... ... £2.15 to £5
" D. 25.-

ROMAN CATHOLIC PORTION.
Compts. B. & A. (northern half) ... £10 to £60
" A. (southern half) ... £2.15 to £5
" D. & E. 25.-

PRESBYTER
Compt. A
" A
" B

BAPTIST AN
Compt. A
" B

Office Hours: 7.30 a.m. to 5 p.m. on Week Days.

New Melbourne Cemetery by CR Heath.
R Nicol, The End of the Road, 1995

systematic manner. The old fashioned mode of building squares with fenced-in gardens should not be followed, but all spaces should be left entirely open as is now done in Victoria Parade, East Melbourne, laid down with grass and planted with shrubs and flowers. The public would soon become accustomed to this mode of laying out the ground and neither shrubs nor flowers would be destroyed. The city should also be surrounded with woods, parks, and recreation grounds.[22]

Charles Bogue Luffman, the principal of Melbourne's School of Horticulture, and later to write *Principles of Gardening for Australia* (1903), engaged most directly with landscape issues. His main recommendations were the preservation and enhancement of natural landscapes and features, cultivation of water features, and 'laying out of gardens around all federal Buildings and in public spaces'. Restating the informal/formal divide, Luffman linked formal city gardens to the 'site, style, and pretentiousness of buildings' in the federal core, with 'adaptation to the natural contour and position of the landscape' outside it.[23]

Sulman's adaptation of his own 'spider's web' model of city design was the best publicised of pre-competition visions for the federal capital. While his 1908 pamphlet on *The Improvement of Sydney* had emphasised architectural and engineering improvements, it also called for upkeep of existing open spaces, reservation of 'additional garden beds, trees or shrubs' wherever possible, and planting avenues with rows of trees, width permitting. These same values infiltrate the treatment in his *The Federal Capital* (1909). In beautilitarian vein, he targeted natural features and landforms unsuitable for development, such as steep hills and creeks, as green elements. Even poorly drained land could be 'turned into a smiling sward that will keep green when the rising ground is burnt a dusty brown'. The most formal element were 'parkways' – linking outer parklands to the city's nucleus to 'bring every inhabitant within a few minutes' walk of green trees and grass, and to provide a quiet space where children may play and obtain fresh air'. This American method was deemed preferable to the European boulevard model which risked wide, dusty streets.[24] The radial lines of Sulman's spider's web found their way into several competition entries in 1911–12, possibly even Walter Burley Griffin's. The most literal use of this model, however, was by Charles Heath in his fan-shaped scheme for Fawkner Cemetery in Melbourne, the rigidity of the geometrical treatment leavened by 'the different treatment of the various avenues and by arranging the tree-planting so as to give views of varying character'.[25]

Entries in the federal capital competition demonstrated a richness of approaches to beautification using parks, gardens, terraces, and belts of trees. The amounts of open space proposed were significantly above contemporary norms. Griffin's winning scheme took the breath away in the comprehensiveness of its features, its innovative design, and the quality of presentation. This was landscape planning at a dramatic scale, but with an eye for detail. The inventory of state-of-the-art aesthetic features included magnificent tree-lined streets and vistas, broad formal parkways 'banked with foliage', garden frontages in residential quarters, outer suburbs laid out with Olmstedian informality, botanical gardens and forest preserves, foreshore drives, a lake for active recreation, and 'mountains, retained in their natural state as nearly as possible, as parks, and forest and game preserves'.

The contemporary importance of the Griffin plan in these terms lay in making systematic sense of many of the 'softer' city beautiful ideas which had matured through the first decade of federation. The legacy was the legend of the 'bush capital'. Developed by his successors and a procession of parks superintendents starting with Charles Weston, this was translated into gateway boulevards like Northbourne Avenue, magnificent street plantings in the inner suburbs, and subsequently an impressive metropolitan open space system which keeps hills free from development.[26]

Hyde Park

Hyde Park is Australia's oldest park, the major example of formal landscaping in Australia, and with a complex history that is 'a saga in itself'.[27] Its present day character derives mainly from Norman Weekes's winning entry in a 1926 design competition in the wake of damage caused to the 16-hectare park by the building of Sydney's underground railway. The park was ripe for the economical cut-and-cover method of construction and installation of two underground stations. Excavation began in 1916; by the early 1920s the park was a construction site. The Sydney Parks Preservation Society protested the disruption caused. Sydney City Council resolved to hold a competition for 'a comprehensive lay-out and beautification scheme'. The assessors were the town clerk, WG Layton, John Sulman, and Alfred Hook of the University of Sydney. Two main caveats were to be observed: 'reasonable economy' and 'particular attention … in regard to suitable tree planting for colour and shade'. As noted, Sulman expanded these considerations into more general guidelines to help guide the adjudication process.

By the closing deadline of 1 November 1926, 14 entries were received, including plans by John D Moore, David L Davidson, and Leslie Wilkinson. Winner of the £150 first prize was Norman Weekes who had studied with Patrick Abercrombie at Liverpool and had come to Sydney for the city surveyor's job. After many years in private practice,

Competition-winning design for Hyde Park by Norman Weekes.
Building, March 1928

he later became the senior planning bureaucrat with the NSW Department of Local Government. Weekes had already aired his opinions
about Hyde Park to the Institute of Architects of New South Wales:
'There is no doubt that the day when Hyde Park could remain in its
natural state like Centennial Park … has passed; the day is arriving
when it should take on a formal character in conformity with the formality of city life'.[28]

The impressive draftsmanship of the entry is attributed to Raymond McGrath (1903–1977). In design terms, Weekes took his cues
primarily from European practice. The main north–south avenue on
the axis of Macquarie Street reinstated the central walk evident from
the 1850s, but in the form of a vehicular parkway crossing Park Street
via a bridge. An obelisk was suggested as a major ornamental feature
at the northern end, balanced by a new city library at the southern
end. The plan was chock-a-block with elaborate entrances, pergolas
and water gardens. The park's eastern boundary was extended to incorporate College Street and extend parkland all the way to St Mary's
Cathedral and the Australian Museum. What *Building* described as a

Hyde Park and the Anzac Memorial.
Building, August 1932

'one connected and harmonious scheme' literally made the park part of the city.[29]

Weekes' entry determined the subsequent form and character of Hyde Park but not without other interventions. Sulman and his fellow judges sought to eliminate what they saw as flaws by restricting the park to its historic boundaries and resisting any attempt to introduce vehicular traffic. Other experts made inputs, including the city engineer, Alfred Garnsey, who pressed for simplification. Two major elements came later but were assimilated with ease by the axial lines of the Weekes plan: the Archibald Fountain and the Anzac Memorial.

JF Archibald, founding editor of *The Bulletin*, had bequeathed funds for a monument to commemorate the association between France and Australia in World War I. Hyde Park provided an ideal solution when the first-choice Botanic Gardens proved unsuitable. A logical site was the junction of the main and cross avenue from St James station to St Mary's Cathedral, where Weekes had placed his obelisk. The art deco fountain, completed here in 1932, was one of the last works of the French sculptor François Sicard, who had won many honours, including a prize from the École Des Beaux Arts. BJ Waterhouse and expatriate Australian architect Hubert Corlette collaborated on architectural aspects.[30]

Weekes also modified his plan to accommodate a war memorial on the site of the proposed library. The siting and design of a war memorial in Sydney was contested for a decade. Sir Bertram Mackennal's cenotaph in Martin Place was a state government venture, engineered by the Labor premier Jack Lang. Meanwhile public subscriptions were accumulating for an Anzac Memorial elsewhere. Numerous sites were suggested in the press and professional journals, including Martin Place (noted in chapter 7), Fort Denison and a 'multum-in-parvo affair' combining triumphant arches, campanile, cenotaph, offices and display of war artifacts in Cook Park.[31] The memorial trustees formally evaluated at least ten sites before choosing Hyde Park. It was a controversial choice because of the loss of parkland. JS Purdy, City Health Officer and former president of the NSW Town Planning Association, led a rearguard action with the slogan 'Hands off the breathing spaces of the people'. But beaux arts architect Gordon Keesing supported the decision: 'No encroachment of the park is intended; no more than the

Lincoln memorial is an encroachment on the Park in Washington'.[32]

The 1930 design competition attracted 117 competitors. The assessors were Alfred Hook and Leslie Wilkinson from Sydney University plus EJ Payne, the public trustee. Dr Mary Booth, the president of the Anzac Fellowship of Women and a member of the Town Planning Association of New South Wales, led and almost won the fight for a purely commemorative rather than a utilitarian structure incorporating offices, favoured by the Returned Sailors' and Soldiers' League. The design brief still required a dual-purpose structure costing £75 000, but with more limited office space than envisaged by the *Anzac Memorial (Building) Act 1923*. The winning entry by the Sydney architect Bruce Dellit resolved the artistic and the functional in the 'most satisfactory manner possible, for, by skilful layout, the two sections of the building have been virtually segregated without distortion of the planning'.[33] Wilkinson declared the winning design 'six-sevenths aesthetic and one-seventh utilitarian'.[34] Its distinctive art deco ziggurat form was a break from tradition but included classical elements. Attracting most attention at the exhibition of entries at Farmers Department Store in July 1930 was a perspective drawing by Dellit – the 'only drawing of its nature' – which placed the memorial as the centerpiece of a formal park landscape evocative of how it and the Archibald Fountain delivered 'tension and climax' to Weekes's design.[35]

Foreshore parks

Of all the targets of town planning reform, acquisition and improvement of open space were usually considered the most feasible by civic authorities. Outcomes, often with an urban beautification rationale, were expressed in the form of new playgrounds, playing fields, and golf courses; resumption of market gardens (without demurring to the social dislocation involved); infill of mangrove swamps; the general cleaning up of eyesore sites; and foreshore reclamation.

In Perth, the State Gardens Board spent two decades reclaiming and improving the Perth city foreshore from Claremont to the Causeway in association with the Department of Public Works. The estimated value of both new and improved property alone was estimated at £168 000.[36] At Victor Harbor, south of Adelaide, Charles Reade prepared

Manly Beach beautification competition entry.
Building, January 1930

a general scheme of development integrating foreshore improvement with sea wall and promenade, improved park facilities, band rotunda, a Soldiers Memorial Garden of Honour, and a memorial to commemorate the meeting of Matthew Flinders and Nicholas Baudin in Encounter Bay in 1802. Looking ahead some 10 to 15 years, the plan sought to avoid piecemeal development without being prohibitively expensive.[37] An extension plan by Walter Scott Griffiths in 1922 to the mouth of the Hindmarsh River inserted yet more elements confirming the evolution of a seaside resort: car park, amusement ground, bowling green, additional tennis courts, kiosk and 'built-in fireplaces'.[38]

Where strengthened local government legislation gave councils greater land development powers, many used them to pursue beautification schemes and acquire and improve open space in the 1920s. This was the case in New South Wales with the *Local Government Act 1919,* introduced by JD Fitzgerald.[39] The Depression interrupted or curtailed the grand schemes but some work continued under employment-relief schemes. In a distinctively Australian way, beachside improvements responded to popular demands. 'The craze to beautify is spreading like an epidemic', reported *Building* in April 1924. Bondi, Manly, Clovelly and Balmoral were all infected.

A major blueprint for the modern development of Bondi Beach was a 1924 design by Robertson and Marks in a competition judged by John Sulman, George Sydney Jones, engineer RJ Boyd, and the local mayor. The first stage was to include a kiosk and surf sheds, lavatory blocks, a bandstand, and an efficient circulation plan for pedestrians and vehicles.[40] LM Graham's winning plan in the 1930 Manly foreshore design competition preserved 'all the natural beauty that the area possesses in its avenue of trees' and envisaged new buildings 'to harmonise with the surroundings'.[41] The winning entry for Randwick Council's Clovelly Bay Improvement Competition held the same year envisaged a total transformation of the bay into an Olympic-style aquatic venue with terraced grandstands capable of accommodating 30 000 people. There was also an 'arched bridge' across the ocean front to eliminate circuitous traffic flows and link into the marine drive proposed by the NSW Town Planning Association. Charles Coulter won third prize.[42] Mosman Council's Balmoral Beautification scheme from the late 1920s was criticised by a beach defence committee, which argued for trees rather than 'stern concrete'.[43] The council architect, Alfred Hale, still managed to supervise a complete waterfront ensemble: English-style promenade and seawall, bridge to a small island, neo-classical band rotunda, and a bathers pavilion (now a restaurant).[44]

Boulevards and memorial roadways

Bold eulogised American parkways to delegates at the 1918 town planning conference in Brisbane: they were an 'attractive feature' of many cities and 'any person privileged to drive along these beautiful parkways cannot fail to be an ardent advocate of such an admirable method of city beautification and recreation'.[45] His own city went further than most in adapting these ideals. Bold himself was a pivotal figure in Perth City Council's Endowment Lands residential development project from the late 1920s. A visionary scheme drawn up by local surveyor-planners Carl Klem and Percy Hope called for new coastal and suburban communities to be separated by an inviolate green belt to prevent sprawl but to be interconnected by two landscaped arterial roads. With ribbon development prohibited, motorists would enjoy 'a speedy run' while the 'natural beauties of the tuart country' would be preserved.[46] The inspiration for these roads ultimately derived from the Kansas City and Denver parkway systems. The original idea was for multi-channel rights-of-way accommodating fast, through, and slow, pleasure, traffic.[47] When the northerly Boulevard and the Plank Road (now Oceanic Drive) to the south were first opened in the late 1920s, they formed a clockwise one-way loop system to the coast because of their narrow width.

The memorial roadway was a distinctively Australian form of war commemoration.[48] Avenues of honour were popular in Victoria after Ballarat led the way in 1917. *Building* was not completely convinced of this form of commemoration, commenting on the Brisbane to Redcliffe project in 1923:

> Constructing new roads in this fashion savours very much of utility ... Road making has been so long the function of governing authorities that it seems to be making a virtue of necessity to construct a road under the guise of a memorial, no matter how beautiful that road may become.[49]

But various cities had their own tales to tell. In Adelaide, concerted moves to redevelop Bay Road between the central city and the major seaside resort of Glenelg into a beautiful boulevard commenced in the 1910s. Albert Conrad at the 1917 town planning conference held in Adelaide suggested development as a 'National Highway'. This could 'transform the present regulated thoroughfare into an avenue of use and beauty ... tracks could be defined for vehicle, train, and equestrian traffic, bordered with trees and plantations, and embellished with suitable memorials'.[50] A Bay Road committee of local authorities along

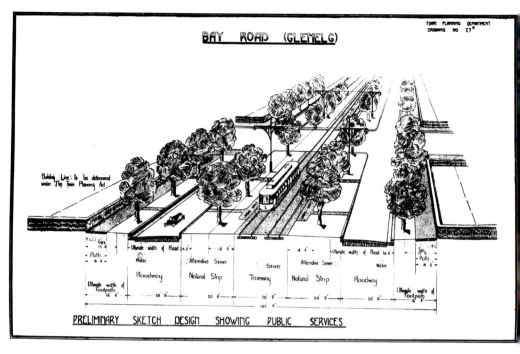

Converting Bay Road, Adelaide into a boulevard. *CC Reade, Planning and Development of Towns and Cities in South Australia, 1919*

Memorial gateway entrance project, Anzac Parade, by Norman Weekes. *Architecture, November 1925*

with the Town Planning Association of South Australia kept on the case.[51] The government town planner drew up a plan in 1919. The imminent arrival of the Prince of Wales in 1920 gave 'fresh stimulus' to the idea.[52] An Anzac Memorial Highway League was formed and pastoralist Sir Walter Kidman offered £500 in support of beautification. In 1925 the Anzac Highway was officially named in honour of Gallipoli veterans and Kidman's largesse applied to extensive plantings of Norfolk Island pines. Construction of a dual highway separated by a central plantation commenced in 1938. Commemorative public art and signage with an Anzac theme came much later.[53]

Improving Randwick Road

A major Sydney parkway story was the transformation of a portion of Randwick Road, the main outlet to the south-eastern suburbs, into a memorial roadway. In sifting through various improvement proposals in 1908–09, the Royal Commission favoured practical proposals that delivered an aesthetic bonus as opposed to any merely decorative schemes; the right balance had to be struck between art and commerce. Its environmental recommendations touched several bases. It urged the preservation of the natural beauty of Sydney Harbour foreshores and sanctioned town planning controls to correct open space deficiencies in future suburban development. With its main gaze on traffic movement, it also endorsed contour drives around waterways and along the heights 'for the benefit and recreation of the citizens' as well as suggesting that main roads be 'converted to boulevards' through tree planting where possible. Little directly came of these views, although, unrelatedly, Sydney would later get scenic drives through national parks and roads dubbed parkways. However, the commission's endorsement of 'the desirability of improving the approaches to our parks' by means of American-style parkways did come to fruition.

Lying southeast of the central business district were the city's main sporting facilities: the Sydney Cricket and Sports Ground, Randwick Racecourse, the Showground, the playing fields of Moore Park, and Centennial Park. Part of the original vision for Centennial Park was a physical link with the wider city. An extension of Grand Avenue outside the park boundaries to provide a 'principal approach' to the park

Anzac Parade, Sydney, 1920s.
Mitchell Library, State Library of New South Wales

through Moore Park from Randwick Road was completed in 1888, but the effect was undermined by the state of Randwick Road and the narrow, congested connections into the city proper. Most determined to turn this around through widening Oxford and Flinders streets to form a continuous wide thoroughfare all the way from Macquarie Street to Moore Park was the lord mayor and prominent businessman, Allen Taylor.[54]

'Fresh from a world's experience', Taylor presented evidence to the royal commission in January 1909.[55] Compulsory acquisitions for the great avenue were estimated to cost in the order of £100 000 but would produce 'one of the features of Sydney'. Taylor saw it as 'an immense advantage for many reasons', not the least of which was the traffic congestion caused by major sporting events. He foresaw an instrument to improve surrounding districts and 'dovetail' into other 'beautiful' boulevards.[56] The commission considered the proposal as 'not one of pressing urgency' while still applauding the general idea of better approaches to parks and 'more especially the Centennial Park'. It was thus left to Taylor to convince his council of its merit; and the month after the commission reported he was exhorting his fellow councillors into action:

> This opportunity should not be lost of procuring this fine outlet to the eastern districts. This would prove a great boon and give the City one of the most beautiful avenues in Australia, which is so much needed, and, further, bring us in direct touch with all our pleasure resorts and the neglected Centennial Park, the beauties of which are overlooked through the fact that it is almost impossible unless at a great risk to reach such delightful grounds. I feel that I am more than justified in appealing to the good judgment of the Council not to lose this opportunity of beautifying our City, which can be done now at such a moderate cost.[57]

Thus commenced a seven-year process of land resumptions on the Flinders Street section and also efforts to secure financial assistance from other stakeholders to widen Randwick Road, a timely opportunity for which had arisen with closure of the old zoo on the corner of Cleveland Street. Much of the work devolved to a later lord mayor, Richard Meagher (1916–17), who wanted his city to follow Melbourne's lead: 'one cannot come from Melbourne to Sydney without noticing that Sydney is very much behind as far as any broad and artistic avenue is concerned'.[58] Meagher was unable to obtain financial assistance from either the Royal Agricultural Society or the Kensington Racing Recreation Club, but just when the scheme seemed lost in August 1916 he secured an increased pledge from the Australian Jockey Club of £3000. Beautification called for new tree plantings and a median strip of flower-beds in the widened section north of Cleveland Street on the approach to Centennial Park. Meagher suggested the road be renamed Anzac Parade, 'a name associated with so many distinguished memories'. R H Brodrick, the city building surveyor and architect, designed and supervised construction of a small memorial sandstone obelisk at the entrance to the new road, which was officially opened by the lady mayoress of Sydney on 15 March 1917. The obelisk still stands, having been relocated several hundred metres south to accommodate an entrance to the Eastern Distributor motorway.[59]

Melbourne

Various improvement narratives intertwine key threads of a city beautiful-informed approach to civic beautification in Melbourne, but the roots are older. Melbourne Town Council had pursued a vigorous policy of parkland reservation from its incorporation in 1843, 'urged on by extraordinary conceits of space and splendour'.[60] But progress was slow and *Melbourne Punch* described Victoria's capital in the 1850s as 'the grimy, dust-ridden city of an unbeauteous plain'.[61] In the late 19th century, the Kalizoic Society tried to keep alive the interrelated causes of beauty and environmental improvement mainly through rhetoric rather than action, and Federation improvers extended their endeavours. By the early 1900s the achievements lay mainly in scattered projects in city and suburb – the wide roads entering the city centre, public reserves in inner suburbs such as Carlton, and shade trees in Collins Street and suburban thoroughfares. The ongoing crusade of local beautification was sustained by concerned members of the public, committed professionals, progress associations and progressive councils.

More exotic proposals were cooked up by the professionals. For example, the architect Walter Butler fancied a remodelled and monumentalised Treasury Gardens as a 'sort of miniature Bois de Boulogne ... where thousands may assemble amidst attractive and elevating architectural surroundings'.[62] The most extraordinary vision was the 1901 proposal to transform Melbourne's Eastern Hill into a 'monumental zone' by expatriate Victorian sculptor Charles Summers, son of the creator of Melbourne's famous Burke and Wills Memorial.[63] The old Model School site with frontage to Victoria Parade would become 'park-like' in character, ensuring a 'purified and beautified' approach to Carlton Gardens. A dual commemoration of Queen Victoria's reign and the opening of the first federal parliament, the new park was variously described as 'Victoria Federal Square' and 'Commonwealth Square'. Summers' vision included a central ornamental fountain, garden edging, a band pavilion, and a cordon of pedestals with busts of important colonial figures. A domed pavilion 'of classical design and symmetrical proportions' encasing a seated statue of the monarch surrounded by statues of leading political, scientific and cultural figures of her reign was also proposed. This

'View of Melbourne ... showing Yarra Boulevard now in progress and a forecast of the City in 1905'.
EW Cole, Greater Melbourne and the Federal Capital, 1899

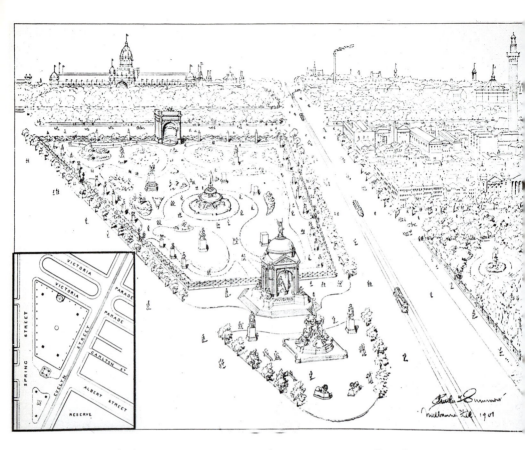

Charles Summers's monument park project on Eastern Hill, Melbourne.
C Summers, Proposed Monumental Zone, 1901

'*al fresco* Walhalla' [sic] would make Melbourne 'the Paris of the Antipodes'.[64] Bernard Hall, the director of the National Art Galley, was unconvinced that the 'beautiful theory' of this sculpture garden would lead to anything but vandalism.[65] It was very much a sculptor's conception, a theme park for statuary with the prospect of a lifetime's commissions. It foundered on even more practical shortcomings. Summers unconvincingly sold its utility as an educational project where a younger generation could learn the lessons of history from an 'assemblage of sculptured worthies' and thus 'worthier objects of ambition than to be a champion cyclist or football player'.

Results of park and landscape planning on the ground were more modest, but not unimpressive. By the early 1900s the results of the drive to greener streets were being welcomed by visitors. Even Victoria Parade, lampooned 'the worst of all muddles' by *Melbourne*

Punch in 1858, was a 'royal route' with its central plantations and rows of shade trees:

> Rockeries, elms and lawns to the poor, pent Collingwood folk are veritable Godsends in the long summer evenings. Here the tired factory hands may step from the reek of foetid workrooms, lay their tired limbs upon genuine grass-plots, and win peace from the friendly stars above.[66]

A major public works project pointing towards larger beautification possibilities was a flood mitigation scheme on the Yarra River between the Princes and Church Street bridges. This involved widening, deepening and straightening the river and improving its banks. Authorised by the 1896 *Yarra Improvement Act*, work commenced the same year under the direction of Carlo 'Charles' Catani (1852–1918), chief engineer of Victoria's public works department. The idea of a park promenade along the lines of Rotten Row in London's Hyde Park was credited to JW Taverner, the minister for public works. But it was the Florentine Catani who enlarged the original engineering conception to provide for tree plantations and a broad swathe of boulevard divided for horse riders, people on foot, and garden plots.[67] Plantings followed the advice of William Guilfoyle of the adjacent Botanic Gardens. There was also a cycle track, following representations by the Victorian League of Wheelmen, stressing the importance of exercise, and an old footbridge was replaced by the reinforced concrete Morell Bridge.[68] Ignoring complaints from upstream municipalities about wasting their funds on beautification, Catani argued that while flood-control works would only be enjoyed by a limited number, the amenity of the general public would be dramatically increased by his broader scheme. He later turned his attention to reclaiming and improving the St. Kilda beach waterfront in the manner of a European-style seaside resort, with split-level esplanade, dance halls and theatres, bathing pavilion and formal gardens.

Catani's Yarra landworks resulted in Alexandra Avenue, named in honour of Queen Victoria's daughter-in-law and officially opened by her husband, the Duke of York, on their visit to Melbourne for the Commonwealth celebrations in May 1901. The celebrations were a key factor in 'beautifying of the city and suburbs' and the conversion of 'vacant ground and rubbish heaps' into 'public gardens and grass plots'.[69] The Alexandra Gardens were similarly claimed in 1904 as a by-product of these events. The city centre viewed from the gardens was said to be 'a vision of wonderful charm, yet it was all man-made scenic beauty, a triumph of human endeavour'.[70] By 1908 the Yarra's south bank resembled 'an aquatic park comparable with the best stretches of Thames side'.[71] The southern gateway to the city across Princes Bridge was further remodelled by Melbourne City Council coterminously with the transformation of the south bank by the state public works department. The immediate approaches of St Kilda Road were widened and ornamental reserves created a new 'decorative garden setting'.[72] Under the direction of the city surveyor, AC Mountain, the council continued the work of the public works department in developing the Queen Victoria Gardens. These were designed by an expert committee that included Catani, and the sweeping treatment was designed to be viewed from St Kilda Road.

The Commonwealth celebrations also marked a decisive stage in the evolution of St Kilda Road. The making of modern St Kilda Road is a complex history with many different actors involved over a long period.[73] Up to the 1850s it was a track through scrub, but Ferdinand Mueller's planting of blue gums along one side of the road is claimed as the first attempt at a fundamental scheme of street landscaping in Australia.[74] By the early 1870s road boards, councils and the colonial government incrementally made piecemeal improvements which saw a proper road formed. The arrival of elite institutions, such as Melbourne Grammar School, Wesley College and Government House, helped seal the road's upwardly-mobile status. Its significance as a gateway to the city even in the 1870s was recognised when St Kilda council urged the city council to continue a planting scheme to create 'an approach from the south, which, for magnificence and beauty, might in time, vie with the world-famed avenues, which adorn many of the capitals of Europe'.[75] The process of expunging eyesores and cleansing the area of 'larrikins and dead-beats' accelerated with the approach of Federation.[76] An elaborate early scheme featured then-fashionable regularly spaced plantations and rockeries. At the time of the 1901 royal procession, the road had already been transformed 'into a noble boulevard', largely by the engineer AC Mountain and Donald

St Kilda Road. *Proceedings,*
First Australian Town Planning Conference, 1917

Campbell, Melbourne City Council's inspector of treeplanting and reserves. When JD Fitzgerald was not talking up Paris as the model city, he had only to look to the Victorian capital – 'splendid, spacious, substantial, ornate, marvel of rapid and solid growth'. Melbourne was a city that had 'carried the process of urban "parkification" to an extraordinary pitch of perfection'. St Kilda Road in particular was an inspiration. 'Why cannot Sydney, too, have its flower-beds placed in the centre of great fluxes and refluxes of men, in the midst of a great traffic and a great commerce?'[77] By the 1920s, St Kilda Road was famous as 'one of the best in the world for beauty and utility'.[78]

The opening of the Shrine of Remembrance confirmed St Kilda Road's status as Australia's premier boulevard. Debate and controversy in the site selection, funding, and architecture of a major war memorial for Melbourne played out against a backdrop of political instability. The story captures broader questions about the appropriate commemoration of war and the politics of design in the city beautiful era.

A diversity of sites was considered before and after a 1920 report for the Victorian government advised that:

> the memorial must be placed at a prominent point in the City, where it would be under direct observation of many passers-by; it should be surrounded by a large open space of architectural and monumental setting and scale; and it should be situated at the intersection of axial communication lines.[79]

In 1918 the city council considered the idea of a memorial carriageway or avenue of honour, but could not come up with a satisfactory site. In 1919 William Lucas devised a complex at the southern end of Exhibition Street comprising an amphitheatre, terraces, and museums with landmark column, but both the out-of-the-way location and its relatively small scale were criticised.[80] AJ Macdonald incorporated memorial elements in his south bank civic centre, as noted in Chapter 6. And in the mid-1920s a proposal for an 'Anzac Square' in front of Parliament House gained strong support until the huge cost of the resumptions needed to make it work became apparent. Eventually,

a site on St Kilda Road, near Alexandra Avenue, was endorsed for a war memorial in the form of an 'an arch of victory crowned by statuary'.

Such a feature would form 'a fitting finish to the avenue and a noble entrance to the city proper'.[81] Walter Butler prepared a sketch to form the basis of a public competition. But concerns were raised about the impact on traffic, trams and pedestrians, and the potential of such a structure to 'block the fairway and destroy the vista'.[82] Two alternative south bank sites were more closely scrutinised: one near Queen Victoria Gardens close to the river and 'the Grange' further south, which would form 'a terminal vista from one of Melbourne's main and important streets'.[83]

The most impressive unofficial proposal was by Harold Desbrowe-Annear with the assistance of fellow architect Percy Meldrum, in July 1921. Annear was an eclectic, and for his war memorial plan he married a 'truly renaissance layout' with the kind of classical forms used in his Springthorpe Memorial in Kew Cemetery (1897) and the Princes

Aerial perspective of war memorial and civic centre project by Harold Desbrowe-Annear. *For Every Man His Home, March 1922*

Bridge arch for the Commonwealth celebrations (1901).[84] On the Grange site ('a monumental site of pre-eminent value') later selected for the Shrine, he envisaged a Melbourne version of the Arc de Triomphe. This was more than beaux-arts park planning. The arch ('a central feature of telling amplitude') brought out the quality of a major city axis extending north along St Kilda Road, across the river through the CBD and all the way to the kink in Swanston Street, then occupied by the Carlton brewery. Here Desbrowe-Annear envisaged a new civic centre. The existing town hall would be modified into shopfronts and a large new auditorium. A public square 'of quite suitable dimensions' would be created at Flinders and Swanston streets. On the south side of the Yarra, Desbrowe-Annear planned a new museum and art gallery and an amphitheatre which anticipated the present Myer Music Bowl. Replanning of the radial routes focussed on the arch would also help correct 'very faulty street planning' in the vicinity.[85] This ambitious proposal brought together many earlier ideas and themes. While the central feature was unapologetically artistic – the arch form would never be mistaken for a factory or smokestack – it was presented in a package which promised many significant functional improvements.

In June 1921 Melbourne City Council and the Victorian government finally agreed upon matching funding for a memorial of £100 000, with the balance of £150 000 from community subscriptions. In August a National War Memorial Committee headed by the lord mayor, John Swanson, and including Frank Stapley was established and a public appeal launched. Undoubtedly helped by Desbrowe-Annear's advocacy, the Grange site in the Domain was finally confirmed. It would be described as 'probably the finest site that Melbourne can offer'.[86]

An architectural competition launched in November 1922 attracted 83 entries and the winner was announced in December 1923. Desbrowe-Annear stuck to his memorial arch and picked up a minor prize in association with Meldrum and Stephenson. The winning entry, by returned soldiers Philip Hudson and James Wardrop, envisaged a rather a stern pavilion of mixed Greco-Egyptian influences. Reaction to the winning design was mixed. *Building* praised the incorporation of an 'evergreen Hellenic' portico, saying the whole conception breathed 'the spirit of serene and reverent repose'.[87] Second-place-getter William Lucas went off to exile in Canberra after virtually accusing the winners of plagiarising monuments in Birmingham and Washington. Blamire Young accused the design of 'inarticulate stutterings' and a hostile campaign was waged by the Melbourne *Herald*.[88]

Four years elapsed before construction started, time enough for critics to revisit the question of whether Melbourne would be better served by a more utilitarian memorial. Tax and ratepayer associations were particularly prominent in the debate. Numerous suggestions surfaced: homes for returned soldiers; a hospital; a laboratory for scientific research; a new Yarra bridge; and a junior technical school. Enthusiasm waned when the real costs of such options were calculated and popular sentiment returned to the original guiding idea of an artistic 'memorial for memory's sake', seemingly serving no practical ends other than to inspire and uplift.[89]

The foundation stone was laid in June 1928 and the Shrine was dedicated by the Duke of Gloucester in 1934 in front of a crowd of 300 000. It was arguably the first major monument erected in Australia – 'an awesome monument, built on a scale rarely equalled in the modern world', according to its biographer.[90] Here, finally, was the distinctive man-made feature that Melbourne had long aspired to, its neo-classical nuances and parkland setting also in line with the preferred architecture of the city beautiful movement. Its immediate precinct defined the 'regularising aesthetic' which had propelled the whole prior history of city improvement.[91] The wider spatial setting had even more planning significance. Its siting defined a major visual axis for central Melbourne that had been dreamt about for decades, miraculously using the existing street system. If it was all a little over-the-top, it was clearly by way of 'overcompensating for perceived earlier deficiencies'.[92]

The final report of the Metropolitan Town Planning Commission in 1930 briefly noted construction of the Shrine, commending its fine site, but the commission remained fixated with road proposals. It did however like the idea of extending the character of existing green boulevards such as St Kilda Road and Alexandra Parade in Collingwood with more 'tree-planted thoroughfares'. But it was Alexandra Avenue, a project which had created interest abroad, that became the desired model.[93] Returning from an overseas study tour on which he talked to Frederick Law Olmsted Jr and Arnold Brunner, as well as visiting Riverside Drive in New York and the parkways of Kansas City, James Morrell had already cast it as a model for a 'national parkway' to be extended upstream to Studley Park along the banks of the Yarra.[94] He elaborated this later as a roadway 'for personal rather than commercial' traffic.[95] The commission similarly endorsed further extension, which had commenced with a section completed by Prahran council in 1918.

From a metropolitan perspective, the commission considered that Melbourne's physical geography lent itself to the development of a regional park system at minimum expense, based largely around river and creek valleys. New parkways planned as 'valuable additions to the road system of the metropolis' formed part of this vision. Landscaped for beauty and opening up interesting views, they could

The axis of St Kilda Road from the Shrine of Remembrance to Melbourne city centre, 1956. *Noel Freestone*

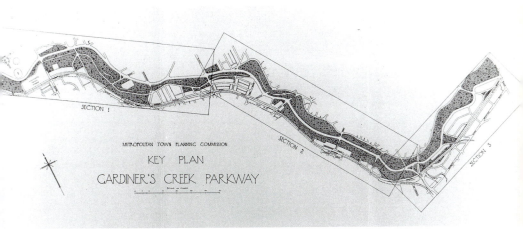

Gardiner's Creek Parkway project. *Plan of General Development, Melbourne, 1929*

also increase the accessibility of open space and augment property values. Recommendations were made for several parkways following the course of the Plenty and Maribyrnong Rivers, plus Gardiners and Darebin creeks. The Yarra would be flanked by twin roads, one an extension of Alexandra Avenue and a parallel road on the north side of the river. The making of the Yarra Boulevard carved out in the 1930s by unemployed workers for basic sustenance payments ('susso') followed the spirit rather than the detail of the commission's thinking. Considerable funds were made available to the Victorian government by the leading retailer Sidney Myer.[96] Related proposals were floated, including a boulevard link from Port Melbourne to the city in time for the Victorian centenary.[97] 'Any excuse to beautify a city is better than none', declared *Building*.[98]

Conclusion

Tree planting, park design, foreshore improvement and creation of parkways generally added up to a culturally, politically and economically acceptable approach to civic art that could be related to wider metropolitan ideals. An American scribe wrote in the *Shire and*

Municipal Record that 'the beautiful street is not a luxury, but absolutely essential to the successful development of the city beautiful' and to obtain the best results utility 'cannot be divorced' from beauty.[99] There was little dissent from the general mantra, although the specifics of how that was to be realised in particular places could prove more controversial.

There are revealing contrasts with overseas experience. The balkanization of local government explains the muted enthusiasm for big city and metropolitan park systems. The ideal of the residential parkway was impeded by a development industry dominated by subdividers and small-scale builders. Despite these constraints, the aesthetic interventions surveyed in this chapter continue to deliver significant amenity values to the present day. While Australians may have eschewed really grand manner planning, at the intersection of the sacred and the secular – where the war memorial movement and the city beautiful idea found common ground – was a chemistry that produced several impressive cultural landscapes, notably the Shrine of Remembrance in Melbourne, the southern section of Hyde Park in Sydney, and Anzac Square in Brisbane (see chapter 7).

CHAPTER 10

The everyday landscape

In a speech to the Royal Institute of British Architects (RIBA) reported in the Australian press, the architect WR Lethaby summed up a near-universal problem of the early 20th century city:

> We have to consider our towns and streets as they are in fact. Our disorderly railway stations must be taken for granted no longer; we must improve lamp posts, drain ventilators and railings; all must be made clean, smart and decent. We must aim at the stricter control of public advertising, at smoke prevention, and at better street cleaning, and help forward all minor improvements.[1]

This denoted an exhaustive agenda for the city beautiful. Across the Atlantic, American advocate CM Robinson enumerated countless ways 'to make beautiful what has been so long the commonplace in civic life'.[2] The surveyor GH Knibbs, in a paper 'The Theory of City Design' to the Royal Society of New South Wales had the same message. The treatment of water fountains, fire alarms, letter boxes, lamp standards, public toilets and 'other furniture of modern streets, all need to be considered in the design, so as to be made harmonious with their surroundings'.[3] In addressing the little things, emphasised the American engineer Frank Koester, the cohesiveness of the streetscape was still a paramount consideration:

However well a city may be planned, its avenues laid out and its parks provided in liberality, it will fail of realizing its full advantages, unless its streets are properly embellished, kept clear of nuisances and given proper attention in every detail ... A rigid policy of exclusion of all unnecessary objects and the ornamentation or concealment of those that must remain should be followed.[4]

Previous chapters have emphasised large scale planning exercises arising from one-off spatial master plans of one kind or another usually under government leadership at federal, state, and central city levels. There was also a wider field of initiatives aimed at encouraging or regulating a higher artistic standard in the workaday built environment. It all came back to better educating the public and tunnel-vision professionals on the place of beauty in civic life, its role in city planning, its relevance to the utilitarian, and appropriate ways of negotiating the line between encouragement and enforcement. William Morris Hughes wrote in 1908 that while it was all very well for a city to abandon itself to the grand embellishments of civic celebration, deep down 'the beautiful city and the beautiful home are for every day, and it is upon these that national and individual character depend'.[5]

This penultimate chapter looks at a range of more day-to-day and micro-scale planning aspects of beautification from architectural, engineering and community standpoints. It considers moves toward regulating street aesthetics, building height and the design of local public monuments. It highlights ways in which engineering structures were aestheticised and considers the broader nature of street and suburban beautification during the reign of the city beautiful.

Cityscape problems

The muddle in the central city was of particular concern. Eyesores were easy to spot. Ragged cornice lines and prominent sidewalls meant an incongruous assortment of adjoining buildings, each expressing its 'own character and purpose'.[6] Ugly telegraph and light poles were blights. Perth's town clerk, William Bold, returned from a world tour convinced that the WA capital had the 'greatest number' of unfinished poles 'of any city which I visited'.[7] Sydney's lord mayor, Thomas Hughes, had vigorous correspondence with the Commonwealth Postmaster-

General's Department about poles being erected 'in their raw condition in many instances with the bark on and with ugly knotty projections'.[8] Inartistic shop fronts and awnings were problematic, as were a clutter of unimaginatively designed and poorly sited furnishings. Advertisements and billboards further assaulted the eye. The indecorous hoarding was a bête noire of US city beautiful thinking, and in Australia could similarly 'stand for the burden of urban ills that weighed a modern city down'.[9] Even some statues inherited from the 19th century turned out to be poorly located and required removal for road works.

This 'jumble of effort' contrasted starkly with overseas icons. The great streets of the world such as the Rue de Rivoli in Paris and Regent Street in London displayed 'continuity in the horizontal sweep of features, from base to skyline of facades'.[10] Arcaded business streets like Bologna's had both 'artistic value' and were 'necessary utilitarian structures'.[11] A city like Washington generally got it right. Its new government triangle of buildings, masterminded by Edward H Bennett in the late 1920s, displayed 'an air of dignity and vision' through 'the general systematic arrangement, the street trees and the wide spaces'. Here there were no skyscrapers 'nor any modern eccentricity in design' with a 'classic feeling' predominating.[12]

How to secure this same pervasive harmony, continuity, and decorum for Australian cities? The architect John Barlow summed it up as well as anybody: 'we will never have a beautiful city while each one is permitted to build as he chooses'.[13] For all the grand schemes, civic centres, efforts at public education, and recommendations of royal commissioners that might produce sporadic benefits, the universal bottom line was seen to lie in regulations which would give both local councils greater powers and their architectural advisers wider influence. CM Robinson encapsulated a threefold value of better building regulations:

> They are based on the principle that it is as proper to curb the freedom of the individual for the good of the community in matters of public art as it is in those of public health or safety. Accordingly, they undertake to limit the height of all structures (generally hygienic considerations are involved in this requirement), to secure in their appearance some degree of harmony with their neighbours, and then to require the plans for public buildings to receive the approval of artists.[14]

The impact of these strands in Australia can be conveyed in turn.

Limiting the skyline

The height of buildings became an issue in the early 1900s when new construction standards and the invention of the elevator combined to make possible the skyscraper. Big commercial cities bore the initial brunt as historically cohesive skylines were punctured by new buildings. Professional journals reproduced articles by American commentators adopting different views reflecting a wider community schism. Polarised attitudes to Manhattan encapsulated the debate: it was either the acme of modern capitalist civilisation or its nadir.

Many practical reasons were cited for restricting the height of buildings: fire-fighting technology would not be able to cope; enormous wind pressures would be created; the health, lives and safety of the community would be endangered; city streets would become sunless chasms clogged by extra workers; the public transport system would groan from increased demand. Counter arguments stressed impedance of economic progress, restriction of development rights, and stifling of creative endeavour and technological progress. The clash was between humanitarian and commercial values, or what one NSW politician described as 'a sentimental point of view' and the utilitarian.[15]

The former, perhaps surprisingly, prevailed. Helping win the day was the compelling observation that New York was not the world and that major commercial cities like London, still a major urban reference point for most Australians, prospered without skyscrapers. Aesthetic considerations underlay much of the debate. Rampaging skyscrapers conflicted with the rationality and order of the beaux arts city; they were seen as destructive of architectural beauty. The NSW politician Dr Richard Arthur put this viewpoint in the state parliament:

> From the aesthetic point of view, it is a crime to have buildings of all heights and shapes in our streets. In the cities of the old world, the beauty and picturesqueness of which are matters of pride, attempts are always made to bring about uniformity with regard to the height of buildings, and I think something in that direction might be

Shock of the new: the New York World Building transplanted to Sydney streets. *Art and Architecture, March–April 1906*

attempted here. We have one of the most beautiful situations for a city, and it would be a pity if we did not attempt to make the most of our advantages, instead of allowing the city to be disfigured by the erection of monstrosities.[16]

Many architects agreed. John Sulman saw uniformity of height as eminently desirable in commercial areas because it might then facilitate some coordination of design.

Introduced because of inaction by the Sydney City Council, the NSW *Height of Buildings Act 1912* restricted building height to a maximum of 150 feet (45.7 metres). It was an effective albeit primitive measure, lacking the sophistication of overseas controls relating building height to street width. Melbourne was even more conservative, with new council building regulations in 1916 specifying a maximum height of 132 feet (40.2 metres) for buildings of steel and concrete in streets over 33 feet wide and 110 feet (33.5 metres) for others.[17] Brisbane also set a height limit of 132 feet, a 'happy medium' according to the city architect, AH Foster.[18]

Regulating beauty

From the early 1900s to the late 1930s architectural journals put the case for greater aesthetic control of city building development. To secure the planning ideal of a beautiful city, piece by piece, architectural development had to be firmly guided. This did not mean draconian controls and rigid uniformity but rather, in the opinion of the Queensland Town Planning Association, a set of checks and balances to 'match the building tones of adjoining buildings'.[19] As with the question of building height, the architectural profession was not unanimous on the idea of such 'censorship'. There were concerns that architectural freedom would be curtailed, individual property rights restricted, and building development retarded. 'Officialism in architectural control' should not be 'overdone', cautioned the architect George Sydney Jones.[20] The architect, town planner and Melbourne lord mayor, Frank Stapley, felt that overly standardised street architecture would produce 'monotony and failure'.[21] A Melbourne critic put this sentiment to rhyme:

Control of design, what futility;
What unparalleled, crass imbecility;
'Twould result in designs
On stereotyped lines
And the architect's mental sterility.[22]

There was however a good deal of enthusiasm for committees of experts to review architectural and development plans. Foreign precedent was forceful. The position of the RIBA was well known. In January 1904 the journal *Art and Architecture* reported on the RIBA's president, Aston Webb's, plea for a board of control to regulate all matters affecting 'the artistic interests of the city'. Advisory commissions in North American cities such as Washington, New York, Boston, San Francisco and Toronto were regarded as beacons of discernment, as were comparable bodies in European cities. The dream goal was 'a consistency of aesthetic building, such as Paris achieves'.[23]

Various names were suggested, including councils of taste, boards of aesthetic control, art commissions, and art juries. The different labels in part reflected advocacy of different models. GS Jones promoted two formulas. One was a board of professional experts; the other a more community-based guild or society advancing the cause of civic art through public education. The board of experts was most needed to assist councils and state governments 'in all matters of civic art, including city improvements, the control of street effects, continuity of line in buildings, and also to assist in the setting apart of special sites for special buildings'.[24] John Barlow had long supported such an independent board with 'the artistic faculty sufficiently developed to appreciate the aesthetic as well as the practical utility of local environments'.[25] The publishers of *Building*, George and Florence Taylor, malevolently promoted the same idea in their campaign against Walter Burley Griffin, to eliminate his 'meaningless, restless and frequently inane juxtaposition of all styles and idiosyncrasies'.[26]

Architects saw themselves as the main custodians of public taste in the everyday environment. At professional meetings through the interwar period they regularly passed motions to secure for themselves a greater say in aesthetic control. A common complaint voiced by Sydney architect James Peddle was that despite regulations for control of height, safety, structural soundness, lighting, and ventilation, nothing explicitly covered aesthetics: 'a walk of half a mile almost anywhere in or around Sydney, or other towns in the State, should convince the most hardened utilitarian that the case for intelligent aesthetic control of design in our streets is established'.[27] Leslie Wilkinson agreed:

> The design of our street buildings must go hand in hand with city planning. The good of the city must take precedence over the good of the individual, although both will benefit by skilful control. We do not want monotony, but we do want order, with the spice of emphasis and contrast which makes the beautiful street picture.[28]

War memorials

A timely opportunity to progress the cause came through the design of memorials to commemorate the sacrifices of local communities during World War I. Refined aesthetic taste was offended by the many inartistic memorials which began to proliferate in a rush of what the historian Ken Inglis dubbed 'anarchic amateurism'.[29] The professional mindset preferred abstract memorials and cenotaphs; popular sentiment favoured diggers on pedestals. New South Wales and Victoria went furthest by establishing state advisory bodies after the example of a comparable initiative by the Royal Academy of Art in Britain to assist local authorities and fundraising committees.[30]

Victoria established a state War Memorials Advisory Committee in 1919. Chaired by Professor Walter Baldwin Spencer, its membership included several individuals with planning connections, such as the architects Frank Stapley, James Morrell, William Campbell, and Geelong-based GR King. Early on, the committee adapted principles laid down by the Royal Academy of Art, notably that in siting a memorial, 'the approaches to it, and its immediate surroundings should be carefully considered'.[31] While this advice resonated in the selection of a site for the Shrine of Remembrance, on the broader front the committee 'was hardly ever consulted'.[32]

In New South Wales, a clause in the *Local Government Act 1919* required that 'monuments shall not be erected in public places or public reserves unless and until the design and situation thereof shall have been approved by the Minister'. To assist this process the large New South Wales War Memorials Advisory Board was appointed.

Membership was a virtual who's who of the prominent professionals whose interests bridged architecture, art and civic improvement. Sulman, whose younger son Geoffrey was killed in action in 1917, was made president. The architect BJ Waterhouse succeeded Robin Dods, also an architect, as vice-president. Among other appointees and their constituencies were the architects GS Jones and JF Hennessy (Institute of Architects of New South Wales), Leslie Wilkinson and the engineer JJC Bradfield (Town Planning Association of New South Wales), artists Lionel Lindsay and Vic Mann (Art Gallery of New South Wales), and Julian Ashton and Sydney Ure Smith (Society of Artists).

The board could not actually undertake designs but organised a competition for generic memorials of different kinds. The winners included architects John Crust, John D Moore, Gordon Keesing and Bruce Dellit and their designs were reproduced alongside other images of suitable memorials in an advisory bulletin.[33] Design competitions were also held for several communities. For example, the monument for the Blue Mountains town of Leura was conceived as part of a broader civic beautification including parkland and a memorial drive.[34] In its first six months of operation the board approved 18 and disapproved 11 memorials. Sulman later recalled that over 200 projects came to the board in its early years, 'most of which we had to re-design'.[35] There was a name change in 1921 to the Public Monuments Advisory Board, acknowledging the broader territory to regulate. Despite the scale of intervention, the design and siting of commemorative structures in NSW were not 'notably different from elsewhere in the nation'.[36]

Other government bodies

There were precious few other successes. In Adelaide, the government town planning department pursued the direction established by its first head, Charles Reade, in concentrating upon comprehensive municipal planning schemes and subdivision control. Town design and parkland improvement was more 'a side line'.[37] In Brisbane, the mandate of the newly appointed city planner, William Earle, in 1925 was confined primarily to zoning questions and rarely strayed into the aesthetic turf of the city architect. In Canberra the bureaucrats held sway, but just before World War II the National Capital Planning and Development

Committee was established with representation of Sydney improver veterans, the architects BJ Waterhouse and R Keith Harris, and Melbourne architect Percy Meldrum. In the southern capital itself, the Royal Victorian Institute of Architects eventually established its own advisory board to promote 'the symmetrical appearance of the city's buildings' without restricting 'the individuality of architectural design'.[38] A medal for street architecture was also inaugurated in the late 1920s.

In NSW there was a modest breakthrough with the appointment in 1918 of a Town Planning Advisory Board, another initiative by John Fitzgerald when minister for local government. Sulman was again made president, alongside public servants John Garlick and JJC Bradfield, another architect Arthur Pritchard, and real estate developer Richard Stanton. They were joined in 1919 by the surveyor-general, John Broughton, and Housing Board architect William Foggitt. Their brief was wide and their activities limited, but they did encompass aesthetic aspects. The board's first annual report mentions

Rose Bay reclamation
project by the NSW
Town Planning
Advisory Board.
Building, October 1920

advice on colonnading of city streets, picturesque housing scheme layouts, conflict between war memorial and street beautification in Mittagong, and a town extension scheme for the country town of Wyalong.

There was also a reclamation project at Rose Bay in Sydney Harbour, in line with the foreshore improvement projects mentioned in the last chapter. The primary aim was to solve a practical problem – the 'untidy and insanitary condition of the beach' arising from decomposing seaweed. The solution provided an aesthetic opportunity to add 'materially to its attractiveness as a summer evening resort, and rendering possible the holding of aquatic carnivals at night'. The total costs of works and resumptions was estimated at £190 000 but an estimated 9000 feet of new residential building frontages would be created, plus 12 acres of new parkland, and augmentation of 'the natural beauty of the bay'.[39] The scheme has been attributed to Bradfield, who was making a more dramatic mark elsewhere on Sydney's urban landscape.

Urban infrastructure

The most literal manifestation of 'beautility' at the local level was in the artistic design and placement of utilitarian structures such as bus and tram stops, bridges, water-towers, drinking places, pumping stations, reservoirs, sewer vents, public conveniences, and electricity substations. There had been some showcase 19th century examples in Sydney. The Egyptian obelisk at the Hyde Park end of Bathurst Street is a ventilation shaft from an 1850s council sewerage scheme. Nicknamed the 'Mayor's Scent Bottle', *Building* praised it as 'a remarkable illustration of how utility and ornament may be combined' but complained that the Water Sewerage and Drainage Board had not followed the lead throughout the city.[40] Another coup was the roofing of Reservoir No. 1 in Centennial Park in 1899 and its laying out with tennis courts, with a picturesque pavilion also serving as a ventilating shaft. Enclosed by decorative iron fencing, the whole ensemble was a 'pleasurable experience'.[41]

York Street North improvements, The Rocks, by the NSW Housing Board.
Proceedings, First Australian Town Planning Conference, 1917

City beautiful thinking sought to extend this aestheticisation of the mundane. Few progressive improvers would have disagreed with Frank Stapley's summation:

> Town Planning does not ignore the artistic, but, on the contrary, it is considered an essential condition that the engineer and the architect should work together. If an electric light pole is required there is no reason why it should not be of pleasing design. Amongst Town Planners there appears to be a doubt in the minds of some that to attempt to introduce the artistic will delay the adoption of the utilitarian Town Planning schemes. This is a mistake, as the best results can only be obtained by considering the artistic with the utilitarian in all cases except those which are essentially utilitarian such as water and sewerage, but even in this work there are instances such as those afforded by the construction of dams, bridges, towers, etc where the artistic should not be omitted.[42]

Bridges provided conspicuous opportunities to marry art with engineering to serve practical needs. JT Noble Anderson, a participant at the 1901 Federal Capital Congress, maintained that 'a bridge should always be designed so as to harmonise with its surroundings' and cited the Pont Alexandre III in Paris in vindication of the saying that 'utility should combine with ornament'.[43]

An authoritative statement of general principles was compiled by Romeo Lahey, a Queensland-based engineer-surveyor who had studied planning at the University of London immediately after World War I and submitted the first masters thesis on planning to the University of Sydney in 1921. The central precept was bridges as 'monuments to civilization' needed to be 'clothed with the attribute of beauty'. Certain 'fundamental principles' covered symmetry, style, general and artistic form, dimensions, ornamentation, and scale. Reflecting the broader creed of the city beautiful, he argued that the worst sin was to 'attempt to disguise functions by added ornament. It is equally blameworthy to let artistic ideas of form overrule the static principles underlying the design'.[44] Road and bridge authorities began to invite architectural input. Leslie Wilkinson worked on some 17 bridges for the NSW Department of Main Roads to ensure that they were 'designed to accord with aesthetic requirements'.[45]

Judging by its prominence in architectural reports, the major

Electricity substation, Grosvenor Street, Sydney.
Building, November 1912

Church Street Bridge, Melbourne.
Building, March 1925

Melbourne showpiece of the 1920s was the rebuilt Church Street Bridge connecting Richmond and South Yarra. Bridges were an indispensable link for a river city, and this bridge, designed by TR Ashworth and Harold Desbrowe-Annear in association with the engineer JA Laing, was portrayed as a true marriage of engineering and architecture, the utilitarian and the ornate. Opened in 1924 at a cost of £102 000, the graceful reinforced concrete bridge with its spandrel arches, classically-inspired pylons and bracketed lanterns was seen to possess both a 'harmony of form' and a 'harmony with its surroundings'.[46] However, good design outcomes were still hit-and-miss. A new bridge across the Yarra at Spencer Street in 1930 was condemned as the most 'tragic example of ugliness' ever perpetrated in Victoria.[47]

Bradfield's Sydney

The greatest bridge of the era was the Sydney Harbour Bridge.[48] It was a collaborative project in planning and design which evolved over decades, but the key player was JJC Bradfield. The 1924 contract for its construction was awarded to Dorman Long, and the same year Bradfield submitted his doctorate of science dissertation on the bridge and the metropolitan rail system to the University of Sydney. This provided an expansive treatment, encompassing wide issues of city growth and town planning while also maintaining that 'aesthetics had to be given more than ordinary consideration' in the design of the bridge.[49]

Critics of early cantilevered proposals could see only a huge eyesore spanning the harbour. John Sulman would not countenance the despoliation of the natural beauty of the harbour, and vigorously promoted a tunnel. This was a source of lingering tension with Bradfield, one of his first students at the University of Sydney. The arch form somewhat leavened these concerns. This was strongly supported by the Town Planning Association, of which Bradfield was a member, with its council opining that 'it would be more pleasing in appearance, and as it is estimated to cost less, and to afford better approaches, it is hoped that it may be adopted and carried out as soon as possible'.[50] Florence Taylor even burst into poetic rapture:

Arching upwards,
Spanning o'er
Sydney's Harbour
Shore to Shore

Curving onwards
Graceful line
Sweeping heavens,
Most Divine

Noble Structure,
Stout of frame,
Yet reposeful
All acclaim.

You're the grandest
Work extant
In your setting
Elegant.[51]

There were precedents to show it could work. The final design is astonishingly like the rail-only Hell's Gate Bridge (1917) in New York, the largest steel-arch bridge in the world when completed. Its impressive pylons, designed by the architect Henry Hornbostel, were 'simple masses of stone', which replaced a more 'effusive' earlier treatment on the recommendation of the New York Arts Commission.[52] The Sydney pylons were designed by Thomas Tait, a partner in the architect Sir John Burnet's office. Burnet, earlier selected to serve on the adjudication committee for the aborted competition to design Canberra's parliamentary buildings, had studied at the École des Beaux Arts in Paris in the 1870s. The pylon design recalls Lutyens' cenotaph in Whitehall, London, while their arch form above the train and tram tracks on the bridge deck also evoke the triumphal arches of the imperial city beautiful.[53]

Bradfield's vision for engineering extended well

Classically-inspired
entrance to Central
Railway Station, Sydney

Southern Gateway to Sydney
from Harbour Bridge, revised
Bradfield plan with twin
'parklets'. *Art in Australia 1932*

Gateway treatment to the Sydney Harbour Bridge approaches,
North Sydney, 1930s. *Mitchell Library, State Library of New South Wales*

beyond nuts and bolts. He believed that major public works were part technical, part propaganda, and needed to be sold to the community. He used countless speeches, technical papers, and above all imagery to express artistic city redevelopment possibilities. His vision for Sydney was extraordinary and in Charles Coulter he found a competent architectural artist to visualise his ideas.

Bradfield did not acknowledge Coulter's work in his thesis but had done so in 1921: 'his excellent perspectives have enabled me to place before you pictorially the ideas I wished to express'.[54] Beauty and utility combined in all aspects of Bradfield's Sydney. The bridge was the vital cog in a reorganised and electrified city railway scheme. The first section opened from Central to St James Station in December 1926, and then on through Wynyard in March 1932 to coincide with the opening of the bridge. Bradfield carefully considered the 'aesthetic treatment' of the railway, below and above ground. All visible structures would be 'in architectural harmony with their surroundings, and all surplus lands will be made into street gardens or miniature parks'.[55] The railways' engineering department was congratulated for 'keeping up the architectural traditions of the city by attention to artistic design and details'.[56]

Bradfield's most visionary proposals concerned the approaches to the bridge. He put forward his own views for rearranging traffic flows on the city side, a topic of considerable professional interest in the 1920s. The major challenge was articulating bridge traffic into and from York, Clarence and Kent Streets. There were various ideas, all connected with major new building development, and featuring archways, peristyles, portal buildings, fountains, and parklets. The 'true classic spirit' was said to pervade the 'colonnade and archway' plan.[57] On the north side, as well as sweeping new road and rail approaches and a grand station at North Sydney, the harbour foreshores from Lavender Bay to Milson's Point were to be redeveloped in Italian Renaissance style with residential flats and other buildings overlooking ornamented cliffs, a park with picturesque walkways, and 'a little statuary on the waterfront'. This was not 'a visionary scheme' for beautification, he contended, but 'a practical proposal which the North Sydney Council or other authority could well carry out with substantial profit to the promoters of the enterprise'.[58]

Bradfield's attention to detail carried through to the little things. Lighting not only imparted 'considerable beauty to the structure at night'. The actual fittings were 'by day … one of the Bridge's most delightful ornamental features'.[59] Coulter had a hand in the refined art deco designs for the lamp standards. Advertising hoardings were banned from bridge roads, the approaches being named the Bradfield Highway. The weakest link in the entire conception was arguably the treatment of Circular Quay, where a station in the location endorsed by the royal commission two decades earlier was destined to 'block all glimpses of blue water'.[60]

The suburb beautiful

The city beautiful aimed at more fundamental objectives than mere prettification. But efforts of home-owners, women's groups, chambers of commerce, progress associations, vigilance committees, local councils, sometimes government authorities and even more occasionally private businesses to expunge obvious eyesores and exploit beautification opportunities expressed a civic sensibility which could be applauded by the professionals.

It wasn't city planning in the comprehensive sense but it was not unconnected with wider campaigns of civic improvement. Much to the chagrin of campaigners like Charles Reade, scattered projects at the local level were often what defined planning in practical terms. In suburban Melbourne on the eve of World War I, 'the matter of town planning, or town beautification as it really amounted to at first, became a rallying point for citizen activists'.[61] For the exhibition at the 1918 Town Planning Conference in Brisbane, local authorities such as North Sydney sent photographs of miscellaneous local improvement activity – street designs, tree plantings, and gardens – which 'told a story of municipal endeavours and attempts at pursuing the city beautiful theme'.[62] After an inspirational trip abroad, the new town clerk of Sydney announced in 1924 that 'city beautification is to me one of the most important civic functions'.[63]

This was expressed in different ways, but often in tree planting, provision of open space and foreshore improvements – as we have seen. The accent was on beautification rather than conservation when creek valleys were cleaned up, low-lying land reclaimed, and cemeteries redeveloped. For many suburban communities, aesthetic treatments were even more utilitarian in the kerbing, guttering, asphalting and lighting of roads, building of footpaths, and maintenance of nature strips.[64] Arguably the city beautiful idea was expressed most widely in the beautification of residual or reclaimed spaces associated with roadworks. Their transformation into garden beds and seats, rockeries, garden beds, grottos, ponds, and so on, made them 'a delight to the eye and a tonic for the jaded mind'.[65] In Hobart, a special 'reserves rate' struck by the city council helped transform many desolate, vacant corners into 'areas of beautiful flowers' and such improvements could be partly 'traced to the increased attention being paid to town planning principles'.[66]

What became known as 'the aesthetic side of engineering' was recognised by progressive councils as a good investment 'inasmuch as it attracts visitors, creates better selling values, and insures that erection of a better class of dwelling; properties are more easily sold

Street tree planting efforts of the Wahroonga Progress Association.
Art and Architecture, November 1905

'Waste space beautified' in Mosman.
Mosman Council, Annual Report, 1922–23

and fewer homes are vacant'.[67] Council attempts to involve residents in working bees and joint ventures had variable results. Mosman in Sydney was one of those councils that offered prizes for house and street beautification.[68] These forms of suburban and town betterment segued into the tidy towns movement. The Country Womens' Association of New South Wales started a 'Beautiful Towns Competition' in 1927. All towns were advised to seek expert technical advice on plantings. The architect Norman Weekes judged the inaugural contest, won by Orange.[69] In South Australia, the 1936 centenary celebrations saw 165 towns receive town beautification grants totalling £7449.[70]

The other connection was with the garden suburb movement when new communities boasted exotic layouts featuring numerous open spaces, memorials, public buildings, gateway features, and axial streetscapes. Garden competitions proliferated and the banning of front fences encouraged the transformation of an ordinary street into 'wide garden-lined boulevard'.[71] The call went out to councils to pay 'more regard to the artistic merits of the layout' when approving new subdivisions.[72] GS Jones in his presidential address to the Institute of Architects of NSW in 1913 appealed to the beautilitarian instincts of the real estate industry:

> Owners themselves, as shrewd business men, must surely see that they would obtain far higher prices than usual if their plans of subdivisions were schemed to secure design and order and beauty in the ultimate effect of their properties when built upon. Utilitarianism, in this matter at least, has dominated things too long, and land owners who think of subdividing and selling their properties would do well, in their own interests financially, to remember that the vast majority of the purchasing public are now alive to the fact that land, which is part of a scheme having as its ultimate aim beautification of the whole, is worth more money and is worth holding longer than land which is not part of such a scheme.[73]

This kind of idealism evaporated with the Depression as did many grander initiatives to inculcate civic pride through beauty. However, even 'susso beautification' arrived with its own aesthetic: rough-hewn stonework in Sydney and rustic basalt borders in Melbourne.[74] Such small-scale activity through the 1930s maintained a connecting thread to a movement which promised so much more in the early 1900s.

Formerly the unsavoury 'Sewer Road', Blair Street's landscaped median
now marks the path of the main Bondi Beach sewer line

Conclusion

The city beautiful strand of the early planning movement made its
mark on the Australian landscape in sundry rather than necessarily
spectacular ways. Its influence was felt in height controls, the location
and design of public monuments, the architectural treatment of
utilitarian structures, and artistic local public works. In the late 1920s
the New South Wales Town Planning Association prided itself on
encouraging attention to the civic bric-a-brac of urban development:
'roadside trees and gardens, benches and flag poles, filling stations,
lights, signs, small buildings, roadside design, club houses, band
stands, bathing sheds, parks, railway station gardens, information
booths, memorial fountains and many other questions'.[75] Where
beauty was concerned, the scope of the town planning imagination
had shrunk:

> To-day is the day of the town planner. He, hitherto, has been suffered
> as a sort of idealist who sang of the "city beautiful" yet when his songs
> were interpreted they were invariably found to begin and end with

schemes of glorious resumptions of expensive city property for the purpose of creating "magnificent tree-lined boulevards". The Town Planner to-day has come to earth. He realises that town planning does not consist so much of glorious resumptions as of the securing of healthy and comfortable living conditions; that the city can be made artistic by the elimination of ugly telegraph and lampposts and by neater footpaths and more artistic shop fronts.[76]

In large measure, the planning function had, for a time, seemingly reduced to 'beautifying of the commonplace'.[77]

CHAPTER 11

New themes, old traditions

The concerns of city planners worldwide had moved on from the city beautiful as a central organising concept well before the Depression extinguished most of the lingering idealism. World War II ushered in new agendas and methodologies based on functionalist objectives. The United States had begun to turn away from the city beautiful ideal much earlier. The US architect Arnold Brunner had warned the American Civic Association Convention in 1910 that 'to the average citizen the "city beautiful" suggests the city impossible'.[1] Professionals began to repudiate the movement. With the new accents on efficiency and economy, beauty was at best a by-product. By the 1920s the balance between the yin of beauty and the yang of utility sought by city beautiful improvers was well and truly out of kilter as aesthetic concerns were perceived to overrule practicalities. As Emily Talen concludes, the pioneering plan makers 'never actually accomplished the goal of integrating beauty and science'. While the cause of civic art would linger, and indeed be revived by the end of the 20th century, a new hard-nosed and comprehensive paradigm of pragmatic city planning emerged. For all its sumptuousness, the Chicago Plan showed the way in expressing the coming 'domination of practicality over aesthetics'.[2]

This final chapter summarises the Australian experience. The city beautiful in Australia attempted to graft an artistic sensibility onto what were then the core professional skills of the planner, architecture, engineering and surveying, with mixed success. But the discussions, debates and experimentation involved helped shape the nature of planning through its formative years. And while a civic renaissance was not to be, there were enough important legacies to remind us today of a vital and distinctive phase in the history of urban development in Australia.

Continuities and discontinuities

That phase essentially ended in the 1930s. We perhaps should be grateful that many of the more cold and mannered visions exemplified by the 1909 Royal Commission for the Improvement of the City of Sydney and Its Suburbs were not realised. There were always formidable obstacles to the wider realisation of city beautiful dreams. Beyond traditional Australian apathy towards 'utopian' schemes, the costs of implementing proposals were usually regarded as prohibitive by politicians already nervous about government's direct involvement in urban development. Local government, fragmented into a patchwork of small authorities, also impeded the realisation of metropolitan dreams such as park and parkway systems. The power of private capital to frustrate reconstruction involving freehold property was well established. Even when aesthetic-based reform was sold as functional, cost-effective improvement, it ultimately failed to directly address more pressing and practical planning needs like better roads, improved subdivision plans, and adequate housing. On the other hand, many of the good ideas associated with the city beautiful movement need to be acknowledged: open space and environmental improvements, the importance of integrated design, and a commitment to enhancing the public realm.

There were some achievements on the ground. Although Walter Burley Griffin's holistic vision for Canberra had been degraded, the symmetry and balance in the landscape composition of the central area had at least crystallised sufficiently to hold out prospects for further possibilities, even if it was only the 'beauty dreamers' who cared.[3] The Sydney Harbour Bridge opened minus John Bradfield's shoreline of grotto gardens but its overall form was the most extraordinary synthesis of beauty, utility and modernity. New roads, parks, tree plantings, waterside promenades and street beautification works were outcomes from coordinated local efforts. University campuses also bore testimony to city beautiful thinking, but generally out of the public eye. The civic and park complex of Johnstone Park in Geelong is one of the most impressive early achievements of an integrated city beautiful set-piece in Australia. Many community war memorials became artistic landmarks, and the completion of major capital city structures such as the Anzac Memorial in Sydney's Hyde Park climaxed broader efforts toward civic improvement in those cities.

The dedication of the Shrine of Remembrance in Melbourne represented the highpoint of a protracted search for a major civic-artistic intervention to transcend the limitations of the city's street grid. The economic value of the Shrine was perhaps ultimately realised in tourism dollars. It became a landmark that would be marketed as capturing the essence of Melbourne at the 1956 Olympic Games and beyond. Like Adelaide before it, by the 1930s Melbourne was relaxing more confidently in its self-made environmental qualities. The time was now right for a local businessman to copyright a picture postcard series of 'Melbourne The City Beautiful'.[4]

It was not a comprehensive victory. The Depression was a watershed. Stillborn dreams, failures to seize opportunities, and unfinished business were apparent everywhere, but certainly keenly felt in Sydney. By the 1930s aesthetic reformers were reflecting soberly on how little had been achieved. The artist and publisher Sydney Ure Smith felt Sydney was headed for second-rate status: progressive in a commercial sense but 'hopeless artistically'.[5] The architect David King lamented a failure to realise one cherished city beautiful goal: 'There is not one Public Building in our City terminating a vista at the end of any Main Thoroughfare'.[6] In a wide-ranging address, the architect BJ Waterhouse, who had been in the thick of civic improvement activities since the 1920s, expressed bitter disappointment that after a half-century of development there was not one new important building 'well sited in an appropriate and beautiful setting'. No theatre, no opera house, no municipal art gallery, no 'stately law courts', no city square 'expressive of city dignity', and no 'Minister of Civic Control'.[7] In Sydney as in other cities many of the particular urban spaces and civic aspirations which had obsessed the early planners are still problematic. Melbourne at least has achieved a closure of sorts with Federation Square, its unsettling architecture miles away from the beaux arts traditionalism that had earlier animated the struggle to define a 'central focal point of the city'.

By the 1930s such goals had already been re-situated within the changing nature of the city, organisation of professional practice and evolving culture of planning. Indeed, this transformation was well underway even before World War I. The need for a metropolitan scale of urban management intensified, and within that more expansive frame of reference the significance of early architectonic touchstones such as city-centre 'portals' was lost. Architectural practice shifted its priorities, with an inexorable move away from 'the gentlemanly pursuit of a professional art' to 'the pragmatic and efficient provision of buildings for commerce and industry'.[8] Planners also took on these imperatives. The architect-planner John Sulman may have retained a soft spot for the triumphal arch that he made the fulcrum of his vision for a new Sydney in 1908 as a way of elevating the city 'from the realm of the material into that of the ideal'. By the 1920s, however, structures in such strategic locations would not only be seen as obstructions to 'modern traffic' but their 'solidity and mass [could] clash with the architecture of the surrounding buildings'.[9]

The shift of planning ideology away from the order of the city beautiful towards a more pragmatic agenda in the interwar period is very evident. Professional town planning institutes began to replace the former community associations state-by-state before merging into a federal body in 1951. By the 1940s planner-architects were rushing to disown their earlier aesthetic impulses. In Melbourne, John Gawler divided planning into the aesthetic and the practical. Only the latter paid dividends, with road systems and land use zoning the key areas.[10] From Perth, Harold Boas proclaimed that 'Town Planning has long since ceased to be The City Beautiful – it is today an exact science dealing with the flow and volume of traffic and the physical layout of our cities'.[11] And in Sydney the newly arrived professor of town and country planning, Denis Winston, defined planning as the 'general

Temporary commemoration of the Federation
arch of 1901, Melbourne, 2001

development and control of physical environment for the convenience, health and happiness of the greatest number':

> The Town Planner used to be thought of as merely a specialized kind of architect who dealt with the "beautification", as it was called, of streets and squares. He was expected to give a sort of cosmetic treatment of paint and powder to the wrinkled, dirty, and often diseased face of the town. To-day, as in medicine, so in town planning, we attempt to go to the root of the problem and aim at prevention rather than cure.[12]

Fatally weakened through these endorsements of a new kind of scientific endeavour was the historical connection between planning and architecture. The old verities about the importance of civic design, art and improvement dissolved. The continuing etiolation of 'artistic sensibilities' and re-emphasis on utilitarian-led planning evident through much of the post-World War II period was not unrelated to the rise of social science-based educational curricula with 'very little visual content'.[13]

Broader forces encouraging the same thinking were also at work in Australian society. These are exemplified by changes in the national

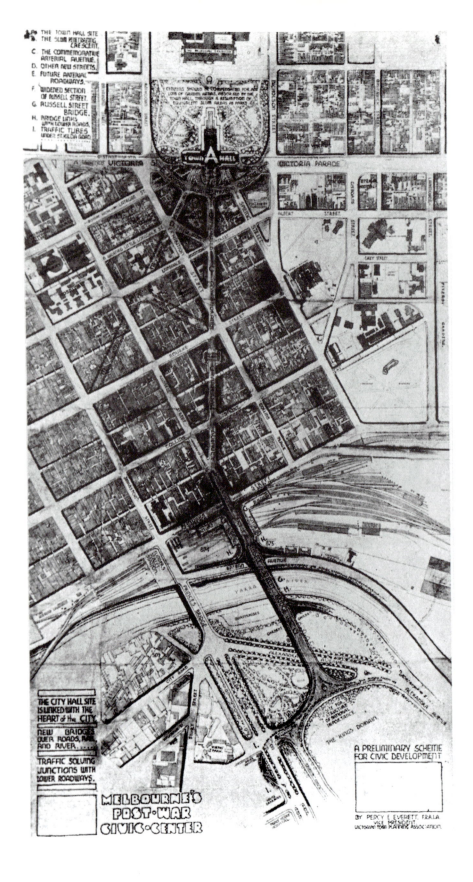

A. THE TOWN HALL SITE
B. THE SLUM PENETRATING
   CRESCENT.
C. THE COMMEMORATIVE
   ARTERIAL AVENUE.
D. OTHER NEW STREETS.
E. FUTURE ARTERIAL
   ROADWAYS.
F. WIDENED SECTION
   OF RUSSELL STREET.
G. RUSSELL STREET
   BRIDGE.
H. BRIDGE LINKS
   WITH LOWER ROADS.
I. TRAFFIC TUBES
   UNDER ST.KILDA ROAD.

CITIZENS SHOULD BE COMPENSATED FOR ANY
LOSS OF GARDEN AREAS INVOLVED BY THE
TOWN HALL THROUGH A RESUMPTION OF
EQUIVALENT SLUM AREAS AS PARKS.

TOWN HALL

VICTORIA PARADE

ALBERT STREET.

GREY STREET.

THE KINGS DOMAIN

THE CITY HALL SITE
IS LINKED WITH THE
HEART of the CITY

NEW BRIDGES
OVER ROADS, RAIL,
AND RIVER.

TRAFFIC SOLVING
JUNCTIONS WITH
LOWER ROADWAYS.

A PRELIMINARY SCHEME
FOR CIVIC DEVELOPMENT

MELBOURNE'S
POST·WAR
CIVIC·CENTER

BY PERCY E. EVERETT, F.R.A.I.A.
VICE PRESIDENT
VICTORIAN TOWN PLANNERS ASSOCIATION.

mood toward war memorials. In contrast to World War I, from the late 1940s utilitarian memorials, in the form of town halls, community and returned servicemens' clubs, swimming pools, sports grounds, war veterans' homes, marine drives, and hospitals and medical clinics, were widely preferred. The historian Ken Inglis reports a 1944 Gallup poll showing 90 per cent of Australians voting for practical memorials: 'monumentality was out of fashion'; it was 'the triumph of utility'.[14]

The everlasting civic centre

While planning had shifted away from its artistic connotations, there was one enduring form which had crystallised in the city beautiful era: the civic centre. The planned grouping of public buildings serving the everyday needs of civic society has been one of the most enduring ideals of modern planning. There was a rush to build civic centres in post-war Britain, with an enduring predominance of beaux arts layouts and neo-classical architectural styles.[15] In the US the civic centre was the capstone of many post-World War II reconstruction plans, and by the 1960s convention centres and performing arts complexes were common in civic renewal projects. Suburban communities and small towns constructed their own public building groupings in a more 'modest display of civic propriety.'[16]

Major civic centre proposals were featured in both the official 1954 metropolitan master plans for Melbourne, prepared by the Melbourne and Metropolitan Board of Works, and for Perth (1955) by the town planners Gordon Stephenson and Alastair Hepburn. The 1940s was an active decade for schemes suggesting new settings for the Melbourne Town Hall. The idea of rebuilding it on the site of or near the Exhibition Building was taken up enthusiastically by, among others, Percy Everett. By then vice-president of the Town and Country Planning Association of Victoria, Everett ventured a visionary scheme linking the north and south banks of the Yarra River with new axial avenues and bridges. The Exhibition Gardens would accommodate a new town hall and associated buildings. Victoria Parade was remodelled into a crescent

Melbourne civic centre project by Percy Everett.
Building, April 1943

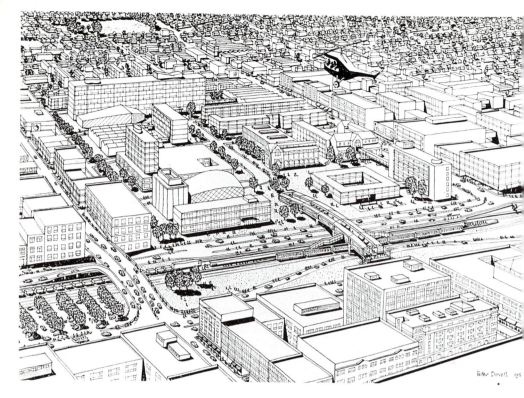

Cultural centre project, Perth.
Plan for the Metropolitan Region, Perth and Fremantle, 1955

and new radial avenues were pushed into the city, eliminating nearby slums as well as improving accessibility and visual links to the central business district.[17] Unifying such schemes was the portrayal of a city 'in a state of flux and change' with no hint of 'nervousness in the idea that a radical rearranging of the city was imminent and necessary' in a climate favouring bold post-war reconstruction.[18] The Board of Works plan developed ideas of the Town Planning Commission from the 1920s to propose the western side of Spring Street opposite Parliament House as a new 'civic focal point'.[19]

The proposal in the Perth plan was to group 'civic and cultural buildings' north of the railway with modernisation and expansion of art gallery, library and museum buildings. This was the just one in a sequence of proposals going back to the days of the architects G Temple Poole and William Hardwick that subsequently involved a remarkable cast of international and Perth names, including Harold Boas, John Oldham, and the American architectural firm Skidmore Owings and Merrill. A significant step towards realising the long-standing idea was the opening of a new Art Gallery of Western Australia in October 1979 as part of a larger cultural and educational zone.[20]

The chimerical dream of a Sydney civic centre would linger into the post-war years in both state and local government circles. Florence Taylor had largely given up on the idea of a new town hall and instead developed a proposal for a new cultural centre in the Domain, complete with opera house, museum and conservatorium.[21] From 1952–55 the Sydney City Council seriously contemplated the idea of its city engineer, Alfred Garnsey, for a civic centre incorporating the existing Australian Museum and Sydney Grammar School around the three southern flanks of Hyde Park.[22] The case for such a complex echoed overseas recognition that 'a Civic Centre is not a luxury nor purely an exhibition of civic pride, but has a real economic value by attracting tourists (potential shoppers), facilitating administration (by co-ordinating governmental buildings) and rehabilitating inner city areas'.[23] The council later turned its attention to Macquarie Street, but neither scheme materialised.

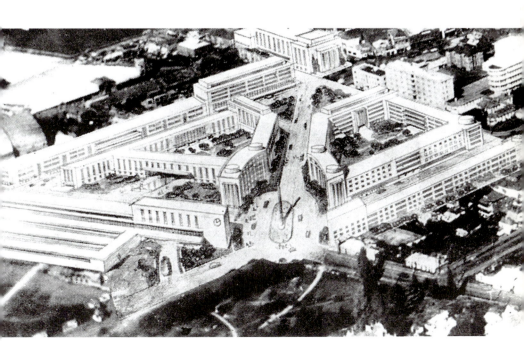

Redevelopment proposal for Wapping, Hobart.
City of Hobart Plan, 1945

Central places for peripheral people: United Nations Plaza,
San Francisco civic centre

The City of Hobart Plan of 1945 prepared by Fred Cook, formerly of the Melbourne Town Planning Commission, recommended a new civic centre development comprising a consolidation of existing public buildings near Franklin Square with a massive new government secretariat building: 'Imagine the Government offices and other congruous uses housed in a large, imposing block of buildings … with lawns in front, displaying a worthy façade to all entering the port'.[24] This complemented a proposed redevelopment of the 'old and decadent' area of Wapping on the opposite side of the central city with a 'traffic circus and transport interchange square' as a new gateway to the city from the north. An ambitious mixed-use centre was also proposed for the postwar reconstruction of Darwin.[25]

Civic centres featured in many other postwar city, suburban and country town plans. The architect and town planner Karl Langer inserted a string in his schemes for the Queensland towns of Mackay, Kingaroy, and Dalby in the 1950s. Denis Winston's comments at a public meeting in Orange, NSW, in July 1958 on civic centres as a community focal point hark back to the rhetoric of the city beautiful:

> In Australia we have had few opportunities of seeing how inspiring and enjoyable a group of buildings can be when well designed to harmonise with each other and properly landscaped with lawns and trees. Such a group is not only practical and convenient but can become a focus for loyalty and inspiration for a more vigorous civic life and a symbol of the quality of citizens and their representatives alike.[26]

Globally, latter-day interpretations of civic centres reveal the weakness of the classic city beautiful idea of a citadel of administrative, institutional and high culture buildings. Most unfortunate is the revival of the bombastic-authoritarian capital city style, which reaches its nadir in Bucharest, Pyongyang, Yamoussoukro and Ashkhabad.[27] Many American centres had a 'haughty detachment' from everyday life – 'an air of disdain rather than dignity.[28] They became vast, deserted 'hollow cores' surrounded by bureaucratic bunkers.[29] The vacuum has often been filled by vagrants, homeless people and drug dealers.[30] The monolithic cultural centres conceived in the 1960s, some designed in neo-beaux arts style, were problematic. In her book *The Death and Life of American Cities* (1963) the Canadian critic Jane Jacobs made the most devastating and influential critique of this style of cultural precinct. She blamed it on the city beautiful allied to garden city thinking. Monofunctional urban districts were 'a pitiful kind of planning', 'woefully unbalanced' and 'tragic' in their effects, undermining urban vitality by 'isolating' uses. They represented an ill-conceived policy of 'decontamination', rupturing public institutions from the fabric of the existing city. The problems are more evident in the United States than Australia, where the civic centre idea remained a virtual theoretical project until after World War II, but precincts created in the 1950s and 1960s can suffer, like business centres, from a lack of vitality, especially after normal business hours. Recent revitalisation efforts have aimed at creating more people-friendly, mixed-use centres with active street frontages.

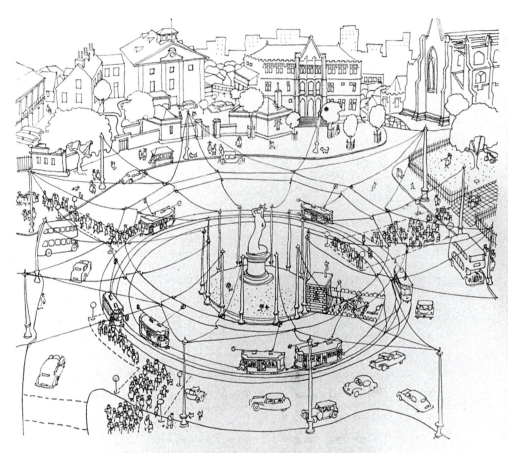

THE FIFTH COLUMN

"Here is developing a part of our City of whose charm and quiet dignity, future generations will be justifiably proud. . . .

"It is a fitting thing that the Queen-Mother should look down upon this place."

(Extract from a speech delivered at the unveiling of Queen Victoria's Statue, Queen's Square, Sydney.)

Stop Press

To this scene add six or seven prefabricated bus (or tram) shelters as featured in our Fifth Column for October, 1950.

The continuing quest for better civic design,
post-war Sydney. *Architecture, January–March 1951*

Continuities and the revival of urban design

The surge of activity and interest in urban design since the 1980s has created a renewed interest in the city beautiful as a pioneering visual paradigm of good city form. Revival of the visual content in planning, largely suppressed from the 1920s onwards through the embrace of scientific methodologies, was a slow, protracted battle. Seers included the town planner Thomas Sharp and architect Trystan Edwards in Britain, and the urban planner Ed Bacon and landscape architect Christopher Tunnard in the United States. A consistent message was the rupture of the historic link to architecture and consequent neglect of the third dimension of urban environments. Writing in 1953 for an Australian audience, Tunnard stated that planning had to be lifted 'out of the plane of workability and expediency ... surely our concept of the City Beneficial must include some aspects of the City Beautiful'.[31]

Tunnard's sentiments were echoed by Australian architects like Donald Ward who sought to recapture the 'magnetic quality' of urban places by putting 'poetry into planning, art into engineering'.[32] The challenge was taken up in the 1960s by bodies such as the Civic Design Society in Sydney, with University of Liverpool planning alumnus Elias Duek-Cohen, a central figure, and the Civic Trust of South Australia in Adelaide, which was formed to encourage a better civic environment through public education and debate.[33] The backlash against the stereotyped and ugly landscapes of urban and suburban modernism in the 1960s (the architects Robin Boyd and Don Gazzard playing leading roles) provided a broad foundation for the recent renaissance of urban design. The most epochal moment came in 1996 with the establishment of a national Urban Design Taskforce by former prime minister, Paul Keating.

This evolution reflects an international reinstatement of aesthetics in city planning.[34] As taken on board by local authorities and through state agencies, urban design vigilance is mediated through a complex apparatus way beyond the advisory committees and review panels envisaged by the civic art pioneers. Guidelines, design competitions, master plans, and development control plans provide instruction for better appreciating the interrelationship of buildings and structures in urban and suburban landscapes.

Respecting city traditions:
The Market Square development in Washington, DC

When it ventures into the place-making and place-marketing aspects of an improved urban environment, the rhetoric of the new design is not unlike that of the old civic art. The visual appreciation of the urban environment is stressed and the quintessential 'bird's eye view' associated with the city beautiful has made a big comeback. The aesthetic however is usually radically different. There is no longer the reliance on beaux arts geometry, symmetry and formal groupings. A more lively mix-and-match approach sensitive to site, streetscape and sustainability rules.

Nevertheless, a 'second coming' of the city beautiful has been observed in the United States as cities have sought to enhance design and amenity through resuscitating their own historic city beautiful plans for public plazas, malls, parks, riverfronts, and recovery of dead freeway land.[35] Where formal civic spaces and centres are the target, the overall conclusion appears to be that 'the most felicitous way to relate new construction to Beaux Arts classicism is to carefully insert more of the same'.[36] The 'New Urbanism' also demonstrates an indebtedness to city beautiful thinking. New urbanism is associated with community planning based on compactness, walkability, liveability, mixed uses, and high design and development standards. Its principal practitioners, such as the architect and urban designer Peter Calthorpe, have acknowledged the impact of the city beautiful, particularly in its historic contribution to the formal design of residential estates.[37] The impact comes not only in a similar penchant for modified classical street grids, parkland systems, and attention to gateways and vistas but also in the valuation of the public realm through community centres and spaces.

Respecting the legacy of the city beautiful

In the US the city beautiful movement, for all its class-consciousness and struggle for credibility against the demands of the commercial world, has left a pervasive impact, at the small and large scale. According to Jon Peterson, its influence on building and advertising codes, clean streets, provision of utilities and planning instruments is so commonplace that it is easy to overlook.[38] Witold Rybczynski

It seemed like a good idea at the time: Forrest Place, Perth, 1997. Perth City Council has recommended demolition of the pedestrian walkway and the redesign of Forrest Place.

cites the bigger projects – such as union stations, public libraries and parkways – as attractive and valuable outcomes. He argues that the original cores of the city beautiful college campus are 'the most fully realized examples of the civic art ideal' and proof that Americans 'could build beautiful urban places'.[39]

In Australia, the landscapes connected to the influence of the city beautiful movement before World War II similarly range from humble street gardens and parklets to more formal precincts and corridors variously recognised in heritage terms at local, state and federal levels, although not explicitly because of the city beautiful connections canvassed in this book. The fate of some of these urban spaces has belied their importance to the nation's urban development. Forrest Place in Perth and Anzac Square in Brisbane remain two of the most important city beautiful products but their heritage significance has been diminished by intrusive development. Like all the urban spaces discussed in this book, they have a life way beyond their formative years and city beautiful origins, but latter influences have not always been benign.

The outstanding opportunity to fully realise the early vision of Forrest Place as a genuine civic square came when the 50 year lease for the Padbury retail buildings was set to expire and the Commonwealth agreed to the transfer of property to the state. Yet the denouement was not all that happy. Fuelled by rhetoric of a new civic heart for Perth, from the mid-1960s a series of urban design studies and ideas connected the fate of Forrest Place with broader ideas for improving pedestrian flows in the city and functional linkages across the barrier of the railway to the emerging cultural complex to the north.[40] A 1986 development plan was the blueprint for the demolition of the Padbury Building, widening of the street, redevelopment of Boans department store into the Forrest Chase Shopping Centre, erection of Albert Facey House on the old Customs House site, and a network of upper-level pedestrian walkways and overpasses, the most destructive being a link across the northern end of Forrest Place. Forrest Place was pedestrianised in 1978 and further transformed into a multi-level street mall with steps and recessed courts.

While the project architect sought visual connections between old and new in terms of building forms and relationships, their subtlety

University of Adelaide, lower campus redevelopment in spirit of the historic WH Bagot scheme. The axis of the library lawn links to a new park, providing a green connection to the Adelaide Botanic Gardens.

was to be lost in the modernist brutality of the setting.[41] A contemporary observer lamented: 'How is it possible that such an important development can, after 90 years of gestation, go so wrong'.[42] The values driving this scheme derived from the high modernist obsessions of the 1960s: technological fixes, grade separation, and circulation efficiency.[43] These problems are more widely recognised now and a solution may finally be at hand. But for the time being, while its special qualities and history are not totally denied, Forrest Place is perhaps defined less by the public values which made it possible than by its orientation to a retail mall.[44] This lingering distortion of public values perpetuates the dilemma of successfully integrating commercial and civic values foreseen before World War I.

Clearly 'the most substantially intact example of formal planning and design at such a scale in the centre of Brisbane', Anzac Square offers a more complete environment.[45] But there is now a surrounding clutter and scale of development which detracts from the sense of repose sought originally. The building of the new federal office tower on the site was a disastrously unsympathetic intervention. A 1970s subway connection into Post Office Square under Adelaide Street realised the longstanding idea of a connection between the post office and the railway station but the visual connection is obscured and the southern boundary of the

Federation Place: A new symbolic entrance to Centennial Park in Sydney

square compromised. Upper-level pedestrian ways now hang off the flanking buildings and the view north towards the railway station is monstered by a towering office block and hotel behind. It could have been much worse, and more directly intrusive plans for car parks and retail redevelopment were resisted.[46]

Recognition of the social and design history of places encourages more sympathetic approaches to infill, extension and contiguous development. This can be a long time coming. Sydney City Council decided in 1940 to accept the lord mayor's recommendation to extend Elizabeth Street in accordance with the city engineer's 'Trafalgar Square' scheme but 'owing to war conditions it was not … considered that the resolution will be carried into effect until the conclusion of hostilities'.[47] The new headquarters building for Qantas in the late 1950s half-realised the vision of a semicircular place, but a modernist slab erected opposite for a Commonwealth Government Centre in 1962 destroyed the symmetrical scheme, despite a 'spirited debate' among architects and planners as to the merit or otherwise of conforming to the original concept. The architect Peter Webber interpreted the incident as 'a salutary warning' for a style of baroque formality disconnected from similarly olde world autocratic powers of implementation.[48]

Rules of decorum can also have a moral suasion, and here not all was lost for when the unloved Commonwealth building was demolished to make way for the Chifley Tower (1993). The complementary curvature of its podium was ultimately a good mannered gesture to the thinking of lord mayor Norman Nock and engineer Alfred Garnsey in the 1930s.

Another Sydney example tacitly acknowledging a city beautiful past was the Centenary of Federation project to formally reinstate the western entrance to Centennial Park. Several leading Australian architectural firms were asked to present their ideas. While it has not resolved all the circulation and landscaping concerns in the vicinity, the realised scheme for Federation Place by Alexander Tzannes (who in 1988 also designed the classical dome structure commemorating the federation ceremony in Centennial Park) offers a modern reinterpretation of the triumphal arch as a gateway structure, enhancing the existing boulevard right of way (now, Federation Way) to provide a better link between Anzac Parade and Moore Park.

The most ambitious attempt to correlate urban design needs and opportunities with historical influences drawing on the city beautiful idiom is the Griffin Legacy project of the National Capital Authority, launched in 2002. Underpinned by considerable historical research aimed at tracking down 'lost' Griffin drawing and documentation, the final report provides a detailed reconstruction and interpretation of the original 1912 plan. The centrepieces of the Griffins' vision for central Canberra are still palpable. Ken Taylor describes the view from Old Parliament House north as 'a compelling axial landscape statement of order and symmetry'. The contrast between the formality of Anzac Parade and the gum trees of Mount Ainslie is a 'powerfully compelling dynamic tension … one of the great landscape axes of the world'.[49] While much has been irrevocably compromised by insensitive, albeit well-intentioned, development, there remains an extraordinary number of good Griffin ideas which are capable of realisation today.[50]

The Griffin Legacy project reasserts the primacy of the original design as the most important reference mark in guiding future development without naively proposing the building of the 1912 city. It seeks to extend the legacy through eight major initiatives:

- Protecting significant physical elements of the Griffin Plan through heritage controls and conservation management
- Affirming the Griffin Plan as the primary organising framework

for urban form and landscape, including a maintenance of the 'City Beautiful values which underpin Canberra's quality of life'

- Enhancing the urbanity and vitality of the central national area through reinstating undeveloped proposals of the Griffin Plan, such as Constitution Avenue as a cosmopolitan main street
- Linking better the 'federal city' and the 'municipal city' through reducing physical barriers and enhancing connectivity
- Extending the city to the Lake Burley Griffin and develop a variety of waterfront activities
- Reinforcing the city's main avenues as multi-use boulevards
- Interconnecting national attractions with high-quality pedestrian and public transport links
- Promoting the Griffin Legacy through scholarship, exhibitions and public programs.

Planning no longer seeks to conjoin just beauty and utility; its predominant characteristic is complexity and its justification is the simultaneous resolution of multiple objectives.[51] Implementation is another matter, but the Griffin legacy project, for a city which best exemplifies the city beautiful in the Australian popular and professional imagination, captures exceptionally well how earlier moves toward healthy, convenient and beautiful cities can be reinserted and adapted into new preoccupations with sustainable, productive and liveable ones.

Conclusion

An early aesthetic ethos helped to catalyse planning consciousness in Australia in theory (with many projects mooted) and practice (learning from the reality check of implementation). In historical terms, the city beautiful era in Australia was important in first defining and expressing the dominant values of modernist urban planning in the 20th century. Despite the frequent recourse to the classicism of the beaux arts, underlying values of specialisation, order, efficiency, uniformity were statements of modernity.

The Australian brand of a global movement was a rather eclectic one, drawing on American and British influences. There are strong

Circular Quay proposal from the Sydney
'Living City' project, 1994. *Sydney City Council*

parallels with Canada in how a pervasive enthusiasm for civic art cedes
to more restrained treatment as part of the shift toward pragmatic
comprehensive planning, and with a national capital the touchstone
for debates on how best to accommodate beauty in planned settings.

The nexus with the development of the town planning profession
saw an Australian model of the city beautiful driven largely by
professional concerns and interests. As radically reshaped as the urban
spaces might have been in a physical sense, their intent was almost
invariably a conservative reflection of establishment values. Local
communities helped to shape outcomes and sporadically kept alive
the ethos of urban beautification. But there was not the same national
prominence and networking of citizens associations as characterised
the American response. On the other hand, intersection with the war
memorial movement did shape a distinctive response in global terms,
as commemoration could be linked to the cause of improvement. Most

of the notable projects surveyed in this book have a war memorial connection if not centerpiece.

For a short time in the 1900s, the city beautiful movement seemed to best express the aspirations of urban reformers and progressive civic authorities. Today, the recovery of the ideas, nuances and projects of that movement enables us to better appreciate connections between what might otherwise be seen as isolated improvement projects from the early 1900s to the 1930s. Interlinked by values, ideology, and personalities, they represent a cohesive yet largely forgotten era in the history of Australian urban development and design.

'Extending the City to the lake': proposal for reinstating Griffin's intentions for Canberra National Capital Authority. *The Griffin Legacy, 2004*

Notes

Chapter 1: Introduction

1　A. Sutcliffe, *Towards the Planned City*, Basil Blackwell, Oxford, 1981, p. 103.
2　R. Freestone, 'Town Planning', in G. Davison, et al (eds), *The Oxford Companion to Australian History*, Oxford University Press, Melbourne, 1998, pp. 645–46.
3　R. Freestone, C. Garnaut and A. Hutchings, 'A Bibliographic Guide to Recent Literature in Australian Planning History', *Planning History*, 41(1), 2002, pp. 21–34.
4　P. Hall, *Cities of Tomorrow*, Blackwell, Oxford, 3rd ed, 2002, p. 206.
5　C.M. Boyer, *Dreaming the Rational City*, MIT Press, Cambridge, 1983, p. 46.
6　See for example: E.C. Rafferty, 'Orderly City, Orderly Lives: The City Beautiful Movement in St Louis', *Gateway Heritage*, 11(4), 1991, pp. 40–62; R.A.M. Stern, et al, *New York 1900*, Rizzoli, New York, 1983; T.J. Noel and B.S. Norgren, *Denver: The City Beautiful and its Architects, 1893–1941*, Historic Denver, Denver, 1987; H.A. Kantor, 'The City Beautiful in New York', *New York Historical Society Quarterly*, 57, 1973, pp. 149–71; W.H. Wilson, *The City Beautiful Movement in Kansas City*, Lowell Press, Kansas City, 2nd ed, 1990; G.A. Brechin, 'San Francisco: The City Beautiful', in P. Polledri (ed), *Visionary San Francisco*, Prestel, Munich, 1990, pp. 40–64; S. Leckie, 'Brand Whitlock and the City Beautiful Movement in Toledo, Ohio', *Ohio History*, 91, 1982, pp. 5–36.
7　W.H. Wilson, *The City Beautiful Movement*, Johns Hopkins University Press, Baltimore, 1989.
8　J.A. Peterson, *The Birth of City Planning in the United States, 1840–1917*, Johns Hopkins University Press, Baltimore, 2003.
9　S.V. Ward, *Planning the Twentieth Century City*, John Wiley, Chichester, 2002.
10　Hall, *Cities of Tomorrow*, p. 216.
11　G. Stelter, 'Rethinking the Significance of the City Beautiful Idea', in R. Freestone, (ed), *Urban Planning in a Changing World*, E & FN Spon, London, 2000, p. 99.
12　W.H. Wilson, 'The Ideology, aesthetics and politics of the City Beautiful Movement', in A. Sutcliffe (ed), *The Rise of Modern Urban Planning 1800–1914*, Mansell, London, 1980, p. 166.
13　Quoted in W.A. Saw, 'Some Aspects of Town Planning', *Journal and Proceedings of Royal Society of Western Australia*, 5, 1919, p. 42.
14　This listing consolidated from Wilson, *The City Beautiful Movement*, p. 75ff, and 'The ideology, aesthetics and politics of the City Beautiful Movement', pp. 165–98.

15   Stelter, 'Rethinking the Significance of the City Beautiful Idea', p. 107.
16   *Sydney Mail*, 3 March 1909, p. 8.
17   E. Talen, *New Urbanism and American Planning*, Routledge, New York, 2005, p. 122.
18   Wilson, *The City Beautiful Movement*, p. 83.
19   Quoted in G.P. Landow, *The Aesthetic and Critical Theories of John Ruskin*, Princeton University Press, Princeton, 1971, Chapter 2, online at <http://www.victorianweb.org/>
20   Quoted in M.H. Lang, *Designing Utopia*, Black Rose Books, Montreal, 1999, p. 20.
21   D. Hume, *Treatise of Human Nature* (1739) Dent, London, 1964, Part 3, Section 1.
22   *Building*, April 1915, p. 59.
23   *Building*, November 1912, p. 128.
24   M. Scott, *American City Planning since 1890*, University of California Press, Berkeley, 1969, p. 68.
25   Quoted in Talen, *New Urbanism and American Planning*, p. 75.
26   *Western Architect*, April 1910. From 'Urban Planning, 1794–1918: An International Anthology of Articles, Conference Papers, and Reports', by J.W. Reps, <http://www.library.cornell.edu/Reps/DOCS/homepage.htm>
27   *Building*, April 1911, p. 15.
28   'Introduction', in J. Nolen (ed), *City Planning*, D Appleton and Co., New York, 1917, pp. 17–18.
29   Peterson, *The Birth of City Planning in the United States*, p. 206.
30   J. Nolen, *The Place of the Beautiful in the City Plan*, National Conference on City Planning, 1922, p. 12.
31   *Building*, September 1917, p. 13.
32   Wilson, 'The ideology, aesthetics and politics of the City Beautiful Movement', p. 173.
33   *Building*, April 1911, p. 13.
34   *Building*, September 1932, p. 21.
35   *Garden Cities and Town Planning*, January 1916, p. 5.
36   *Building*, April 1911, p. 19.
37   D. Stevenson, *Cities and Urban Cultures*, Open University Press, Maidenhead, 2003, p. 77.
38   R. Freestone, *Model Communities*, Thomas Nelson, Melbourne, 1989.

Chapter 2: America and the world

1   J.W. Simpson, 'Preface', *Transactions of the Town Planning Conference*, London, October 1910, Royal Institute of British Architects, London, 1911, p. iv.
2   D.J. Olsen, *The city as a work of art*, Yale University Press, New Haven, 1986.
3   P. Pregill and N. Volkman, *Landscapes in History*, John Wiley, New York, 2nd ed, 1999, pp. 564–65.
4   C. Zueblin, 'The Civic Renascence: "The White City" and After', *The Chatauquan*, December 1903, p. 373.
5   C.M. Robinson, *The Improvement of Towns and Cities*, G.P. Putnam's Sons, New York, 1901, p. 131.
6   E. Morrison, *J. Horace McFarland*, Pennsylvania Historical and Museum Commission, Harrisburg, 1995.
7   R.A. Walker, *The Planning Function in Urban Government*, University of California Press, Los Angeles, 1941, p. 15
8   E. Bellamy, *Looking Backward*, Penguin American Library, New York, 1982, p. 55.
9   Quoted in R. Prestiano, *The Inland Architect*, UMI Research Press, Ann Arbor, 1985, p. 171.
10   L.F. Perkins, 'Municipal Art', *The Chautauquan*, February 1903, reproduced in Reps, Urban Planning, 1794–1918, <http://www.library.cornell.edu/Reps/DOCS/homepage.htm>
11   M. Manieri-Elia, 'Toward an "Imperial City": Daniel Burnham and the City Beautiful

Movement', in G. Ciucci, et al., *The American City*, Granada, London, 1980, p. 40.

12 J.A. Peterson, *The Birth of City Planning in the United States, 1840–1917*, Johns Hopkins University Press, Baltimore, 2003.

13 K. Schaffer, 'Fabric of City Life: The Social Agenda in Burnham's Draft of the Plan of Chicago', in *Plan of Chicago*, Princeton Architectural Press, 1993, p. xii.

14 Peterson, *The Birth of City Planning in the United States*, p. 219.

15 J.A. Peterson, 'Two Faces of the City Beautiful: Daniel H Burnham and Charles Mulford Robinson', Paper presented to the Society for American City and Regional Planning History Conference, Chicago, 1993, p. 5.

16 Peterson, *The Birth of City Planning in the United States* pp. 154–55.

17 C.M. Robinson, *The Improvement of Towns and Cities*, GP Putnam's Sons, New York, 1901, p. 166.

18 J.M. Mayo, *War Memorials as Political Landscape*, Praeger, New York, 1988, p. 90.

19 W.H. Wilson, 'The ideology, aesthetics and politics of the City Beautiful Movement', in A. Sutcliffe, (ed), *The Rise of Modern Urban Planning 1800–1914*, Mansell, London, 1980, pp. 182–83.

20 N.P. Lewis, *The Planning of the Modern City*, John Wiley, New York, 1916, p. 162.

21 F. Koester, *Modern City Planning and Maintenance*, McBride-Nast and Co, London, 1915, p. 30.

22 W.C. Leedy, 'Cleveland's Struggle for Self-identity', in R.G. Wilson and S.K. Robinson (eds), *Modern Architecture in America*, Iowa State University Press, Ames, 1991, pp. 75–105.

23 D.V. Mollenhoff and M.J. Hamilton, *Frank Lloyd Wright's Monona Terrace*, University of Wisconsin Press, Madison, 1999.

24 W.H. Wilson, 'The Billboard: Bane of the City Beautiful', *Journal of Urban History*, 13, 1987, pp. 394–425.

25 'South Dade: City Beautiful', *Abitare*, 276, July–August 1989, pp. 144–51.

26 L.M. Roth, 'Company Towns in The Western United States', in J.S Garner (ed), *The Company Town*, Oxford University Press, New York, 1992, p. 180.

27 Quoted in J.D. Fairfield, *The Mysteries of the Great City*, Ohio State University Press, Columbus, 1993, p. 126.

28 J. Nolen, *The Place of the Beautiful in the City Plan*, National Conference on City Planning, 1922, p. 6.

29 R. Wojtowicz, *Lewis Mumford and American Modernism*, Cambridge University Press, Cambridge, 1996, p. 28.

30 Peterson, *The Birth of City Planning in the United States*, p. 217.

31 J.E. Draper, *Edward H Bennett, Architect and City Planner, 1874–1954*, Art Institute of Chicago, Chicago, 1982. p. 41.

32 H. Bartholomew, 'The Principles of City Planning', *American City*, 26, 1922, p. 457.

33 H. Bartholomew, *A Comprehensive City Plan: Memphis*, Tennessee City Plan Commission, 1924, p. 129.

34 R.A.M. Stern et al, *New York 1930*, Rizzoli, New York, 1983, p. 31.

35 C. Schorske, *Fin De Siecle Vienna*, Vintage Books, New York, 1981.

36 D.P. Jordan, *Transforming Paris*, The Free Press, New York, 1995, p. 354.

37 Z. Celik, 'Bouvard's Boulevards: Beaux-Arts Planning in Istanbul', *Journal of the Society of Architectural Historians*, 43, 1984, pp. 341–55.

38 A. Almandoz (ed), *Planning Latin America's Capital Cities 1850–1950*, Routledge, London, 2002.

39 G.H. Yetter, 'Stanford White at the University of Virginia', *Journal of the Society of Architectural Historians*, 40, 1981, p. 325.

40 T.S. Hines, *Burnham of Chicago*, University of Chicago Press, Chicago, 1979.

41 A. Balfour and Z. Shiling, *Shanghai*, Wiley-Academy, Chichester, 2002.

42 J.W. Cody, *Building in China: Henry K Murphy's "Adaptive Architecture, 1914–1935*, Chinese University Press, Hong Kong, 2000.

43 J.L. Cohen, *Scenes of the World to Come*, Flammarion/Canadian Centre for Architecture, Montreal, 1995.

44   A. Sutcliffe, *Towards the Planned City*, Basil Blackwell, Oxford, 1981, p. 197.

45   T. Hall, *Planning Europe's Capital Cities*, E & FN Spon, London, 1997, p.333.

46   P. Hall, *Cities of Tomorrow*, Blackwell, Oxford, 3rd ed., 2002, p. 201.

47   S.D. Helmer, *Hitler's Berlin*, UMI Research Press, Ann Arbor, 1985.

48   C.C. Collins, in W. Hegemann and E. Peets, *The American Vitruvius*, Princeton University Press, 1988, p. xx.

49   Quoted in M. O'Malley, 'The most beautiful capital in the world', *Canadian Heritage*, 12(1), 1986, p. 37.

50   D. Gordon, 'A City Beautiful plan for Canada's capital: Edward Bennett and the 1915 plan for Ottawa and Hull', *Planning Perspectives*, 13, 1998, p. 274.

51   W. Van Nus, 'The Fate of City Beautiful Thought in Canada, 1893–1930', *Historical Papers/Communications Historiques*, 1975, pp. 191–210.

52   E. von Baeyer, 'The Battle Against Disfiguring Things', *Bulletin, Society for the Study of Architecture in Canada*, 11, 1986, pp. 3–9.

53   G. Stelter, 'Dreaming the Impossible Dream: The Grand Tradition in the Modernization of Canadian Cities, 1905–1915', Paper presented to the Society for American City and Regional Planning History Conference, Chicago, 1993.

54   Van Nus, 'The Fate of City Beautiful Thought', p. 205.

55   C. Miller, 'The City Beautiful Movement in New Zealand and the Saga of the Auckland Civic Centre', in C Garnaut and S Hamnett (eds), *Fifth Australian Urban History/Planning History Conference: Conference Proceedings*, University of South Australia, 2000, pp. 276–84.

56   J.F. Munnings, 'The City Beautiful', *Official Volume of Proceedings of the First New Zealand Town-Planning Conference and Exhibition*, Government Printer, Wellington, 1919, p. 159.

57   C. Miller, 'Did the City Beautiful Movement Exist in New Zealand? A Preliminary Conclusion', in C.L. Miller and M.M. Roche (eds) *Proceedings of the 8th Australasian Urban History/Planning History Conference*, Massey University, Wellington, 2006, pp. 323–36.

58   *Art and Architecture*, May–June 1910, p. 88.

59   S.V. Ward, *Planning and Urban Change*, Paul Chapman Publishing, London, 1994, p. 37.

60   C. Crouch, *Design Culture in Liverpool 1880–1914*, Liverpool University Press, Liverpool, 2002, p. 156.

61   T. Mawson, *The Life and Work of an English Landscape Architect*, Charles Scribner's Sons, New York, 1927.

62   *Architecture*, March 1923, pp. 41–45

63   A.J. Youngson, *Urban Development and the Royal Fine Art Commissions*, Edinburgh University Press, Edinburgh, 1990.

64   D. Schubert and A. Sutcliffe, 'The "Haussmanization" of London?: The planning and construction of Kingsway-Aldwych, 1889–1935', *Planning Perspectives*, 11, 1996, p. 141.

65   T. Mawson, *Civic Art*, B.T. Batsford, London, 1911, p. 42; cf., S.D. Adshead in the *Town Planning Review*, 1, 1910, pp. 148–50.

66   J. Sulman, *An Introduction to the Study of Town Planning in Australia*, NSW Government Printer, Sydney, 1921, pp. 68, 70.

67   *Building*, March 1913, p. 95.

68   L. Weaver, *Houses and Gardens by Sir Edwin Lutyens, RA*, Country Life, London, 1925, p. 302.

69   Sutcliffe, *Towards the Planned City*, p. 163.

Chapter 3: The Australian scene

1   C.C. Reade, 'Foreword', in *Official Volume of Proceedings of the First Australian Town Planning and Housing Conference and Exhibition Adelaide 1917*, Vardon and Sons, Adelaide, 1918, p. 6.
2   J.S. MacDonald, 'City of Cheap Finery', *The Argus*, 31 May 1913.
3   City of Adelaide, *Mayor's Report*, 1904, p. 9.
4   Quoted in M.J. Webb, 'Urban Expansion, Town Improvement and the Beginning of Town Planning in Metropolitan Perth', in J. Gentilli (ed), *Western Landscapes*, University of Western Australia Press, Perth, p. 375.
5   *The Australasian*, 1 October 1850, pp. 137–46.
6   *Town and Country Journal*, 31 December 1895. p. 27.
7   R. Free, *Lloyd Rees*, Lansdowne Press, Melbourne, 1972.
8   *Australasian Builders and Contractors News*, October 1887, p. 1.
9   A.M.S. Roberts, 'City Improvement in Sydney: Public Policy 1880–1900', PhD thesis, University of Sydney, 1978.
10   R. Freestone and S. Veale, 'The Street Beautiful: Triumphal Arches and Urban Improvement in Sydney 1888–1925', *Public History Review*, 4, 1995, pp. 25–40.
11   *Australasian Sketcher*, 12 March 1884, p. 34.
12   T. Bonyhady, *The Colonial Earth*, Miegunyah Press, Melbourne, 2000.
13   J. Keily, 'Study on Unity of Design Planning New Towns and New Suburbs', *Transactions and Proceedings, Victorian Institute of Surveyors*, 3, 1891, pp. 88–104.
14   J. Sulman, 'The Laying Out of Towns', in his *An Introduction to the Study of Town Planning in Australia*, NSW Government Printer, Sydney, 1921, pp. 214–16.
15   G.H. Knibbs, 'The Theory of City Design', *Journal and Proceedings of the Royal Society of New South Wales*, 35, 1901, pp. 62–112.
16   *Building*, May 1916, p. 110.
17   *Architectural and Building Journal of Queensland*, 11 March 1929, p. 79.
18   *Building*, April 1917, p. 83.
19   C.B. Luffmann, 'The Agricultural, Horticultural, and Sylvan Features of a Federal Capital', in *Proceedings at the Congress of Engineers, Architects, Surveyors, and others interested in the Federal Capital of Australia held in Melbourne*, J.C. Stephens, Melbourne, 1901, p. 45.
20   J. Sulman, 'The Cities of Australia and Their Development', *Proceedings of the First Australian Town Planning Conference Adelaide 1917*, p. 60.
21   *Journal of the Royal Victorian Institute of Architects*, 5, 1907, p. 84.
22   W.M. Campbell, 'The Streets of Melbourne from an Architectural Point of View', *Journal of the Royal Victorian Institute of Architects*, 1, 1904, pp. 179–88.
23   'Report of the Executive Commissioner for New South Wales to the World's Columbian Exposition, Chicago, 1893', NSW Government Printer 1894, p. 19.
24   *Memorial Volume, Dedicatory and Opening Ceremonies*, Chicago, 1893, p. 105.
25   Quoted in F. Somers, 'The Life and Works of John Bede Barlow', B.Arch. thesis, University of New South Wales, 1970, p. 76.
26   *Building*, October 1912, p. 81.
27   *Building*, May 1924, pp. 42–48; cf., Wilkinson in *Architecture*, June 1929, pp. 132–41.
28   Sulman, *Town Planning in Australia*, p. 147.
29   *WA Mining, Building and Engineering Journal*, 26 October 1912, pp. 18–19.
30   *Art and Architecture*, vol. 4, 1907, p. 128.
31   Sulman, *Town Planning in Australia*, p. 142.
32   R.F. Irvine, Report of the Commission of Inquiry into the question of the Housing of Workmen in Europe and America, *NSW Parliamentary Papers*, 1913, Vol 2, p. 48.
33   K.S. Inglis, *Sacred Places*, Melbourne University Press, Melbourne, 2nd ed, 2005, pp. 282–83.
34   S. Petrow, 'Making the City Beautiful: Town Planning in Hobart c1915 to 1926', *Tasmanian Historical Research Association, Papers and Proceedings*, 36, 1989, p. 104.
35   *Building*, November 1924, p. 52.
36   G.S. Jones, 'Australia and Civic Art', *Proceedings of the First Australian Town Planning Conference Adelaide, 1917*, p. 51.

37   G. Taylor, *Town Planning with Common-Sense*, Building Limited, Sydney, 1915, p. 107.
38   Draft of Town Planning Bill, c1915, State Library of Tasmania.
39   R.F. Irvine, *Town Planning: What it Means and What it Demands*, Town Planning Association of N.S.W., Sydney, 1914, p. 4.
40   J.S. Battye, 'The City Beautiful', 1934, Radio Talk No 4, 638A, Bold Papers, Battye Library.
41   *Building*, April 1917, p. 90.
42   *Liberty*, 1 March 1934, p. 7.
43   *Building*, April 1915, pp. 83–84.
44   *Building*, April 1915, p. 112.
45   R. Freestone and B. Hanna *Florence Taylor's Hats*, Halstead Press, Sydney, 2007.
46   D.M. Bluestone, 'Detroit's city beautiful and the problem of commerce', *Journal of the Society of Architectural Historians*, 47, 1988, p. 262.
47   J.D. Fitzgerald 'Town planning and civic beautification', *The Lone Hand*, 14, 1914, p. 448.
48   J.D. Fitzgerald, 'The Science of Town Planning: Its Universal Application', *Building*, December 1913, p. 96.
49   R.K. Clark, 'The City Beautiful: Promise and reality', *The Architect*, 10(2), 1969, pp. 40–44.
50   C.T. Stannage, *The People of Perth*, Perth City Council, Perth, 1979, pp. 298–99.
51   J. Willis, 'Conscious design: The Melbourne University Architectural Atelier 1919–1947', *Fabrications*, 13(2), 2004, p. 49.
52   *Australian Dictionary of Biography*, Vol 12, p. 138.
53   Jones, 'Australia and Civic Art', p. 50.
54   *The Salon*, September 1916, pp. 53–54.
55   D. Rowe, 'Building a National Image: The Architecture of John Smith Murdoch, Australia's First Commonwealth Government Architect', PhD thesis, Deakin University, 1997.
56   D. Rowe, 'John Smith Murdoch and the Early Development of Canberra', *Fabrications*, 6, 1995, pp. 24–37.
57   American Park Association, #2777, Scrapbooks, Box 24. Kroch Library, Cornell University
58   M. Heilbron (ed), *Inventing the Skyline: The Architecture of Cass Gilbert*, Columbia University Press, New York, 2000. p. 181.
59   G.A. Taylor, *Town Planning for Australia*, Building Limited, Sydney, 1914, p. 35.
60   *Building*, October 1913, p. 51.
61   Somers, 'John Bede Barlow'.
62   R. Mackay, 'Robert Charles Given Coulter 1864–1956', B.Arch thesis, University of New South Wales, 1971.
63   G.S. Keesing, 'The Atelier System of Architectural Study', *The Technical Gazette*, 4, 1914, 22–25.
64   A Brown-May and S. Swain (eds), *The Encyclopedia of Melbourne*, Cambridge University Press, Melbourne, 2005, p. 28.
65   H. Edquist, 'Harold Desbrowe-Annear and the City Beautiful', *Transition*, 59–60, 1998, pp. 46–57.
66   F. Stapley, Presidential Address, *Official Volume of Proceedings of the Victorian Town Planning Conference*, Ballarat, 1919, p. 17.
67   *The West Australian*, 26 August 1911, p 14.
68   *Journal of the Royal Victorian Institute of Architects*, 11, 1913, p. 76.
69   *Architectural and Building Journal of Queensland*, June 1924, p. 44.
70   Sulman, *Town Planning in Australia*, pp.148, 152.
71   W.E. Bold, *Report on Tour Round the World*, 1914, Perth City Council, p. 51.
72   Report of the Royal Commission for the Improvement of the City of Sydney and Its Suburbs, 1909, *New South Wales Parliamentary Papers*, Vol 5, p. xxiv.
73   *Building*, January 1909, p. 55.
74   *Building*, January 1910, p. 36.

75 *Building*, April 1911, pp. 19, 17.
76 *Architectural and Building Journal of Queensland*, March 1927, p. 42.
77 *Building*, June 1914, p. 99.
78 *Building*, April 1915, p. 58.
79 Jones, 'Australia and Civic Art', p. 51.
80 *Building*, November 1921, p. 44.
81 L.A. Curtis, 'Town Planning as Applied to New Cities and the Remodelling of Ill-Designed Ones', *The Surveyor*, 27, 1914, p. 6.
82 *Journal of the Royal Victorian Institute of Architects*, July 1917, p. 95.
83 *Architecture*, December 1917, p. 147.
84 J.D. Fitzgerald, 'Sydney: The Cinderella of Cities', *The Lone Hand*, 1, May 1907, p. 60.
85 *Building*, November 1914, p. 72.
86 Presidential Address, *Official Volume of Proceedings of the Second Australian Town Planning Conference and Exhibition, Brisbane, 1918*, pp. 30, 36.
87 *Building*, June 1917, p. 27.
88 *Building*, April 1915, p. 112k.
89 Taylor, *Town Planning with Common-Sense*, p. 19.
90 *Building*, April 1923, p.130.
91 *Building*, May 1922, p. 32b.
92 F. Stapley, 'Town Planning', *Australian Municipal Journal*, July 1921, p. 32.
93 J.D. Fitzgerald, 'New Cities for Old', *Property Owner*, April 1921, p. 2.
94 Sulman to J.D. Fitzgerald, 21 September 1908, Fitzgerald papers, MSQ252, Mitchell Library.
95 Quoted by Somers, 'John Bede Barlow', p. 51.
96 *Building*, April 1917, p. 90.
97 *Building*, January 1917, p. 99.
98 A.J. Brown, 'Martin Place: Unified Architectural Treatment', 11 October 1933, TC 3812/30, Sydney City Council Archives.
99 *Sydney Mail*, 20 May 1908.
100 G. Davison, 'Public Life and Public Space: A lament for Melbourne's City Square', *Historic Environment*, 1(1), 1994, p. 5.
101 *Building*, January 1924, p. 70.
102 SA Acting Government Town Planner, *Annual Report*, 1920–21, p. 10.
103 *Building*, January 1924, p. 69.
104 G.A. Taylor, *There! A Pilgrimage of Pleasure*, Building, Sydney, 1915, p. 211.
105 F.W. Fitzpatrick, 'The Thrall of the Axis', *Building*, July 1915, p. 78.
106 J.W. Barrett, *Eighty Eventual Years*, J.C. Stephens, Melbourne, 1945, p. 94.
107 *Proceedings of the First Australian Town Planning Conference*, p. 7.
108 *Proceedings of the Second Australian Town Planning Conference*, p. 22.
109 *Proceedings of the Second Australian Town Planning Conference*, p. 182.
110 Town Planning Association of N.S.W., Report of Council, 1928, Mitchell Library.
111 *Australian Dictionary of Biography*, Vol 7, p. 336.
112 R. Robertson, 'WE Bold: The Town Clerk', in L. Hunt (ed), *Westralian Portraits*, University of Western Australia Press, Perth, 1979, p. 178.
113 W.A. Saw, 'Some Aspects of Town Planning', *Journal and Proceedings of Royal Society of Western Australia*, 5, 1919, p. 40.
114 *Building*, May 1923, p. 134.

Chapter 4: The federal capital

1 K. Fischer, *Canberra, Myths and Model*, Institute of Asian Affairs, Hamburg, 1984; D.L. Johnson, *Canberra and Walter Burley Griffin: A Bibliography of 1876 to 1976 and a Guide to Published Sources*, Oxford University Press, Melbourne, 1980; R. Pegrum, *The Bush Capital*, Hale and Iremonger, Sydney, 1983; P. Reid, *Canberra Following Griffin*, National Archives, Canberra, 2002; J. Reps, *Canberra 1912*, Melbourne University Press, Melbourne, 1997.

2   *Building*, July 1915, p. 60.
3   J. Sulman, *The Federal Capital*, John Sands, Sydney, 1909, p. 7.
4   G.A. Mansfield, W.L. Vernon, J. Barlow, and G. Knibbs, 10 August 1900, in 'Report of the Commissioner on Sites for the Seat of Government of the Commonwealth', October 1900, *NSW Parliamentary Papers*, 1900.
5   *Art and Architecture*, 5, 1908, p. 206.
6   *Art and Architecture*, 8, 1911, p. 209.
7   G.S. Jones, 'Some Thoughts Concerning the Federal City', in *Proceedings at the Congress of Engineers, Architects, Surveyors, and others interested in the Federal Capital of Australia held in Melbourne*, J.C. Stephens, Melbourne, 1901, p. 22.
8   F.B. Gipps, 'Lake George (New South Wales) as a site for the Federal Capital of Australia', *Royal Geographical Society of Australasia (Victoria)*, 19, 1901, p. 38.
9   P. Harrison, *Walter Burley Griffin, Landscape Architect*, National Library of Australia, Canberra, 1995, p. 4.
10   'Federal Capital Sites. Reports respecting proposed sites at Mahkoolma, Canberra, and other sites in the Yass (Lake George) District. Report upon suggested site for the seat of government of the Commonwealth at Mahkoolma', W.L. Vernon, April 1906, *Commonwealth Parliamentary Papers*, 1906, Vol. 2, p. 5.
11   'Mr. Hamlet the Past President of the Royal Society of N.S.W. on Modern Chemistry and the Federal Capital', *Australian Technical Journal*, 4(10), 1901, pp. 298–99.
12   J. Young, *The Proposed Federal City for the Commonwealth of Australia, in New South Wales*, Batson and Co., Sydney, 1905, p. 5
13   Sir J. Forrest, 'Federal Capital: Proposed Sites', *Commonwealth Parliamentary Papers*, Vol. 2, 1907–1908, p. 3.
14   Jones, 'Some Thoughts Concerning the Federal City', p. 22.
15   *Proceedings at the Congress*, p. 7.
16   *Building Engineering and Mining Journal*, 5 October 1901, p. 311–12.
17   G.H. Knibbs, 'The Theory of City Design', *Journal and Proceedings of the Royal Society of New South Wales*, 35, 1901, pp. 62–112.
18   *Building Engineering and Mining Journal*, 5 October 1901, p. 312
19   *Building, Engineering and Mining Journal*, 7 December 1901, p. 387.
20   G.V.F. Mann to W.H. Ifould, Letter with Sketch Plan, 30 January 1924, A027/9A, Mitchell Library.
21   *The Surveyor*, 14, 1901, p. 136.
22   Report of the Commissioner, October 1900, p. 28.
23   *Sydney Morning Herald*, 30 December 1911.
24   M.H. Haefele, 'Ideal Visions of Canberra', MA thesis, Australian National University, 1995, p. 32.
25   G. Gregors, 'The Capital City Design Theory debate 1890–1910', in R. Freestone (ed), *The Australian Planner*, School of Town Planning, University of New South Wales, 1993, p. 193.
26   J. Davis, 'Federal City for Commonwealth of Australia', 31 December 1906, Series A100/1, Item A1907/238, National Archives.
27   J. Sulman, 'The Federal Capital of Australia', *Transactions of the Town Planning Conference, London, October 1910*, Royal Institute of British Architects, London, 1911, pp. 604–05.
28   Quoted in *Building*, December 1911, p. 70.
29   B. Maybeck to W.M. Hughes, PM, 5 January 1920, CRSA199, Department of Home Affairs, 22/1013, National Archives.
30   C.H. Caswell scrapbook, MS4058, National Library.
31   A. Benson, 'Canberra Design Competition of 1911: Contender for second place', *Canberra Historical Journal*, 3, 1979, pp. 8–13.
32   L.A. Curtis, 'The Federal Capital Designs', *The Surveyor*, 25, 1912, p. 169.
33   D. Van Zanten, 'Walter Burley Griffin's Design for Canberra, the Capital of Australia', in J. Zukowsky (ed), *Chicago Architecture 1872–1922*, Art Institute of Chicago, Chicago, 1987, p. 335.

34 'Copy of Federal Capital Design No. 29 by W.B. Griffin', Appendix B, in 'Report from the Select Committee appointed to inquire into and report upon The Development of Canberra', *Commonwealth Parliamentary Papers*, No. 52, September 1955.
35 J. Weirick, 'Walter Burley Griffin, Landscape Architect: The ideas he brought to Australia', *Landscape Australia*, 3, 1988, pp. 241–56.
36 *Building*, July 1912, p. 43.
37 W.B. Griffin, *The Federal Capital: Report Explanatory of the Preliminary General Plan*, Government Printer, 1913, pp. 15, 10.
38 Copy of Federal Capital Design No. 29 by W.B. Griffin', p. 96.
39 W.B. Griffin, in *City Club Bulletin*, February 1914, p. 66.
40 W.B. Griffin, *The Federal Capital: Report explanatory of the preliminary general plan*, Melbourne: Government Printer, 1913, p. 5.
41 Griffin, *The Federal Capital*, p. 1.
42 Quoted in Report from Select Committee, p. 80.
43 'Copy of Federal Capital Design No. 29 by W.B. Griffin', pp. 95, 96.
44 Van Zanten, 'Walter Burley Griffin's Design for Canberra', p. 339
45 'Copy of Federal Capital Design No. 29 by W.B. Griffin', p. 97.
46 C. Vernon, 'Walter Burley Griffin's American Landscape Oeuvre: Prelude to Canberra', Paper presented to the Urban History/Planning History Conference, Canberra, 1995.
47 M. Manieri-Elia, 'Toward an "Imperial City": Daniel H. Burnham and the City Beautiful Movement', in G. Giucci, et al, *The American City*, Granada, London, 1980, p. 113.
48 *Building*, June 1912, p. 48
49 Reid, *Canberra Following Griffin*, p. 23.
50 *Sydney Morning Herald*, 4 March 1914.
51 Caswell scrapbook, MS4058, National Library.
52 Benson, 'Canberra design competition of 1911', pp. 11–12.
53 Caswell scrapbook MS4058, National Library.
54 *Town Planning Review*, October 1912, pp. 166, 167.
55 *Garden Cities and Town Planning*, December 1912, p. 271.
56 F.W. Fitzpatrick, 'The Thrall of the Axis', *Building*, July 1915, p. 78.
57 Report of Board appointed to investigate and report as to suitability of certain designs for adoption in connexion with lay-out of federal capital, November 1912, *Commonwealth Parliamentary Papers*, 1912, Vol 2, p. 2.
58 D. Rowe, 'John Smith Murdoch and the Early Development of Canberra', *Fabrications*, 6, 1995, p. 34.
59 *The Salon*, March–April 1913, p. 266.
60 *Building*, December 1912, p. 42.
61 *Sydney Morning Herald*, 28 November 1912.
62 *Building*, June 1913, p. 47.
63 *Canberra: Capital City of the Commonwealth of Australia*, Government Printer, Melbourne, 1913, p. 31.
64 *Building*, June 1917, p. 27.
65 *Building*, December 1916, p. 49.
66 Federal Capital Advisory Committee, *First General Report*, 1921, p. 7.
67 J. Sulman to Minister for Works and Railways, 22 September 1922, National Archives, CRSA2717, Vol. 3, Folder 2.
68 *Journal and Proceedings of the Royal Society of New South Wales*, 35, 1901, p. 99.
69 D. Rowe, 'Building a National Image: The Architecture of John Smith Murdoch, Australia's First Commonwealth Government Architect', PhD thesis, Deakin University, 1997, Vol. 1, p. 233.
70 K.S. Inglis, *Sacred Places*, Melbourne University Press, Melbourne, 2nd ed, 2005, p. 333.
71 'The Australian War Museum as the Australian National War Memorial', 14 March 1922, CRSA2717, Vol 3, Folder 11, National Archives.

72   Reid, *Canberra Following Griffin*, p. 186; A. Roberts, 'Memorials in the National Capital: Developing a sense of national identity', *Canberra Historical Journal*, No 2, 1990, p. 6; and K. Taylor, 'Anzac Parade: A landscape of memory', *Canberra Historical Journal*, No 38, September 1996, p. 5.
73   'The Australian War Museum as the Australian National War Memorial'.
74   *Building*, March 1927, p. 42.
75   Sulman in Parliamentary Standing Committee on Public Works, 'Report together with Minutes of Evidence relating to the Proposed Australian War Memorial Canberra', May 1928. *Commonwealth Parliamentary Papers*, 1926–27–28.
76   *Building*, November 1941, p. 12.
77   Reid, *Canberra Following Griffin*, p. 177.
78   *Building*, March 1915, p. 11.

Chapter 5: City plans

1   C.C. Reade, *Planning and Development of Towns and Cities in South Australia*, Government Printer, Adelaide, 1919, p. 21.
2   A.W.J. Hutchings, 'The Development of Comprehensive Town Planning in South Australia, 1915–1930: Its Successes and Failures', MPlan thesis, University of Adelaide, 1985, p. 10.
3   R. Gibbons, 'Improving Sydney 1908–1909', in J. Roe (ed), *Twentieth Century Sydney*, Hale and Iremonger, Sydney, 1980, p. 120.
4   J.D. Fitzgerald, 'Sydney: The Cinderella of Cities', *The Lone Hand*, 1, 1907, p. 58.
5   *Sydney Morning Herald*, 10 December 1908.
6   *Building*, September 1907, p. 14.
7   Town Clerk to City Building Surveyor, 20 May 1908, CRS 1147/08, Sydney City Council Archives.
8   E. Irvin, *Sydney as It Might Have Been*, Alpha Books, Sydney, 1974.
9   J. Barlow, 'The City Beautiful', *Journal of the Institute of Architects of New South Wales*, 1(1), 1904, p. 9.
10   Report of the Royal Commission for the Improvement of the City of Sydney and Its Suburbs, 1909, *New South Wales Parliamentary Papers*, Vol 5, p. v.
11   *Building*, July 1909, p. 35.
12   E.W. O'Sullivan quoted in B. Mansfield, *Australian Democrat*, Sydney University Press, Sydney, 1965, p. 292.
13   A. Sutcliffe, *Towards the Planned City*, Basil Blackwell, Oxford, 1981, p. 173.
14   Under Secretary of Public Works Department to Coulter, 13 October 1909, in R.G.C. Coulter, *Book of Me*, National Archives, Series M1535.
15   *Journal of the Royal Institute of British Architects*, 17, 1910, p. 537; *Town Planning Review*, 1910, 1, p. 160.
16   Report of the Royal Commission, p. xxxviii.
17   C.C. Reade, 'Foreword', in *Official Volume of Proceedings of the First Australian Town Planning and Housing Conference and Exhibition Adelaide 1917*, Vardon and Sons, Adelaide, 1918, p. 6
18   Report of the Royal Commission, Minutes of Evidence, p. 69.
19   Report of the Royal Commission, p. lix.
20   J.R. Logan and H. Molotch, *Urban Fortunes: The Political Economy of Place*, University of California Press, Los Angeles, 1987.
21   *Building*, July 1909, p. 35.
22   *Sydney Morning Herald*, 18 March 1911, p. 7
23   *Town Planning Review*, 1910, 1, p. 160
24   *Journal of the Royal Institute of British Architects*, 17, 1910, p. 537.
25   D. Winston, *Sydney's Great Experiment*, Angus and Robertson, Sydney, 1957, p. 26.
26   Letter to the editor from R.C.G. Coulter, 11 May 1915, Newspaper cutting, TC528/13, Sydney City Council Archives.
27   M. Kelly, *Faces in the Street*, Doak Press, Sydney, 1982, p. 12.

28 *Art and Architecture*, March–April 1912, p. 453.
29 *The Salon*, September–October 1912, p. 103.
30 *Building*, July 1909, p. 35.
31 *The Bulletin*, 31 December 1908, p. 6.
32 Report of the Royal Commission, Minutes of Evidence, p. 63.
33 B.J. Opie, 'Frederick Charles Cook', *Royal Australian Planning Institute Journal*, 10, 1972, p. 160.
34 *Building*, April 1923, p. 129.
35 *Morning Post* (Melbourne), 20 November 1925.
36 All three quotations in this paragraph from *Report of the Metropolitan Town Planning Commission*, Government Printer, Perth, 1931, p. 112.
37 Metropolitan Town Planning Commission, *Plan of General Development*, Melbourne, 1929, p. 276.

Chapter 6: Civic centres

1   T. Kimball and H.V. Hubbard, *Our Cities To-Day and To-Morrow*, Harvard University Press, p. 264
2   D.M. Bluestone, 'Detroit's city beautiful and the problem of commerce', *Journal of the Society of Architectural Historians*, 47, 1988, p. 257.
3   P. Abercrombie, *Town and Country Planning*, Oxford University Press, London, 3rd ed, 1959, p. 100.
4   G.S. Jones, 'Australia and Civic Art', *Architecture*, 2(4), 1917, p. 85.
5   W.S. Griffiths, 'Town Planning – Part II', *Shire and Municipal Record*, May 1913, p. 513.
6   J. Sulman, *An Introduction to the Study of Town Planning in Australia*, NSW Government Printer, Sydney, 1921, p. 148.
7   *Building*, May 1922, pp. 32f–32g.
8   *Architecture*, 1941, 41, p. 65.
9   Griffiths, 'Town Planning, Part II', p. 513.
10 W.E. Bold, 'The Distribution of Parks, Playgrounds and Other Open Spaces', in *Official Volume of Proceedings of the Second Australian Town Planning Conference and Exhibition*, Brisbane, 1918, p. 156.
11 W.F. Gates, 'Parks and Playgrounds', *Official Volume of Proceedings of the First Victorian Town Planning Conference*, Ballarat, 1919, pp. 49–50.
12 G.S. Jones, 'The Grouping of Public Buildings', *Architecture*, November 1921, 119–22.
13 Sulman, *Town Planning in Australia*, pp. 70, 80.
14 *Building*, March 1919, p. 87.
15 *Building*, October 1924, p. 138.
16 *Building*, July 1920, p. 61.
17 *Building*, June 1915, p. 96.
18 A.S. Conrad, 'Town Planning Suggestions for Adelaide and the Metropolitan Area', *Official Volume of Proceedings of the First Australian Town Planning and Housing Conference and Exhibition Adelaide 1917*, Vardon and Sons, Adelaide, 1918, p. 89.
19 *The Salon*, May–June 1913, pp. 347–48.
20 *Architectural and Building Journal of Queensland*, March 1927, pp. 41–44.
21 *Building*, July 1917, p. 80.
22 W.M. Campbell, 'The Streets of Melbourne from an Architectural Point of View', *Journal of the Royal Victorian Institute of Architects*, 1, 1904, pp. 179–88.
23 *Australian Municipal Journal*, May 1925, p. 210.
24 Sulman, *Town Planning in Australia*, p. 78.
25 *Australian Municipal Journal*, January 1924, p. 11.
26 *Building*, July 1928, pp.132–36.
27 J. Keily, 'Study on Unity of Design Planning New Towns and New Suburbs', *Transactions and Proceedings, Victorian Institute of Surveyors*, 3, 1891, pp. 88–104.
28 *Building*, August 1920, p. 87.
29 *Building*, August 1920, p. 90.

30   *Building*, May, 1923, p. 136.
31   *Journal of the Royal Victorian Institute of Architects*, 18, 1920, p. 104; Sulman, *Town Planning in Australia*, p.78.
32   F. Koester, *Modern City Planning and Maintenance*, McBride-Nast and Co, London, 1915, p. 23.
33   W.R. Butler, 'Architectural Aspects of Town Planning', *Journal of the Royal Victorian Institute of Architects*, 15, 1917, p.84.
34   J.S. Gawler, *A Roof Over My Head*, Lothian, Melbourne, 1963, p. 20.
35   J.A. Smith, 'A Solution of Melbourne's Civic Centre Problem', *Journal of the Royal Victorian Institute of Architects*, 23, 1925, p. 140.
36   *Building*, March 1923, pp. 42–43.
37   *Building*, May 1925, p. 146.
38   *Building*, June 1921, p. 51.
39   Sulman, *Town Planning in Australia*, p. 78.
40   City of Perth, *Mayor's Report 1909–1910*, p. 16.
41   W.E. Bold, 'Perth Improvement', typescript, 6 November 1911, pp. 3–4.
42   *West Australian*, 26 August 1911, p. 14.
43   M.J. Webb, 'Urban Expansion, Town Improvement and the Beginning of Town Planning in Metropolitan Perth', in J. Gentilli (ed) *Western Landscapes*, University of Western Australia Press, Perth, 1979, p. 376.
44   *WA Mining, Building and Engineering Journal*, 3 July 1915.
45   *WA Mining, Building and Engineering Journal*, 6 July 1917.
46   R.K. Clark, 'The City Beautiful: Promise and reality', *The Architect*, 10(2), 1969, p. 44.
47   W.E. Bold, *Civic Reminiscences 1896–1943*, typescript, Battye Library, 1943, p. 8.
48   Clark, 'The City Beautiful', p. 42.
49   Sulman, *Town Planning in Australia*, p. 78.
50   Clark, 'The City Beautiful', p. 44.
51   City of Perth, *Mayor's Report 1927–28*, p. 13.
52   *Report of the Metropolitan Town Planning Commission*, Government Printer, Perth, 1931, p. 5.
53   *Building*, May 1926, p. 70.
54   Engineer in Chief, Department of Works and Labour, to Town Planning Commission, 17 April 1930. Metropolitan Town Planning Commission Records, AN 93/ACC 955, File 23, State Archives of Western Australia.
55   'Town Planning', Report by the Town Clerk, 19 July 1931, Bold Papers, 638A, Battye Library.
56   *Property Owner*, April 1921, p. 2.
57   Report of the Royal Commission for the Improvement of the City of Sydney and Its Suburbs, 1909, Minutes of Evidence, p. 81, *New South Wales Parliamentary Papers*, Vol 5.
58   Report of the Royal Commission, p. xlvi.
59   Report of the Royal Commission, Minutes of Evidence, p. 228.
60   *Architecture*, August 1938, pp. 192–97.
61   Sulman, Town Planning in Australia, p. 80.
62   *Building*, September 1916, p. 9; cf. *Building*, July 1920, pp. 59–61.
63   *Architecture*, August 1924, pp. 1–8.
64   *Commonwealth Home*, December 1929, p. 29; *Building*, April 1930, p. 92; 'The Main Traffic Avenues of Sydney', by Sir John Sulman 9 April 1928, TC4322/27, Sydney City Council Archives.
65   *Building*, June 1927, pp. 77–78.
66   *Building*, September 1917, p. 13.
67   *Building*, February 1918, pp. 17–18.
68   P.E. Everett, 'Geelong an Example of Community's Pride', in H. Desbrowe-Annear, *For Every Man His Home*, Alexander McCubbin, Melbourne, 1922, pp. 61–63. See also G. Lehmann, 'George R. King – "Kingmaker" in a Regional City', in C.L. Miller and M.M. Roche (eds), *Proceedings of the 8th Australasian Urban History/Planning History*

Conference, Massey University, Wellington, 2006, pp. 245–58.

69   W.H. Wilson, *The City Beautiful Movement*, Johns Hopkins University Press, Baltimore, 1989, p. 294.

Chapter 7: Public spaces

1   *Architecture*, June 1920, p. 180.
2   *WA Mining Building and Engineering Journal*, 19 October 1912, p. 19.
3   M. Webb, *The City Square*, Thames and Hudson, London, 1990, p. 9.
4   T. Mawson, *Civic Art*, BT Batsford, London, 1911, p. 100.
5   R. Unwin, *Town Planning in Practice*, T Fisher Unwin, London, 1909, p. 138.
6   W.A. Saw, 'Some Aspects of Town Planning', *Journal and Proceedings of Royal Society of Western Australia*, 5, 1919, p. 61.
7   J. Sulman, *An Introduction to the Study of Town Planning in Australia*, NSW Government Printer, Sydney, 1921, p. 89.
8   Mawson, *Civic Art*, p. 98.
9   *Building*, May 1910, pp. 59–64.
10   W.S. Griffiths, 'Town Planning – Part II', *Shire and Municipal Record*, May 1913, p. 513.
11   W.H. Morris, 'The City Square: Its Value and Treatment', *Commonwealth Home*, May 1930 (pp. 45–47); June 1930 (pp. 45–47).
12   G. Davison, 'Public Life and Public Space: A lament for Melbourne's City Square', *Historic Environment*, 1(1), 1994, p. 5.
13   *Building*, April 1923, p. 129.
14   *Building*, June 1933, p. 98.
15   Davison, 'Public Life and Public Space'; J. Williams, 'The Search for a Square', *Victorian Historical Journal*, 63(2 & 3), 1992, pp. 50–63. N. Day 'The Struggle to Build a City Square…', *Architecture Australia*, 65(4), 1976, pp. 22–39
16   *Building*, April 1923, p. 130.
17   *Journal of the Royal Victorian Institute of Architects*, 34, 1936, pp. 65–67.
18   *Australasian Builder and Contractors' News*, 16 August 1890, p. 113.
19   B. Hamilton, 'Town Planning Principles and Civic Improvement', *Journal of the Royal Victorian Institute of Architects*, 22, 1924, p. 112.
20   *Journal of the Royal Victorian Institute of Architects*, 26, 1928, pp. 95–99.
21   *Building*, March 1929, pp. 141–42.
22   'Discussion on the Proposed Cathedral Square', *Journal of the Royal Victorian Institute of Architects*, 26, 1928, p. 212.
23   Victorian Town Planning Association, *Annual Report*, Melbourne, 1928.
24   *Sydney Morning Herald*, 13 May 1914.
25   *Commonwealth Home*, February 1930, p. 3
26   *Architecture*, May 1932, pp. 108–116.
27   *Building*, September 1935, p. 32.
28   D. Gazzard, 'The Peoples' Promenade: Martin Place 1860–1985', in G.P. Webber (ed), *The Design of Sydney*, The Law Book Company, Sydney, 1988, pp. 70–93.
29   *Art and Architecture*, July–August 1907, pp. 134–37.
30   *Sydney Morning Herald*, 26 May 1920; J.J.C. Bradfield, 'City Squares and Central Avenue', *Architecture*, June 1920, pp. 187–91; R. Freestone and B. Hanna, *Florence Taylor's Hats*, Halstead Press, Sydney, 2007; *Building*, September 1927, p. 65.
31   *Architecture*, June 1920, p. 180.
32   *Building*, June 1937; 'Minute by the Lord Mayor (Norman L Nock), 10 March 1939', in Proceedings of the Municipal Council of the City of Sydney, 1939. p. 418.
33   *Building*, June 1922, p. 53.
34   Conservation Plan, Credit Union Australia Building, 501 Ann Street, Brisbane, 1991, R. Irving and C. Pratten, p. 6.
35   J. Sulman, 'The Cities of Australia and their Development', *Official Volume of Proceedings of the First Australian Town Planning and Housing Conference and Exhibition Adelaide 1917*, Vardon and Sons, Adelaide, 1918, p. 61.

36   *Brisbane Courier*, 30 October 1923.
37   Parliamentary Standing Committee on Public Works, 'Report relating to the Acquisition of Lands for the Proposed Anzac Memorial Square, Queensland', July 1921, *Commonwealth Parliamentary Papers*, Vol. 5, 1920–21.
38   *Building*, October 1925, p. 151.
39   *Building*, October 1923, p. 145.
40   'Anzac Square, Brisbane', National Archives, CRS A361, DSG23/764.
41   In evidence 7 October 1922, Parliamentary Standing Committee on Public Works, 'Report together with Minutes of Evidence Relating to the Proposed Erection of Commonwealth Offices, Brisbane', October 1922, *Commonwealth Parliamentary Papers*, Vol. 2, 1923–24.
42   *Architectural and Building Journal of Queensland*, November 1924, pp. 27–28.
43   D. Rowe, 'Building a National Image: The Architecture of John Smith Murdoch, Australia's First Commonwealth Government Architect', PhD thesis, Deakin University, 1997, Vol 1, p. 232.
44   *Lest We Forget*, brochure, June 1927.
45   Queensland National Anzac Memorial. An Appeal; Pro-forma Letter from WA Jolly, 25 July 1928; Anzac Square file, Brisbane City Council records.
46   Report of Adjudicators, 3 November 28, reported to Meeting of the BCC Executive Committee, 11 December 1928, Anzac Square file, Brisbane City Council records.
47   *Architectural and Building Journal of Queensland*, 10 January 1929; *Brisbane Courier*, 5 July 1929; Buchanan and Cowper, on the Anzac National memorial in course of erection for the Anzac National Memorial Committee of Queensland, 13 May 1930, Brisbane City Council records.
48   *Architectural and Building Journal of Queensland*, 10 December 1930, p. 11.
49   *Architectural and Building Journal of Queensland*, 7 November 1922, p. 20.
50   *Architectural and Building Journal of Queensland*, 7 September 1923, p. 12.
51   *Architectural and Building Journal of Queensland*, 8 December 1924, pp. 14–15.
52   *Architectural and Building Journal of Queensland*, 10 November 1927, p. 68.
53   *Building*, June 1927, p. 155.
54   *Architectural and Building Journal of Queensland*, 11 March 1929, p. 79.
55   C.G. Hilford, 'Forrest Place Perth: Its Origins, Present Function and Future Role', M.Arch thesis, University of Western Australia, 1971, p. 8.
56   Quoted in Hilford, 'Forrest Place', p. 21.
57   *West Australian*, 24 January 1914.
58   Rowe, 'Building a National Image', Vol 1, p. 242.
59   *WA Mining, Building and Engineering Journal*, 18 October 1923.
60   *West Australian*, 28 July 1922.
61   *West Australian*, 6 February 1923.

Chapter 8: The campus beautiful

1   See series of articles by A.M. Githens in the American journal, *The Brickbuilder*, on 'Group Plans' for fairs, expositions, schools, colleges, and other monumental groups, running intermittently from 1906 to 1913.
2   *Architecture*, October 1918, p. 87.
3   C.R. Boughton and G. Caiger, *A Coast Chronicle*, Board of the Prince Henry Hospital, Sydney, 1963, p. 80.
4   'The New Show Grounds of the Royal Agricultural Society of South Australia', c1924, Heath papers, State Library of Victoria.
5   T. Bender (ed), *The University and the City*, Oxford University Press, New York, 1990, p. 59.
6   Contemporary quotation in C. Brentano, ' "Stately and Glorious Buildings": The Origins of the University of California's Campus Plan', *Planning History*, 16(3), 1994, p. 8.
7   C.Z. Klauder and H.C. Wise, *College Architecture in America*, Charles Scribner's Sons,

New York, 1929, p. 25.

8   W. Hegemann and E. Peets, *The American Vitruvius*, Architectural Book Publishing Co., New York, 1922, p. 111.

9   C.M. Robinson, *Modern Civic Art*, G.P. Putnam's Sons, New York, 1904, p. 275.

10   T. Hines, *Burnham of Chicago*, University of Chicago Press, New York, 1979, p. 226.

11   Quoted in W.T. Booth and W.H. Wilson, 'Carl F Gould: His Planning and Architecture at the University of Washington', *Pacific Northwest Quarterly*, 85, 1994, p. 109.

12   Klauder and Wise, *College Architecture in America*, p. 31.

13   P.V. Turner, *Campus*, MIT Press, Cambridge, Massachusetts, 1984.

14   R.A.M Stern, et al, *New York 1900*, Rizzoli, New York, 1983, p. 405.

15   R.P. Dober, *Campus Planning*, Reinhold, New York, 1963; J.W. Cody, *Building in China: Henry K Murphy's 'Adaptive Architecture' 1914–1935*, The Chinese University Press, Hong Kong, 2001.

16   GE Cherry, et al, 'Gardens, civic art and town planning: the work of Thomas H. Mawson (1861–1933)', *Planning Perspectives*, 8, 1993, pp. 307–332.

17   P.J. Larkham, 'The University and the City', Keynote address, Fifth Symposium of the Planning History Study Group (South Africa), University of Stellenbosch, April 1998, p. 12.

18   J.W.R. Whitehand, 'Institutional Site Planning: the University of Birmingham, England, 1900–1969', *Planning History*, 13 (2), 1991, pp. 29–35.

19   S. Muthesius, *The Postwar University*, Yale University Press, New Haven, 2000.

20   E. Haarhof, 'Modernisation in the Colonies: The Garden City Movement in New Zealand', in R. Freestone (ed), *The Twentieth Century Urban Planning Experience*, Proceedings of the 8th International Planning History Conference, Sydney, 1998, pp. 312–17.

21   C. Rasmussen, 'Universities', in G. Davison, et al, (eds) *Oxford Companion to Australian History*, Oxford University Press, Melbourne, pp. 657–58.

22   Leslie Wilkinson quoted in S. Falkiner (ed), *Leslie Wilkinson*, Valadon, Sydney, 1982, p. 60.

23   S.G Foster and M.M. Varghese, *The Making of the Australian National University*, Allen and Unwin, Sydney, 1996, p. 70.

24   L. Wilkinson, 'University Architecture', in *Report of the Eighteenth Meeting of the Australasian Association for the Advancement of Science*, WA Government Printer, Perth, 1926, p. 612.

25   C. Vernon, 'An "accidental" Australian: Walter Burley Griffin's Australian–American landscape art', in J. Turnbull and P. Navaretti (eds), *The Griffins in Australia and India*, 1998, Miegunyah Press, Melbourne, pp. 2–15.

26   D. Dexter, *The ANU Campus*, Australian National University, Canberra, 1991.

27   G.A. Taylor, *Town Planning for Australia*, Building, Sydney, 1914, p. 50.

28   Wilkinson, quoted in Falkiner, *Leslie Wilkinson*, p. 60.

29   *The Salon*, 2, 1913, pp. 249–51.

30   *Building*, May 1921, p. 78.

31   M.M. Griffin, 'The Magic of America', typescript, New York Historical Society, p.152.

32   *Building*, May 1921, p. 78.

33   *Building*, April 1921, p. 66.

34   Quoted in Falkiner, *Leslie Wilkinson*, p. 67.

35   *Building*, April 1921, p. 64.

36   J. Sulman, *An Introduction to the Study of Town Planning in Australia*, NSW Government Printer, Sydney, 1921, p. 154.

37   G. Jahn, *Sydney Architecture*, Watermark Press, Sydney, 1997.

38   J.W. Hackett to the Senate of the University of Western Australia, 16 November 1914, University of Western Australia Archives.

39   Chancellor J.W. Hackett quoted in C. Vernon, 'Pre-eminence of Landscape: The University of Western Australia, 1914–1927', Perth, 1998.

40   *Architecture*, November 1915, p. 97.

41   Harriet Edquist, *Harold Desbrowe-Annear*, Miegunyah Press, Melbourne, 2004, p. 104.

42   G. and F. Stephenson, 'Planning for the University of Western Australia', *Town Planning Review*, 37, 1966, p. 25.

43   R.J. Ferguson, *Crawley Campus,* University of Western Australia Press, Perth, 1993.

44   J.M. Bagot, *Reveries in Retrospect*, Hassell Press, Adelaide, 1946, p. 53.

45   *Australian Dictionary of Biography*, Vol 7, 1979, p. 133.

46   D. Jones, ' "A Plea for Tradition": The ideas of Walter Hervey Bagot and his Mediterranean landscapes', *Studies in the History of Gardens and Designed Landscapes*, 21, 2001, p. 97.

47   W.G.K. Duncan and R.A. Leonard, *The University of Adelaide 1874–1974*, Rigby, Adelaide, 1973, p. 126.

48   D. Jones, 'A focus for celebration and ceremonial: Bagot's vision for the Library forecourt', *Adelaidian*, 10 April 1995, p. 8.

49   Quoted in Brian Pascoe (ed), *A Guide to the Great Court*, University of Queensland Press, Brisbane, 1992, p. 2.

50   Quoted in J.J.C. Bradfield, 'University at Saint Lucia Lay-Out', p. 7. Address before the Senate and Staff of the University at the Geology Theatre, 22 June 1936, University of Queensland Archives.

51   C.C. Nakkash, 'Original Site Planning University of Queensland', B.Arch thesis, University of Queensland, 1990, p. 20.

52   F.W. Robinson, 'A New University at St. Lucia', p. 6. A paper read before 'Shop Talk' Association of members of Staff at the University of Queensland, on Friday 13 October 1933, University of Queensland Archives.

53   Bradfield, 'University at Saint Lucia Lay-Out', p. 12.

54   Report of the University (St Lucia) Building Committee to the Honourable W Forgan Smith LLD Premier of Queensland, 20 June 1936, University of Queensland Archives.

55   M.I. Thomis, *A Place of Light and Learning*, University of Queensland Press, Brisbane, 1985, p. 165.

56   Bradfield, 'University at Saint Lucia Lay-Out', pp. 21–22.

57   J.C. Hennessy, Letter to W Forgan Smith, 14 September 1936, Chief Secretary's Office, 6514/36, Queensland State Archives.

58   Quoted in Thomis, A Place of Light and Learning, p. 347.

59   G. Stephenson, 'The Physical Planning of Universities', *Australian Planning Institute Journal*, 3, 1965, p. 149.

60   Hegemann and Peets, 1922, p. 115.

61   E.G. Waterhouse, 'The Landscape Treatment of the Campus', *Architecture,* 24, 1935, p. 248.

62   R. Boyd, *The Australian Ugliness*, Penguin, Melbourne, 1968, p. 33.

Chapter 9: Parks, parkways and the street beautiful

1   C.M. Robinson, The Improvement of Towns and Cities, G.P. Putnam's Sons, New York, 1901.

2   G.B. Burnap, *Parks,* JB Lippincott, Philadelphia, 1916, p. 58.

3   City of Adelaide, *Mayor's Minute*, 1908, p. 22.

4   *Art and Architecture,* July–August 1906, p. 149.

5   *Building,* August 1918, p. 85.

6   W.H. Wilson, *The City Beautiful Movement*, Johns Hopkins University Press, Baltimore, 1989, p. 79.

7   J.M. Carrère, 'City Improvement From The Artist's Standpoint', *Western Architect*, 15, 1910, p. 44.

8   Robinson, *The Improvement of Towns and Cities*, p. 165.

9   *Building,* May 1923, pp. 44–52.

10   J. Sulman, *An Introduction to the Study of Town Planning in Australia*, NSW Government Printer, Sydney, 1921, p. 130.

11   *Architecture*, April 1927, p. 1.

12 J.H. Maiden, *A Guide to the Botanic Gardens*, NSW Government Printer, Sydney, 1903, p. 9.

13 I. Hoskins, 'Cultivating the Citizen: Cultural Politics in the Parks and Gardens of Sydney, 1880–1930', PhD thesis, University of Sydney.

14 *Building*, September 1922, p. 72.

15 *Building*, August 1910, p. 50.

16 *Building*, July 1918, pp. 95–97.

17 Mayors Valedictory Address 1910, City of Launceston.

18 Robinson, *The Improvement of Towns and Cities*, p. 313.

19 J. Sulman, 'The Federal Capital', *Transactions of the Town Planning Conference, London, October 1910, Royal Institute of British Architects, London, 1911*, p. 607.

20 Report of the Royal Commission for the Improvement of the City of Sydney and Its Suburbs, 1909, *New South Wales Parliamentary Papers*, Vol 5, Minutes of Evidence, pp. 127–28.

21 'My Work at Harvard' (typescript), c1934, 17/13, Denis Winston papers, University of Sydney Archives.

22 G. Inskip, 'The Federal City: A Few Suggestions', *Proceedings at the Congress of Engineers, Architects, Surveyors, and others interested in the Federal Capital of Australia held in Melbourne*, JC Stephens, Melbourne, 1901, p. 31.

23 C.B. Luffman, 'The Agricultural, Horticultural, and Sylvan Features of a Federal Capital', *Proceedings of the Congress*, pp. 43–45.

24 J. Sulman, *The Federal Capital*, John Sands, Sydney, 1909, p. 18.

25 C. Heath, 'The New Melbourne General Cemetery at Fawkner', no date (c1927), Frank Heath papers, Box 82, State Library of Victoria.

26 K. Taylor, *Canberra: City in the Landscape*, Halstead Press, Sydney, 2006.

27 H. Proudfoot, *Statement of Significance and Historical Analysis*, Prepared for the Council of the City of Sydney, 1987.

28 *Building*, May 1924, p. 44.

29 *Building*, March 1928, p. 86.

30 *Building*, March 1932, p. 32l–32m.

31 *Building*, March 1922, p. 55.

32 *Commonwealth Home*, January 1929, p. 24.

33 *Building*, December 1934, p. 15.

34 Quoted in Proudfoot, *Statement of Significance*, p. 59.

35 Proudfoot, *Statement of Significance*, p. 69.

36 State Gardens Board, *Twenty Years Progress and Policy 1919–1939*, Perth, 1939, p. 26.

37 C. Garnaut, 'The Soldiers Memorial Gardens Victor Harbour: "An Emblem of Love and Reverence" ', *Landscape Australia*, 21(2), 1999, pp. 117–21.

38 SA Government Town Planner, *Annual Report*, 1922–23.

39 P. Spearritt, *Sydney's Century*, UNSW Press, Sydney, 2000, pp. 28–29.

40 *Building*, April 1924, p. 54.

41 *Building*, January 1930, pp. 93–94.

42 *Building*, August 1930, pp. 56–59.

43 *Building*, January 1931, p. 91.

44 G. Souter, *Mosman: A History*, Melbourne University Press, Melbourne, 1994.

45 W.E. Bold, 'The Distribution of Parks, Playgrounds and Other Open Spaces', *Official Volume of Proceedings of the Second Australian Town Planning Conference and Exhibition*, Brisbane, 1918, p. 154.

46 C.H. Klem, 'Report on Tentative Design of Proposed Layout of the City of Perth's Endowment lands and Limekilns Estate', Town Planning Association of Western Australia Records, 641A, J.S. Battye Library of West Australian History.

47 R.K. Clark, 'The City Beautiful: Promise and reality', *The Architect*, 10(2), 1969, p. 43.

48 K.S. Inglis, *Sacred Places*, Melbourne University Press, Melbourne, 2nd ed, 2005, p. 156.

49 *Building*, February 1923, p. 41.

50 A.S. Conrad, 'Town Planning Suggestions for Adelaide and the Metropolitan Area',

Official Volume of Proceedings of the First Australian Town Planning and Housing Conference and Exhibition Adelaide 1917, Vardon and Sons, Adelaide, 1918, p. 91.

51   *Light Journal of Town Planning and Housing*, June 1920, p. 18.

52   *The Mail*, 14 February 1920.

53   C. Garnaut, *'Making modern towns': Charles Reade and the introduction of town planning to South Australia: 1914–1920*, Crossing Press, Sydney, 2007.

54   C. Faro with G. Wotherspoon, *Street Seen*, Melbourne University Press, Melbourne, 2000.

55   *Building*, February 1909, p. 30.

56   Report of the Royal Commission, Minutes of Evidence, p. 168.

57   Sydney City Council, 29 July 1909 Minute, pp 1–2.

58   Lord Mayors Room Conference, 1 June 1916, *TC830/16*, Sydney City Council Archives.

59   Letter to Mayor, Randwick Council 7 March 1917, TC830/16; Obelisk for Anzac Avenue, TC64/17; Anzac Parade – naming of Anzac Avenue – renamed Haig Ave, TC168/17, Sydney City Council Archives.

60   J. Foster, 'The Fitzroy Gardens, Melbourne', *Landscape Australia*, 2/84, 1984, p. 82.

61   *Melbourne Punch*, 19 August 1858.

62   W. Butler, 'Architectural Aspects of Town Planning', *Journal of the Royal Victorian Institute of Architects*, 15, 1917, p. 87.

63   C.F. Summers, *Proposed Monumental Zone*, Melbourne, 1901; *Argus*, 1 March 1901; *Age*, 1 May 1901.

64   *Sun*, 24 May 1901.

65   B. Hall, 'The Beautifying of a City' in *Proceedings at the Congress*, pp. 47–51.

66   J. McClaggan, 'Melbourne Street Gardens', *The Lone Hand*, August 1908, pp. 428–32.

67   G. Whitehead, 'Melbourne's Public Gardens: A Family Tree', *Victorian Historical Journal*, 63 (2 & 3), 1992, pp. 101–17.

68   T. Dingle, 'Carlo Catani and the Creation of Alexandra Avenue', Paper presented to the Australian Garden History Society Conference 2000, Melbourne.

69   *Official Guide to Melbourne for the Visitor*, Fraser & Jenkinson, Melbourne.

70   *Building*, March 1918, p. 92.

71   McClaggan, 'Melbourne Street Gardens', p. 429.

72   G. Whitehead, *Civilising the City*, State Library of Victoria, Melbourne, 1997, p. 53.

73   J.R. Buckrich, *Melbourne's Grand Boulevard*, State Library of Victoria, Melbourne, 1996

74   R.T.M. Pescott, *The Royal Botanic Gardens, Melbourne*, Oxford University Press, Melbourne, 1982, p. 47.

75   J.B. Cooper, *The History of St Kilda 1840–1930*, Melbourne, 1931, p. 142

76   J. Grant and G. Serle, *The Melbourne Scene 1803–1956*, Hale and Iremonger, Sydney, 1978, pp. 198–99.

77   J.D. Fitzgerald, 'Parks and Open Places', *The Lone Hand*, June 1907, p. 200.

78   *Building*, July 1923, pp. 29–30.

79   W.B. Russell, *We Will Remember Them*, Trustees of the Shrine of Remembrance, Melbourne, 1991, p. 11.

80   W. Lucas, 'A War Memorial for Melbourne', *Journal of the Royal Victorian Institute of Architects*, May, 1919, pp. 52–53.

81   *Australian Municipal Journal*, July 1921, p. 32.

82   *Building*, November 1921, p. 45

83   *Building*, March 1922, supplement.

84   G. Wilson and P. Sands, *Building of a City: 100 Years of Melbourne Architecture*, Oxford University Press, Melbourne, 1981.

85   'The National War Memorial', in H. Desbrowe-Annear (ed), *For Every Man His Home*, 1922, pp. 52–53.

86   *Building*, December 1934, p. 20.

87   *Building*, February 1924, p. 3.

88   *Building*, March 1924, pp. 134–36.

89   P. Isaacson, 'The Shrine of remembrance', *Victorian Historical Journal*, 70(1), 1999, p. 47.
90   Russell, *We Will Remember Them*, p. 16.
91   A. Brown-May, *Highway of Civilisation and Common-Sense*, Urban Research Program, Australian National University, 1995, p.7.
92   J. Kerr, 'Casually Picturesque, Consciously Ideal', in J. Davidson (ed), *The Sydney Melbourne Book*, Allen and Unwin, Melbourne, 1986, p. 187.
93   'Alexandra Avenue, Melbourne', *The Red Funnel*, January, 1906, pp. 477–79.
94   J.C. Morrell, *Town Planning*, Report to the Victorian Minister for Public Works, 1915, p. 78.
95   J.C. Morrell, 'The Town Planning Problem of Metropolitan Melbourne', *Proceedings of the First Australian Town Planning Conference Adelaide 1917*, p. 107.
96   K. Otto, *Yarra*, Text Publishing, Melbourne, 2005, p. 131.
97   *Highways*, 15 June 1933, p. 3.
98   *Building*, May 1933, p. 73.
99   *Shire and Municipal Record*, 15 June 1916, pp. 550–51.

Chapter 10: The everyday landscape

1   *Building*, July 1917, p. 76.
2   C.M. Robinson, *The Improvement of Towns and Cities*, G.P. Putnam's Sons, New York, 1901, p. 110.
3   G.H. Knibbs, 'The Theory of City Design', *Journal and Proceedings of the Royal Society of New South Wales*, 35, 1901, p. 89.
4   F. Koester, *Modern City Planning and Maintenance*, McBride Nast, London, 1915, pp. 149, 148.
5   *Art and Architecture*, September–October 1908, pp. 190–192.
6   *Building*, April 1929, p. 133.
7   W.E. Bold, *Report on Tour Round the World*, Perth City Council, 1914, p. 39.
8   City Beautification, CRS28/1499/09, Sydney City Council Archives.
9   A. Brown-May, *The Highway of Civilisation and Common-Sense*, Urban Research Program, Australian National University, 1995, p. 42.
10   *Building*, April 1929, p. 132.
11   *Art and Architecture*, September 1905, p. 222.
12   *Building*, May 1930, p. 88.
13   *NSW Contract Reporter*, 22 November 1910.
14   Robinson, *The Improvement of Towns and Cities*, p. 63.
15   NSW Parliamentary Debates, 14 November 1912, p. 3224.
16   NSW Parliamentary Debates, 14 November 1912, p. 3223.
17   M. Lewis, *Melbourne: The City's History and Development*, Melbourne City Council, 1995, p. 95.
18   *Building*, November 1925.
19   *Architectural and Building Journal of Queensland*, November 1927, p. 24.
20   *Art and Architecture*, March–April 1912, p. 451.
21   *Building*, August 1917, p. 73.
22   *Building*, November 1928, p. 35.
23   *Argus*, 31 May 1913.
24   Report of the Royal Commission of Inquiry into the Question of the Constitution of a Greater Sydney, Minutes of Evidence, *NSW Parliamentary Papers*, 1913, Vol. 2, p. 169.
25   Quoted in F. Somers, 'The Life and Works of John Bede Barlow', B.Arch. thesis, University of New South Wales, 1970.
26   *Building*, December 1916, pp. 59–60.
27   *Architecture*, September 1929, p. 221.
28   *Building*, May 1929, p. 87.
29   K.S. Inglis, *Sacred Places*, Melbourne University Press, Melbourne, 2nd ed, 2005, p. 151.

30   J. McKay, 'Putting the Digger on a pedestal', *Historic Environment*, 3, 1986, pp. 5–19.
31   *Journal of the Royal Victorian Institute of Architects*, March 1919, pp. 9–11.
32   Inglis, *Sacred Places*, p. 150.
33   NSW Department of Local Government, *War Memorials*, Bulletin No 4, NSW Government Printer, Sydney, 1920.
34   *Architecture*, January 1920, pp. 25–26.
35   J. Sulman, 'Town Planning' (manuscript), c1933, p. 17, Sulman Papers, Mitchell Library.
36   Inglis, *Sacred Places*, p. 154.
37   *The Register,* 23 May 1918.
38   *Building*, June 1929, p. 97.
39   Report of the Local Government Department, June 1920, *NSW Parliamentary Papers*, 1920, Vol 3, Part 2.
40   *Building*, September 1919, p. 79.
41   *Building*, June 1919, pp. 81–82.
42   *Australian Municipal Journal*, July 1921, p. 32.
43   *Building*, June 1924, p. 137.
44   R.W. Lahey, 'The Application of Aesthetics to the Design of Bridges', *Architectural and Building Journal of Queensland*, July 1927, pp. 23–30.
45   S. Falkiner, *Leslie Wilkinson,* Valadon, Sydney, 1982, pp. 113–14.
46   T.R. Ashworth, 'Construction and Aesthetics of the Church Street Bridge', *Journal of the Royal Victorian Institute of Architects*, 22, 1924, pp. 138–57.
47   *Building*, April 1930, p. 64.
48   P. Lalor, *The Bridge*, Allen and Unwin, Sydney, 2005.
49   J.J.C. Bradfield, 'The City and Suburban Electric Railways and the Sydney Harbour Bridge', DSc thesis, University of Sydney, 1924, p. 196.
50   *Building*, March 1923, p. 100.
51   *Building*, March 1932, p. 57.
52   R.A.M. Stern et al, *New York 1900*, Rizzoli, New York, 1983, p. 54.
53   Bridgeclimb Display, Southern Harbour Pylon.
54   *Architecture*, October 1921, p. 105.
55   Bradfield, 'The Transit Problems of Greater Sydney', p. 72.
56   *Building,* December 1926, p. 43.
57   *Building*, March 1926, p. 3.
58   Bradfield, 'The Transit Problems of Greater Sydney', p. 265.
59   *Building*, May 1932, p. 19.
60   *Architecture*, July 1929, p 155.
61   P.R. Murray and J.C. Wells, *From sand, swamp and heath ... A history of Caulfield*, City of Caulfield, 1980, p. 31.
62   M. Park, 'Designs on a Landscape: A History of Planning in North Sydney', PhD thesis, University of Technology Sydney, 2003, p. 22.
63   *Building*, November 1924, p. 47.
64   P. Ashton, 'Reactions to and Paradoxes of Modernism: The origins and spread of suburbia in 1920s Sydney', PhD thesis, UTS Sydney, 1999, p. 24.
65   J. Sulman, *An Introduction to the Study of Town Planning in Australia*, NSW Government Printer, Sydney, 1921, p. 142.
66   *Building*, February 1918, pp. 33–35.
67   *Australasian Engineer*, October 1933, p. 18.
68   *Shire and Municipal Record*, July 1924, p. 36.
69   H. Armstrong, 'Street and Roadside Landscaping in New South Wales', MLA thesis, University of New South Wales, 1986, p. 275.
70   Centenary Celebrations, 'Report of the State Organising Director', March 1937, GRG49/1, Adelaide, SA State Records.
71   *Building*, November 1908, p. 52.
72   *Building*, June 1915, p. 92.
73   *Building,* April 1913, p. 58.

74   K. Otto, *Yarra*, Text Publishing, Melbourne, 2005, p. 131.
75   *Building*, September 1927, p. 87.
76   *Building*, May 1918, p. 83.
77   *Building*, April 1927, p. 131.

Chapter 11: New themes, old traditions

1   W.H. Wilson, 'J Horace McFarland and the City Beautiful Movement', *Journal of Urban History*, 7, 1981, p. 328.
2   E. Talen, *New Urbanism and American Planning*, Routledge, New York, 2005, pp. 154, 126.
3   *Building*, April 1922, pp. 138–39.
4   Correspondence from Cyril White, April 1934, A1861/1, Item no 6524, National Archives.
5   *Architecture*, August 1938, p. 181.
6   D.W. King, Report, Martin Place Extension, 29 March 1934, TC3812/30, Sydney City Council Archives.
7   *Daily Telegraph*, 15 October 1943; *Building*, October 1943, p. 16.
8   P. Goad, 'The Business of Modernism', in P. Goad, R. Wilken and J. Willis, (eds), *Australian Modern: The Architecture of Stephenson and Turner*, Miegunyah Press, Melbourne, 2004, p. 31.
9   J. Sulman, *An Introduction to the Study of Town Planning in Australia*, NSW Government Printer, Sydney, p. 159.
10   J.S. Gawler, 'Plan for a Modern City', *The Record*, February 1948, p. 16.
11   H. Boas to Editor of *The Argus*, 31 May 1944, Boas Papers, 881A/9, Battye Library.
12   *Building*, June 1949, p. 30.
13   A.J. Youngson, *Urban Development and the Royal Fine Art Commissions*, Edinburgh University Press, Edinburgh, 1990, p. 101.
14   K.S. Inglis, *Sacred Places*, Melbourne University Press, Melbourne, 2nd ed, 2005, p. 352
15   P. Larkham, 'Rise of the "civic centre" in English urban form and design', *Urban Design International*, 9, 2004, pp. 3–15.
16   S. Kostof, *The City Assembled*, Little Brown, Boston, 1992, p. 81.
17   *Building*, April 1943, pp. 57–60.
18   C. Lyon, 'Unbuilt Melbourne', *Transition*, Autumn 1988, pp. 45–49.
19   Melbourne and Metropolitan Board of Works, *Melbourne Metropolitan Planning Scheme: Report*, Melbourne, 1954, pp. 123–25.
20   K. Sierakowksi, 'The Plans for the Perth Cultural Centre as of January 1, 1986', *The Architect*, 26(1), 1986, pp. 18–19.
21   R. Freestone and B. Hanna, *Florence Taylor's Hats*, Halstead Press, Sydney, 2007.
22   P. Ashton, *The Accidental City*, Hale and Iremonger, Sydney, 1993.
23   Minute Paper City Engineer's Department 4 November 1955, TC1597/46, Sydney City Council Archives.
24   F.C. Cook, *City of Hobart Plan*, Hobart City Council, 1945, p. 72.
25   *Building*, February 1947, pp. 22–24.
26   'City of Orange Civic Centre', 27 August 1958, Series 11/8, Denis Winston papers, University of Sydney Archives.
27   J. Lang, 'Learning from Twentieth Century Urban Design Paradigms', in R. Freestone (ed), *Urban Planning in a Changing World*, E & FN Spon, London, 2000, p. 82.
28   A.B Gallion and S. Eisner, *The Urban Pattern*, Van Nostrand, Princeton, 2nd ed, 1963, p. 82.
29   A. Garvin, *The American City*, McGraw Hill, New York, 1996, p. 80.
30   *New York Times*, 18 July 2004.
31   C. Tunnard, 'Why Has Civic Design Been Neglected', *Bulletin, Australian Planning Institute*, June 1953, pp. 3, 7.
32   'The City Beautiful', Paper presented to the 7th Australian Town and County Planning

Congress, Hobart, August 1962, p. 15.

33   D. Jones, 'The Civic Trust of South Australia', *Australian Planner*, 33, 1996, pp. 153–59.

34   C. Boyer, 'The Return of Aesthetics to City Planning', in D. Crow (ed), *Philosophical Streets*, Maisonneuve Press, Washington, DC, 1990, pp. 93–111.

35   S. Mannheimer, 'The Second Coming of City Beautiful', *Landscape Architecture*, 82, 1992, pp. 60–64.

36   *Architecture* (American Institute of Architects), December 1988, p. 85.

37   P. Calthorpe, *The Next American Metropolis*, Princeton Architectural Press, Princeton, 1993, p. 15.

38   J.A. Peterson, 'The City Beautiful Movement: Forgotten Origins and Lost Meanings', *Journal of Urban History*, 11, 1976, p. 430.

39   W. Rybczynski, *City Life*, Scribner, New York, 1995, p. 140.

40   *Forrest Place: A New Heart for Perth*, Government of Western Australia, Perth, c1988.

41   A. Brand, 'Forrest Place', *The Architect*, 29(4), 1989, pp. 32–34.

42   J.W. Elischer, 'Forrest Place', *The Architect*, 30(3), 1990, p. 10.

43   G. London, 'Forrest Place: A Case Study for an Urban Architecture', *Transition*, 30, Spring 1989, pp. 19–31.

44   J. Gregory, *City of Light*, City of Perth, 2003, pp. 293–94.

45   'Commonwealth Government Offices (Block 'B') Brisbane', A report by the Commonwealth Department of Housing and Construction, January 1979.

46   W.J. Kursey, *History of Anzac Square 1930–1984*, Anzac Square Preservation Society, Brisbane, 1985.

47   Town Clerk of the City of Sydney, *Annual Report*, 1940, p. 88.

48   G.P. Webber, 'The Nature of the City', in G.P. Webber (ed), *The Design of Sydney*, Law Book Company, Sydney, 1988, pp. 6–7.

49   K. Taylor, 'Anzac Parade: A landscape of memory', *Canberra Historical Journal*, 38, September 1996, p. 4.

50   National Capital Authority, *The Griffin Legacy*, Canberra, 2004.

51   J.M. Levy, *Contemporary Urban Planning*, Prentice Hall, New Jersey, 6th ed, 2003.

Select Bibliography

Clark, RK 'The City Beautiful: Promise and reality', *The Architect*, 10(2), 1969, pp. 40–44.

Edquist, H 'Harold Desbrowe-Annear and the City Beautiful', *Transition*, 59–60, 1998, pp. 46–57.

Gibbons, R 'Improving Sydney 1908–1909', in Roe, J (ed) *Twentieth Century Sydney*, Hale and Iremonger, Sydney, 1980, pp. 120–33.

Hall, P *Cities of Tomorrow*, Blackwell, Oxford, 3rd ed, 2002.

Hamnett, S & Freestone, R (eds) *The Australian Metropolis: A Planning History*, Allen and Unwin, Sydney, 2000.

Harrison, P 'The City Beautiful', in his *Walter Burley Griffin: Landscape Architect*, National Library of Australia, Canberra, 1995, pp. 10–15.

Hutchings, A & Bunker, R (eds) *With Conscious Purpose: A History of Town Planning in South Australia*, Wakefield Press, Adelaide.

Lewis, M 'The City Beautiful 1900–1929', in his *Melbourne: The City's History and Development*, Melbourne City Council, Melbourne, 1995, pp. 87–106.

McIntyre, J 'Sulman and the City Beautiful in Sydney', in Freestone, R (ed) *The Twentieth Century Urban Planning Experience: Proceedings of the 8th International Planning History Society Conference and 4th Australian Planning/Urban History Conference*, University of New South Wales, 1998, pp 565–70.

Peterson, JA *The Birth of City Planning in the United States, 1840–1917*, Johns Hopkins University Press, Baltimore, 2003.

Petrow, S 'Making the City Beautiful: Town Planning in Hobart c1915 to 1926', *Tasmanian Historical Research Association, Papers and Proceedings*, 36, 1989, pp. 99–112.

Reid, P *Canberra Following Griffin*, National Archives, Canberra, 2002.

Reps, J *Canberra 1912*, Melbourne University Press, Melbourne, 1997.

Robinson, CM *The Improvement of Towns and Cities*, G.P. Putnam's Sons, New York, 1901.

Stelter, G 'Rethinking the Significance of the City Beautiful Idea', in Freestone, R (ed) *Urban Planning in a Changing World*, E & FN Spon, London, 2000, pp. 98–117.

Sulman, J *An Introduction to the Study of Town Planning in Australia*, NSW Government

Printer, Sydney, 1921.

Sutcliffe, A *Towards the Planned City*, Basil Blackwell, Oxford, 1981.

Ward, SV *Planning the Twentieth Century City*, John Wiley, Chichester, 2002.

Wilson, WH *The City Beautiful Movement in Kansas City*, Lowell Press, Kansas City, 2nd ed, 1990.

——, *The City Beautiful Movement*, Johns Hopkins University Press, Baltimore, 1989.

——, 'The Ideology, Aesthetics and Politics of the City Beautiful Movement', in Sutcliffe, A (ed) *The Rise of Modern Urban Planning 1800–1914*, Mansell, London, 1980, pp. 165–98.

Index